DATE DUE		
Feb24'69		
3s '69		
Jan26'70		
Jun 8 70		
Oct20'71		
May18 '72		

GAYLORD M-2   PRINTED IN U.S.A.

LITERARY WISE MEN OF GOTHAM

LITERARY WISE MEN of GOTHAM

CRITICISM IN NEW YORK, 1815–1860

JOHN PAUL PRITCHARD

LOUISIANA STATE UNIVERSITY PRESS

810.9003
P93L

64537

January, 1969

Copyright 1963 by
Louisiana State University Press

Manufactured in the United States of America by
Vail-Ballou Press, Inc., Binghamton, New York

Library of Congress Catalogue Card Number 63-19231

Designed by E. S. Diman

Published with the assistance of
a Ford Foundation grant.

To the memory of
JENNIE MAE SMITH
Walton, New York,
1874–1952

ACKNOWLEDGMENTS

R esearch for this study was supported in part by grants from the American Philosophical Society and from the Faculty Research Fund of the University of Oklahoma. Through their generous assistance I was enabled to read extensively at the libraries of Columbia University, Harvard University, the University of Wisconsin, the library of the Wisconsin State Historical Society, and the New York Public Library. During a semester spent as visiting professor at the University of Arkansas, I was made free of its holdings in its library. The Bizzell Memorial Library of the University of Oklahoma has been of consistently generous assistance with its own resources and through interlibrary loan. To all these libraries I express my appreciation for their courteous assistance.

I am indebted to a former colleague at Washington and Jefferson College, Dr. George L. White of Roslyn, L.I., for reading an early draft of this work; to my colleague at Oklahoma, Victor Elconin, for a like service; and to Professor Harry Hayden Clark of the University of Wisconsin for critical reading of the final draft and for detailed suggestions. My student secretary, Miss Nina Flanery, made for me an unusually accurate typescript. I am grateful to Mrs. Dorothy C. Clair for courteous and skillful editorial aid in preparation of the manuscript. To my wife, who patiently endured and encouraged the work, I hope that the dedication to her aunt will serve in some sort as repayment.

J. P. P.

CONTENTS

LITERARY WISE MEN OF GOTHAM

LITTLE OLD
LITERARY NEW YORK

Edmund Wilson once remarked that the New York writers of the nineteenth century were more representatively American than their New England contemporaries. His statement was no doubt a barbed irritant aimed at the sensoria of those who accepted as fact Holmes's quip that Boston was the hub of the universe. There can be little doubt, however, that in Wilson's mind his assertion was solidly backed up with fact; nor has he lacked support. Luther Mansfield, for example, placed New York in company with Philadelphia as a literary mediator between New England and the states of the south. This study attempts to describe significant theories and practices in New York literary circles during that period between the second war with England and the Civil War which Van Wyck Brooks has christened the flowering of New England. It sets off New York from Philadelphia because as the decades passed New Yorkers themselves more and more asserted the separation. Although forces at work throughout the United States will necessarily be included in the study, emphasis will fall upon those literary ideas that were peculiar to Gotham or especially active there. Less attention will be devoted to the literary merits of creative works produced in the city. The focus of concern lies rather upon the interpretive and critical articles in the literary magazines which were published in New York. The shifting tides of literary theory and criticism during these forty-five years constitute the major theme for discussion.

The philosophical origins and characteristics of American literary and critical theory have been adequately treated elsewhere, notably in the work of Harry Hayden Clark; and such treatment requires no essential modification to make it apply specifically to New York. The activities of New York theorists and critics have, however, received at the best either inaccurately sketchy or necessarily hasty, superficial treatment because the scholars who handled them were engaged with more general ideas or larger areas. Floyd Stovall in an introductory sketch for a valuable series of studies in the development of American literary criticism, passes swiftly from the founding of the *North American Review* in 1815 to that of the *United States Magazine and Democratic Review* in 1837, and thence to the beginnings of the *Whig Review* eight years later. Lack of space and primary concern with the overall national picture undoubtedly motivated such leaps from decade to decade and from city to city. The periodicals of the intervening years must also be examined before one can safely generalize about American literary periodicals; and the differences between Boston, where the *North American Review* was edited, and New York, the home of the other two, exert as much influence upon their attitudes as the fact that the first was founded by Federalists and the second by Jacksonian Democrats. To say that the *American Magazine and Whig Review* took a stand between these two extreme periodicals, though fairly accurate politically, hardly represents the literary situation, which can be best studied by concentration upon details of the New York picture.

Stovall is correct in locating the site of a genuinely national literary point of view in New York, but it came into existence there many years before the appearance of Walt Whitman's manifesto, as Whitman himself attested. The causes of this nationally representative spirit were various, and include geographical, economic, ethnic, and social forces. Brief consideration of these forces is informative.

During the decades of concern to this study, New Englanders were accustomed to term Boston with suburban Cambridge the Athens of America, having wrested from Philadelphia its prior claim to the title. If one may pursue their classical analogy, it is tempting to advance the proposition that Boston was to New York as classical Athens was to Hellenistic Alexandria. Like most nonmathematical formulas, these analogies must not be pressed too far. There were nonetheless striking parallels between the city at the mouth of the Hudson and the city dominating the mouths of the Nile.

Like its ancient counterpart, New York was admirably situated for commercial and other intercourse with the rest of the world. The Hudson, like the Nile, tapped a fertile hinterland productive of raw materials and returned to their producers the manufactures of the outside world. River and Erie Canal attracted to the city shipping not only from the other states but from foreign nations as well. When railway began to supersede waterway, the Hudson-Mohawk valleys provided a level roadbed to the interior; and the land route via Philadelphia and Pittsburgh to the west also started from New York. Philadelphia's harbor was less commodious and accessible than New York's. As for Boston it possessed no water route to the west, and rugged hills barred the route by land; until the end of our period its railways had to reach the interior via New York. One needs to be reminded of these geographical facts when he considers the literary scene.

As in business, so in immigration. The Europeans who flocked to the United States after the Revolution naturally entered via the commercial routes. Peoples of varied trades, faiths, and social backgrounds flooded New York. Of these the greater numbers by far passed through to settle the new areas farther west, but thousands also remained in New York. These new citizens quickly joined in the business life of the city and almost as quickly infiltrated its literary activities. Here they found themselves more readily accepted than in Philadelphia or New England.

Unlike Boston, New York's citizens were not culturally under the thumb of any Brahmin caste. In nearly all circles except those of the "high society" of merchants or old landed proprietors, aliens were fairly readily accepted. Entering into the life of the city, these new elements quickly added their distinctive tinges to its colorful life. The melting pot fused them with the native American populace into bodies deriving from many cultures. This new fusion affected literary effort too, partly through its tastes in reading, partly through its creative and critical contributions. Besides British additions to the city, more strikingly alien strains came from Ireland, Germany, and France.

The native-born American New Yorkers had themselves been less homogeneous in ancestry than those in Boston even before the floods of immigrants entered. There was first of all the Dutch strain from the first settlers, represented in literature by Gulian Verplanck and the Duyckinck brothers. Many of British extraction were long-established citizens. To these were added people who had come to New York from other American states. Of these the most numerous so far as their literary impact was concerned came from New England. Among others, Samuel Ward the elder had come from Rhode Island in 1791; his family was to contribute to New York letters the epicurean Samuel Ward, and his sister Julia Ward Howe, both of them writers for the *New York Review and Athenaeum.* Later, as Jefferson's Embargo ruined New England shipping, and since the New England farms could not support a large population, mass migrations evacuated the six northeastern states. Although the greater number went westward, many who were less pioneering in spirit, and among them literary men in particular, moved to New York. Among those who will figure prominently in this study who came from New England were first and foremost William Cullen Bryant, but also Rufus Griswold, Fitz-Greene Halleck, and Nathaniel Willis. Others, like Richard Henry Dana, Sr., and James Russell Lowell, while maintaining their New England ties were frequent visitors in New York. From upstate New York came Lewis Gaylord Clark and his brother Willis. From the states to the south came frequent visitors, like the novelist-critic William Gilmore Simms from South Carolina and Edgar Allan Poe from Virginia. Poe made New York his home during the last years of his life. With such American-born citizens or visitors New York further enriched the mixture that entered into the production of her literary attitudes.

The New York amalgam was composed of peoples who, whatever their origin, had been in the great majority of cases drawn to the city on account of its opportunities for business. The business atmosphere pervaded all urban activities, not least the literary circles. To a greater or less degree, but nearly always in appreciable depth, business set its imprint upon the various men who pursued literary activities. Bryant, an outstanding literary influence, established the pattern. Coming to the city with considerable reputation as a poet, he edited for a brief time two literary magazines, and in 1828 began fifty years service as editor of the *Evening Post.* Verplanck had extensive interests in business and property. James Kirke Paulding and Halleck were employed in banks. Although some writers professed to find business degrading to the author, the consensus held that the literary man should support himself by some trade or business and pursue letters as an avocation. Letters and business, at least in this new country, must go hand in hand—a belief, as will appear in later pages, that profoundly affected New York's literary and critical thinking.

In other matters of the mind, too, New Yorkers were free from the dominance exerted upon letters in New England. In Boston, Harvard College had furnished writers who largely controlled literary activity. Even the Concord rebels from Cambridge conservatism were Harvard-trained. Although the Cambridge clique contributed undeniable benefits upon its members, it tended to stifle divergence from Brahmin concepts of correctness; and the transcendentalists generally were not tolerant of other than their own heresies. In New York, on the contrary, there existed no dominant native group of writers. The Columbia faculty, who had taught many of them, did not exert the controlling directive influence of Harvard. But even had they tried to dominate, the native writers were by the late 1820's outnumbered by newcomers from other states or lands. Without either a dictating class or a homogeneous body of litterateurs, the New York literary world lay open to many varieties of opinion; no Olympian group could frown at and wither their pretensions. This freedom made them more liberal and receptive of new ideas and ways than Brahmin Boston generally was, while the hard common sense of their business atmosphere made them at the same time more practical and skeptical than the thinkers at Concord.

New Yorkers were free also from the presence of an inherited Puritanism or the domination of any sectarian-inspired attitude. The New England writers were, it is true, nearly all rebels from the beliefs of the orthodox, who in many cases had only a decadent form of godliness. The "Boston religion," however, with all its humanistic interests, operated against the pressure of long-established Puritan biases that were held by the immense majority whether they were religiously inspired or not. Writers were inescapably affected by such pressure, which could not but color their opinions and their product. New York had indeed a considerable body of conservative Calvinists, as Herman Melville testified; and Calvinism, like Puritanism, was at the time hostile to humanism as a general rule. The city had, too, its peculiar separatist sects. Such movements, however, were in no way able to control or seriously modify the development of New York's literary theory or practice. Attempts of religious groups or individuals to dictate the policies of the *New York Mirror* and the *Knickerbocker Magazine* were indignantly rejected by their editors. The *New York Review*, perhaps the outstanding quarterly published in the city until the *National Quarterly Review* appeared in 1860, was liberally edited under the auspices of the Protestant Episcopal Church. Such freedom from sectarian intrusion, especially when enjoyed by editors who were in many cases devoutly religious men, furnished a healthy climate for expression of opinion that would be unlikely to go to excess but at the same time would be free from possibly inimical jurisdiction.

Under the practical influence of business life and with freedom from literary or sectarian control, New York litterateurs developed a characteristic inquiring attitude toward new ideas that was skeptical in Dryden's affirmative use of the term. They were interested in the new provided it could prove itself, but not in novelty for its own sake. No New Yorker of the accepted literary circles would have devoted such detailed description to the strange reforming movements as Ralph Waldo Emerson in 1840 gave to the New England reformers. Such movements undoubtedly existed in New York, but they would have been dismissed with brief ironic comment, not handled with Emerson's long-drawn-out satire. Sound practice in business, as they knew, required an intelligent skepticism. Aristotle's remark, that most of the projects that men undertake turn out badly, would have met their cordial agreement. New York's unusually free press examined new literary ideas from many angles. The literary men, as members of a new and still experimental society, were not opposed to innovation, but for the same reason they could not afford hasty, unproved enthusiasms.

There was, however, a limit beyond which New Yorkers' tolerance of ideas would rarely go. They shared the common human dislike of adverse criticism. When James Fenimore Cooper wrote of American defects in character, he was no doubt actuated partly by his deep-seated dislike of New Englanders, but the opinions and attitudes with which he was best acquainted were those of New Yorkers. When he charged the British with being thin-skinned but the Americans with being raw and touched to the quick by adverse opinion, he undoubtedly had in mind the unfriendly response of many New Yorkers to his tactless outspokenness. Lowell's remark in *A Fable for Critics*—which was begun and published in New York—that Americans should give more heed to Cooper's strictures upon them, was directed at New Yorkers fully as much as at other Americans. The earnestness with which responsible periodicals tried to soothe their readers, whenever they had been ruffled by British faultfinding, provides further indication of their touchiness. The vehemence of the editorial voices frequently raised on the side of moderation is a measure of the irritation they were attempting to mollify.

The typical Gotham litterateur would have agreed that literature should have aesthetic values, but he was likely to restrict such values to enjoyment or even entertainment. Poe's definition of poetry as the rhythmical creation of beauty contained implications beyond the comprehension of most of them. In the latter years of the period, John Ruskin's books on art aroused their interest but did not fully win their confidence; Robert Browning's treatment of Italian art in "Old Pictures in Florence" and other poems fared little better. Literary activities, as we shall see, were generally classed by New Yorkers as constituting an avocation rather than a profession and seldom as a means of earning one's livelihood. They would have heartily approved the conduct of James Loeb, who in later years combined a business in Wall Street with an active career in scholarship. To them the life of Edmund Clarence Stedman, who after the Civil War sat alternately in the Stock Exchange and on the lower levels of Parnassus, would have seemed well apportioned. Undoubtedly a man might write more, and possibly better (on this point some disagreed), if he could spend his life in literary pursuits; but life in pre–Civil War New York did not easily find a place for such professional activity. New Yorkers pointed with pride to Washington Irving, who had indeed made a comfortable income from his writing for readers on both sides of the Atlantic, but he was one of the few exceptions to the rule. The wise men of Gotham were children of this world; they faced the facts of life in their times, determined to make the best of both the practical and the imaginative worlds, and convinced through necessity as well as through belief that they were better off in so doing.

The United States, New York literary men agreed, needed a national literature as expression of its greatness and as demonstration in words of democratic nationality. In fulfilling both these ends it would not only encourage and instruct Americans at home, but also serve as propaganda abroad. So far as other national needs permitted, men of talent should liberally expend their energies in the development of this literature. The young nation had, however, other uses for her citizens at least as pressing as the production of her literature. Political and economic establishment of the country took precedence, in fact, of a national literature. If literature was the expression of a country, they reasoned practically, there must first be a country to celebrate; until it was firmly based American capacities should not be diverted into other channels, no matter how important or attractive they were. This feeling, although not peculiar to New York, continued to affect the writers of Gotham after it had declined in importance elsewhere.

Demarcation of a literary era by two wars may require some justification. Few would deny that the year 1815 started a new era in American thought and letters. Viewing in retrospect the American of 1815, Henry Adams set a pattern which has been more recently reaffirmed by Van Wyck Brooks. The regenerated American national consciousness at the end of the second war with Britain was further stimulated by violent nationalistic upsurge in Europe following the downfall of Napoleon. By these the already considerable demand for a national literature was greatly reinforced. For concluding the era with the outbreak of the Civil War, New York literary activity itself furnishes the support; there was a near cessation of literary thinking published in New York periodicals. The city's vital energies were diverted to the basic problem of saving the Union. The impending conflict had in fact shadowed the literary output for the preceding decade; such reviews as did appear in the periodicals—and though often of considerable merit their number was sharply reduced—were devoted rather to survey of the American literary situation and to British works than to new American creative or critical work.

A recent collection of essays upon the Victorian intellectual era has selected the year 1859 as the beginning of a new age in men's concerns. In so doing it has naturally fixed upon Darwin's crystallization of evolutionary theory that appeared in the course of that year. It is true, as New York periodicals were quick to notice, that since about 1838, with the improved communications between America and Europe brought about by the steam packets, British and American problems had run more closely parallel and become more nearly contemporaneous than before; whatever affected one country might reasonably be expected to impinge quickly upon the other. Owing to the overwhelming importance in America of the imminent civil conflict, however, Darwin's revolutionary hypotheses were not immediately given the attention they deserved, but were only slightly noticed for several years. The Civil War may, from its powerful effect upon New York activities, including literature and criticism, be justly considered as the conclusion of an era. Some of the threads, such as the realistic trend and the scant aesthetic beginnings in criticism, were picked up again after the war, but the scene as a whole was changed.

Literary and critical theories for these pre–Civil War decades in New York must be sought chiefly in the periodicals of the times. It is not enough to read the utterances of the better-known literary figures, although Bryant and Poe, whose essays have been collected in large part into volumes, must be included in this research. Nor is it enough to limit attention to the quarterlies and the better monthlies among the periodicals, although the level of their articles was usually higher than

of those in the weeklies. The belief in the close relation of literature
to the society that produced it made quick response to current events
a significant part of critical expression, and the less frequent publications could not respond quickly to contemporary stimuli. The weekly
magazines must also be consulted; in the case of the *Mirror*, at least,
the critical quality compares favorably with the best in New York
except in its lack of detailed discussion.

The significance of the periodicals is increased by the anonymity of
most of their contributors. In their day, each magazine spoke with one
voice; even when two opinions on a subject were expressed, as sometimes occurred, the individual authors were unnamed. Even today,
although careful research has discovered the identity of many writers
in the better periodicals, a large bulk of material remains anonymous
and can be cited only as the voice of the publication in which it appeared. Those writers who can be identified were often influential in
their own day, but are nearly forgotten now. Charles F. Briggs, Evert
A. Duyckinck, Charles Fenno Hoffman, William A. Jones, George
P. Morris, George W. Peck—to name a few at random—have passed
into oblivion so far as most American readers are concerned; in their
day, however, some of them possessed a greater influence than those
whose names time has spared. To ignore their beliefs and statements
or the ideas in the still anonymous essays would gravely unbalance the
picture of the New York literary scene.

For this study more than sixty periodicals of the period that were
published in New York have been read. The files of forty-five yielded
materials that have entered into the making of this volume. From these
periodicals collections have been published, most of them before the
Civil War, of essays by Bryant, William A. Cox, Parke Godwin, William A. Jones, and Henry Theodore Tuckerman; but significant essays
by these men were not included in these volumes. Besides the New
York periodicals, materials by New Yorkers appearing in Boston or
Philadelphia magazines have occasionally been used. Some of the
articles in New York periodicals were written by authors from other
areas, but since they were included by New York editors in their
magazines, it is justifiable to assume that they in most cases reflected
New York opinion. Biographies of a few of these New York figures,
and studies of details in the New York picture, have also appeared.
Some citations from periodicals unavailable to the writer or from
volumes missing from the files used have been included in this study.
No one who has undertaken such a compilation of evidence can avoid
the uneasy fear that he may have failed to include pertinent data. He

can only hope, with some apprehension that his hope is vain, that his mass of evidence fairly represents the area that he has tried to study.

Edmund Wilson's remark, with which this chapter began, is amply supported by the evidence: both opportunity and mental habit made New York litterateurs more representatively American than their contemporaries in New England. They were comparatively ignored in their own day, and have been since then, because, as Perry Miller pointedly puts it, New England scholars have taken care of their own. Without disparaging in any degree the literary qualities of the New England authors and critics, one can assert the claims of New York writers to more thoughtful attention than they have received. The creative wise men of Gotham might have done well to put to sea in a sturdier literary bowl, but their thinkers about the function of literature for their own day deserve the attention and respect of all who would know the American spirit in letters.

ONE

THE AUTHOR

True to the romantic fashion of their time, New York literary
men regarded the author as a subject at least as deserving of study
as his product. During the greater part of the period between the two
wars, critics and reviewers referred to him, whether he wrote in
prose or in verse, as a poet. If he wrote prose fiction, he occupied
a somewhat lower eminence than the writer of poems and had to fight
during the first three decades for recognition as an artist. Like the
writer of romance in the Renaissance, he could almost count himself
lucky to enter the sacred precinct by the back door. By Civil War
days, he had for more than a decade been admitted to the literary holy
of holies. Although it would have been daring in a writer to proclaim
the novelist's near equality with the poet, discussions in the periodicals
of the 1850's clearly indicate that the novelist had arrived at the literary
pinnacle to occupy a seat beside the poet.

To this ascent of the novelist several forces contributed. For one
thing, Fenimore Cooper's outstanding success in America and abroad
made New Yorkers eager to give him all the prestige they could. Even
after his personal popularity had waned, critics while lashing his real
or fancied faults still pointed with pride to him as the creator of the
Leatherstocking Tales and the novel of the sea. For another, the visits
of Charles Dickens and William Thackeray, both of whom were

lionized, added to the prestige of the novelist. The novelists Paulding and Cooper had done greater deeds in the estimate of most readers than had New York's poets; Washington Irving's tales were classics. Bryant, though revered as a great poet, had produced no heroic poem as a poet supposedly should, and his position as editor eclipsed partially his literary reputation. Finally, as even conservatives testily admitted, by the late 1830's literature had gone over to the people; and the people preferred to read novels. Popular taste, however the literati may affect to disdain it, is a compelling force upon literary fashion. In New York, without a Brahmin caste which might have tried to dictate its taste, the voice of the public carried greater weight than in Boston. For such reasons as these the novelist by the years preceding the Civil War had scaled the literary heights.

Novelist and poet alike possessed that creative power which Aristotle and later Samuel Coleridge had declared to be essential to the poet. As the 1829 *American Monthly Magazine* (Boston) put it, the novelist by his picturesque view of every subject and his consequent transformation of life into art was as much a maker as the poet. For his lack of such power the 1853 *National Magazine* excluded John Greenleaf Whittier from the roster of bards. The poet, it declared—like our recent New Critics—is not a political economist, an abolitionist, or a theologian; he transmutes these concerns into a new creation. New Yorkers' reactions to the doctrine of artistic imitation will be reported in more detail in a subsequent chapter.

The poet was also accepted as a seer. Occasionally, as in the 1845 *Democratic Review*, his power was called divine and spontaneous, or the effect of divine possession. As a rule, however, New Yorkers were skeptical of poetic claims of inspiration. Like the Renaissance critic Castelvetro, the 1829 *Mirror* dismissed this claim as a primitive aberration; the poet's immeasurably deeper insights were the source of his power, a power so far beyond that of the average man that earlier peoples had presumed it to be divine. The capacities of the man of genius, said the 1841 *New World*, enable him to react to stimuli so nearly instantaneously that to ordinary perceptions he seems to be supernaturally empowered. Boston and Concord elaborated theories about poetic inspiration; the spokesmen for New York saw a more rational explanation of the writer's power. Bryant in 1826 spoke of the poet as begetting poems in moments of daemonic possession, but the context of his statement makes it clear that he conceived of the poet as constantly in control while he created. And in like vein the 1850 *Whig Review*, following the traditional Platonic track recently trod by Poe, represented the poet as desiring the unattainable of which he has occasional glimpses and thereafter endeavoring to express his vision in a grosser actual medium. However ecstatic the poetic experience, the poet was generally considered to be a prophet only in virtue of his greater insights. The Wordsworthian concept of the poet as possessing in greater amount the powers of observation and expression, reiterated by Emerson, was in New York further rationalized by the concept of literature of, by, and for the people.

Although it was generally agreed that the writer was not divinely inspired, it was equally accepted that he possessed genius. In this respect, the ideas of Pope, Addison, and other writers of the preceding century survived. What this power was or what its origin, few writers troubled to inquire; perhaps such discussions as had been written in England satisfied them. It was a power rather widely prevalent among American writers if the popular press was to be believed; the more serious-minded periodicals occupied an ironic position closer to that expressed in Lowell's *Fable for Critics*. There were, however, varying degrees in which writers might possess this power; the later view that a man of genius appears only rarely would have appealed to few in New York.

The 1836 *American Monthly Magazine*, accepting A. W. von Schlegel's placing of the man of genius above ordinary mortals, added that this power was closely related to and intimately affected by the age in which it appeared, a doctrine no doubt deriving ultimately from the New Yorkers' quarter-century of reading Mme de Staël. At the same time, other periodicals saw the local, contemporary influence upon genius in Coleridge's terms. The *New York Review* approved his saying that genius consisted of carrying into manhood the child's naïveté, simple gladness, and receptivity to all sweet influences. The power of genius, he had written in *Biographia Literaria*, was creative. Its possessor originates, does not merely combine; through the secondary imagination he fuses elements into a new creation, does not merely heap up fixities and definites like the man of fancy.

The tendency of New Yorkers to cut down large claims did not permit reverence of genius to stand unchecked. The 1838 *Knickerbocker* sharply reminded its readers that far from being omnipotent, genius was in part the creature of its circumstances; and in New York these circumstances did not permit undisciplined flights into the empyrean. Although in 1841 H. T. Tuckerman saw genius as residing in the author's emotions, the majority went along with the *New World* in relating it primarily to the intellect. By 1852 the *Knickerbocker*, basing its treatment on the connection of genius to the mind, ventured to analyze it.

THE AUTHOR AS THINKER

Genius, the *Knickerbocker* declared, is the result of "a peculiar and felicitous combination of mental faculties, moral qualities, and physical organization." Emotion and intuition do not figure in its composition. Although it may coexist with taste, wit, humor, common sense, facility, or talent—all of them desirable qualities—it is none of these. It is especially to be separated from talent, for it is pre-eminently the creative power. Genius is "the ability to conceive, comprehend, and reproduce truth, beauty, and harmony: talent is the ability to explore, gather up, and reconstruct truth, beauty, and harmony." Genius makes a new organism, talent remakes an old one. Genius is subjective, speculative, and visionary; talent is objective, practical, and matter-of-fact. "Genius conceives and invents: talent finds and remembers." Genius is easy and natural in its works, talent fastidious and accurate. "Talent ascends: genius transcends. . . . Talent arrives at a conclusion: genius has a revelation"—by reason of insight, be it remembered. The capacity of genius grows organically, like a tree—spontaneous, constantly increasing, yet essentially the same. Talent comes by cultivation as a crystallization, each crystal being "separate, severable, and obvious." (The writer has mischievously assigned to talent that crystallizing power which the transcendentalist had used to image the working of genius.) Genius, coming in flashes, often gives but a partial view and may therefore seem eccentric or inconsistent; talent, with less light, glows more steadily. Translated into Coleridgean terms, we have very nearly repeated here his differentiation of the secondary imagination from the fancy. Talent, or fancy, is put firmly into second place, but the poet requires the offices of both.

Coleridge's concept of the primary imagination, by which the poet becomes a partaker of the divine nature, was little considered in the New Yorkers' discussions of genius. Their more worldly, practical approach to problems made it less usable by them than by the speculative New England theorists. It could be accepted like other matters of divinity, without its being much applied in their literary activities.

This imaginative genius, said W. A. Jones in 1849, is one of the three requisites in the great poet; it appears with deep sentiment and curious felicity of expression. It looks steadfastly at its subject, *Holden's Dollar Magazine* agreed with Wordsworth in 1851, but, as the 1840 *New York Review* had echoed both Wordsworth and Coleridge, it expresses the poet's thoughts through the natural objects in which it clothes them. "In every genuine product of art, nature is taken up, and, as it were, recast. . . . We look through the symbols at the thing signified; it acts upon us as a real and living object." In all this thinking the New York writers combined the eighteenth-century tradition of genius with Coleridgean imaginative theory to produce a picture of the poet's creative power that to the majority of them was quite acceptable.

Genius, we have seen, was governed in part by the circumstances under which it appeared. It was also, the New Yorkers insisted, to be trained and disciplined. As editor of the New York *Mirror*, George P. Morris in 1829, defended his practice of editing poems submitted to him for publication: not only was it his paper in which they were to appear; genius without method, a phrase he thought aptly fitted to the best of these poetasters, allowed the imagination to run wild and often needed the checkrein of judgment. The poet, he added a year later, resembled a cultivated plant in need of pruning that, "unaided by study and labour, never produced anything truly great." *Poeta nascitur, non fit* was, according to Morris, only a half-truth; his natural powers of thought and observation as well as insight and expression must be well trained. Too many young writers ambitious of literary fame were unwilling to submit to the labor involved in their training.

Literary theorists in Gotham, as we have seen, with few exceptions agreed in relating the genius of the poet to the mind. The 1817 *American Monthly Magazine and Critical Review* dryly declared that genius precluded a divergency from good sense. Twelve years later, the *Mirror* added the demand that the author devote years to study of books, partly to master the best models, partly to draw ideas from the best sources, to digest them, and to shape them preparatory to their publication. This soundly based knowledge, the 1838 *New York Review* insisted, should cover a wide range rather than be narrowly specialized—a position close to that occupied by Emerson the preceding August. Developing the plea for sound learning, the 1841 *Knickerbocker* warned readers that encouragement of novelty and originality had already macadamized the road to literary pretension and quackery. The quack was the *bête noir* of the literary kingdom, to be hunted down wherever encountered. The *Democratic Review* consistently equated the author with the scholar, and the competent *Literary World* in 1847 decided that the American author should purvey erudition rather than wit. Two years later, W. A. Jones feared that the participation of many legally trained writers might unduly elevate intellectual force in America over sentiment and imagination, but the consensus of writers saw no danger in such dominance of this scholarly attitude.

The American author should be firmly grounded in sound literary models and principles. He was at the same time the product of new times dwelling in a new world; therefore, he must be alert to current and novel kinds of learning. Novelty yoked with soundly based, tasteful learning was not dangerous. In his new habitat he naturally must observe the life around him and must be thoroughly American in thought and attitude; and, as the 1839 *Democratic Review* remarked, he must write what he has seen and thought. As for the influence of nature, he will undoubtedly be affected by it; it was good for him, said the 1829 *Mirror*, but could not make him able to write. A prospective author without access to the proper books should not write at all. Gulian Verplanck inclined to a like view. In reviewing *Yamoyden*, by James Wallis Eastburn and Robert C. Sands, he declared that its young authors had obviously benefited from their concentration upon Milton's minor poems.

Nature had also her defenders as the poet's tutor. Somewhat surprisingly, the church-affiliated *New York Review* placed nature along with the Bible in the front rank of his teachers. The Bible was "the best safeguard for the purity of different languages—the standard by which the lawfulness and good taste of words and phrases are to be tested." The other function usually assigned to Holy Writ was given to nature, "the other chief companion and teacher of men. . . . It is here that errors are rebuked, and excesses discountenanced." The poet instructed solely by nature may have merit. "Uncharitable criticism has stigmatized the rural doctrines of his rhymes, from negative rather than positive charges. But there is often a great deal of real strength and meaning in his couplets." In an age profoundly affected by the various forms of romanticism and a country whose population was largely rural, the advocates of nature as the poet's instructor would have a strong following. In urban New York, however, although rural influence was far from unknown, the advocates of literary study and attention to current movements had the advantage.

The poet must use his literary models with discretion. In a vein like that worked a century earlier by Edward Young, he could by all means imitate them, but should imitate them aright. Imitation was a process still tainted with the Platonic idea of copying, not filled with the Aristotelian concept of creating. The United States was cursed with American would-be apes of one or another British poet. Bryant urged as an antidote that the poet pore upon the works of many British authors instead of devoting himself to one; he might thereby avoid copying mere peculiarities while learning techniques, as Young also had wished the poet to do. New York critics ridiculed in particular the apes of the recently discovered German writers, "somewhat formidable conspirators against clear style" in the eyes of the 1838 *Knickerbocker*. Thomas Carlyle's style was roughly handled in several periodicals, as was his reputed imitator Emerson. The 1841 *Knickerbocker* in particular stigmatized the Concord sage for imitating "the German-English style of Thomas Carlyle, which whoso handleth, not being expert therewith, useth an edged tool, and will assuredly be wounded thereby." Ideas were meant to be expressed, not concealed —a principle that Emerson would do well to impress upon his followers.

German-influenced writers were, however, a lesser peril to American letters than the slavish Anglophile. Although New Yorkers were on the whole less hostile to Britain than those in some other areas, they were as American in sentiment as any; the writer who received their approval must be unmistakably of the Western hemisphere. In varying degrees, but in one consistent tenor, they proclaimed this preference whenever events or the work of some writer brought the matter to their attention. The almost unanimous response, varying only from regret to vilification, with which the New Yorkers responded to what they fancied to be Cooper's un-American attitude after he had returned from abroad, is the most noticeable instance of this feeling. On the extreme of Anglophobia in the earlier years stood James K. Paulding, who in essay and novel alike proclaimed American principles in literature as in all else. In the late thirties and forties, the *Democratic Review* took up the cudgels against British influence. In 1849, one of several years in which anti-British sentiment ran unusually high, it proclaimed: "There must be less worship of British models, less imitation of English writers, and less deference to English criticisms." Less heatedly, Parke Godwin in 1853 declared that the racial melting pot that was America, by grafting upon the earnest northern character the volatile and graceful vivacity of the south of Europe, was producing a "fresh, genial enthusiasm" that was new in the world. The common run of writers might continue to ape the British; it was, however, the consensus of the majority that the abler American authors were becoming more and more distinctively American. The paradoxical situation mourned in 1820 by Paulding—"we were born rich, and yet have all our lives subsisted by borrowing"—seemed to them to be no longer true.

Bryant in his remark that poetry powerfully and vigorously excites thought did not indeed rule out its other effects. The poet in prose or verse was much more than a thinker, more even than Man thinking. He did however, the New Yorkers generally agreed, operate primarily in the realm of the mind. Of this they became more assured as the end of the pre–Civil War era drew near. The good poet, according to the 1849 *Literary World*, impresses readers with his intellectual power while he completely masters their feelings; and in 1856 *Putnam's Magazine*, defending contemporary poets against the charge that they provided more difficult reading than Pope, countered with the suggestion that they had more to say.

This emphasis upon the intellectual parts of the poet was so heavy partly because it was in harmony with the New York atmosphere. It was no doubt the heavier because they were living in an age when the claims of the feelings and of intuitive knowledge were everywhere advanced. A successful business atmosphere plays down the demands of sentiment and treats skeptically a knowledge not based on reason. In the more strictly literary area as well, New Yorkers wanted to stabilize an American literature by curbing its excesses while making it more truly representative of the new country as they envisioned the United States.

Dissatisfied with the spineless run of American literary men, New Yorkers demanded that the writer be earnest and vigorous. The establishment of the new nation undoubtedly made of primary importance the developing of its government, and this could be secure only if the economic structure of the nation were sound. It was right, they believed, that the best effort of Americans should be devoted to politics and business. On the other hand, a strong national literature, which could be made only by strong men, was vitally important. If literature was the expression of a society, a strong national literature indicated a flourishing nation. Other nations with developed literatures of their own, Britain in particular, look down upon the nation without its literary expression. And if the United States was ever to be understood and appreciated abroad, its authors must be its propagandists. The lovers of literature in New York found themselves supported by practical men in their desire for a truly American literature, however extra-literary the reasons of the latter might be.

Although the fear that literature in America was being abandoned to the effeminate existed from the very first, expression of this fear was particularly vocal after 1840. Prior to this time, the virility of the leading New York authors had been little questioned. Bryant, Paulding, and Cooper among her creative writers were masculine natures, as were

lesser lights like Richard Sands and Joseph Rodman Drake. Both these
latter had died early. Irving was admired but tacitly dismissed by many
as old-fashioned. Bryant had turned his energies to a newspaper, and
Cooper had gone into eclipse by reason of his honest but outspoken
tactlessness. Men felt that writers like Willis, who were much in the
public eye, lacked not only talent but virility. Henry Wadsworth
Longfellow and other New England writers were suspect also as
deficient in masculinity. Lowell's assertion that elegance also is force
was not palatable to the majority of New Yorkers interested in literature, any more than was the sham-shaggy at the other extreme.

Mathews ?

On many levels, the demand for strong literary personalities was
heard. Even H. T. Tuckerman, who was about as near to an aesthete
as New York provided, felt in 1841 that the author's mental effort
must be vigorous. In the same year the *Knickerbocker*, evidently convinced that too much energy had been diverted into political and
business channels, listed as one quality of the American author a will
sufficiently strong to resist the lure of these more colorful callings. On
the lower cultural level, *Brother Jonathan* in 1842 warned the author
to ignore all unwisely exerted pressures, especially mercenary attrac-
tions. "Fame, with her trumpet, does not always turn up a trump, and
never comes at the bidding of mere mercenary invokers."

Protests increased with the passing years against abandonment of
authorship to the less virile. One sign of deficient literary energy noted
by the 1847 *Literary World* was the disposition of American writers
to merely emulate British writers. Bryant, it added, was a notable but
rare exception to this lack of initiative; his strength offered a worthy
example to budding writers. The contemporary *American Literary
Gazette* offered as a deterrent to literary milksops the recommendation
that the American author compose only from strong impulse to self-
expression. If the writer is to master our feelings, said the 1849 *Literary
World*, let him display "rigorous straightforwardness of purpose and
a practical energy." To many New York readers of this article, the
operative word was "practical."

In a minor flurry of confidence, the 1852 *National Magazine* declared, "Art in America seems to partake of the steam-power which
pervades all classes and conditions of men." This burst of approval was,
however, drowned out in the chorus of disapprobation. "Our authors,"
declared *Emerson's Magazine* in 1858, "do not grasp their material
with the power of men and women who mean to vitalize it." The statement of the *Democratic Review* in 1839, that the poet who survives
will be manly and unaffected in his verse, was expanded to include the

writer of prose. Virility was felt to be a scarce commodity in both.

The writer's force was expected to show itself also in his gusto or zest for his materials. Perhaps owing to the influence of William Hazlitt, whose essays had many admirers in New York, the quality was frequently cited in the thirties and forties as requisite to his success. With it, said the 1837 *Knickerbocker*, an American writer could show his wares to the best advantage. It would help to atone for his "overweening fondness for superabundant finery in style," which too often, as the *Whig Review* remarked a decade later, along with sound was supposed to supply the lack of sense. W. A. Jones in 1849, and H. T. Tuckerman two years later, listed zest as a vital ingredient in the author; and a few years later Evert Duyckinck deplored its absence from the pallid products of American poets. Elegance, as the 1842 *New World* remarked in criticizing Longfellow's *Ballads*, should be shored up with vigor and boldness. Whitman no doubt took such declarations to heart.

The *furor poeticus*, it was widely agreed, is not really madness. The few exceptions to this rule, declared the 1835 *American Monthly Magazine*, have no doubt given rise to this aberration, which has wrought great harm to the profession of letters. MacDonald Clarke, New York's outstanding example of the unbalanced versifier, produced nothing to support the traditional theory of poetic madness. George Crabbe and Sir Walter Scott were cited by the 1837 *New York Review* as poets who had lived orderly, well-spent lives. In 1840 it added that a "sage and meditative imagination—the rare endowment of 'the vision and the faculty divine'" had uniformly inspired the greatest poets. Such vision, said the 1848 *Knickerbocker*, conveys to poets true and real poetic images that reason must plod to attain; but they come from deeper insight, not from madness or daemonic possession.

Being sane, the poet was usually held equally responsible with other men for his actions as the era advanced. The conservatively pious *Minerva* stood ready in 1824 to condone Byron's lapses in life and poetry: he had atoned for his faults by dying in the cause of freedom and religion and had himself been devoutly religious. The 1833 *Mirror* demanded that men who would foster American genius be tolerant of its waywardness: "applaud and emblazon it. . . . Overlook faults, overlook error . . . if evidence of genius appear, say so." With innocence foreshadowing that of William Dean Howells four decades later, it was asserted that American authors were of higher moral character than their brethren across the Atlantic. The 1836 *American*

Monthly Magazine declared them to be singularly free from drunken-
ness and the company of vicious women. Moral transgression, the
Mirror added two years later, should not be condoned in him; he
could no longer hide behind the aegis of eccentricity. "There is no
necessary connection between genius and gin—between the muse and
the stews—and between attick salt and an attick dwelling." So the
rational mind of New York ruled with decreasing tolerance on writers'
infractions of propriety.

As Victorian standards of conduct spread from Britain to the
United States, the rein upon authors' conduct was steadily tightened.
Although nominally enforcing fairly strict moral codes, the New York
literati had in practice relaxed them to a point unusual in the United
States. Both conduct and conversation were frequently "Rabelaisian,"
at least in the more liberal circles. Victorian prudery, however, showed
its power. "When a spirit of purity is in the man," *Holden's Dollar
Magazine* declared in 1850, "no badness or baseness can be in the artist."
Harper's Magazine indeed tried a year later to mitigate this severity:
although moral standards indeed applied to literary men, they should
be mercifully enforced. Tuckerman, however, insisted that the so-
called infirmities of genius were not indissolubly attached to the author;
and in 1852, reversing the stand taken by *Minerva* in 1825, the *Whig
Review* categorically refused to admit any distinction between the
author's works and his personal character. With little to go on beyond
published utterances on this delicate subject, it is difficult to estimate
how much the printed statements reflected actual sentiment or conceded to external pressures.

This rational attitude toward letters, although it gave primacy to
the author's intellect and training, freely admitted his need to be likewise a man of strong emotions, however much kept in check. As the
1832 *Mirror* put it, the poet's steadiness and principles will let his
emotional capacities develop along with his observation. Tuckerman
remarked in 1850 that the enthusiastic poet delights to place himself
in the presence of whatever interests him, and the 1856 *Putnam's*
asserted that enthusiasm is the basic element in poetry. Both agreed
with the statement of the 1830 *Mirror*, that the outpourings of an
excited mind do not necessarily constitute poetry.

Horace's precept that the performance devoid of emotion fails to
move had the full support of New York critics. Bryant had told his
New York Athenaeum audience that poetry could not consist in
imagery devoid of emotion, and in "The Poet" he had urged the poet
to fix the fleet emotion in verse before it should escape him. Tuckerman

in 1845 had made much of the knowledge that comes with moments of high emotion, and had urged his readers to accept it even though it might be beyond their reason to appreciate. The poet could, said the 1851 *Literary World*, express the profoundest emotions of the heart; they were not only elemental in human nature but also sage and meditative. *Putnam's* a few years later heard the poet's heart beating in sympathy with his time and the noblest human aspirations; his was the language of enthusiasm, of the passions and the affections. The emphasis upon the emotional appeal of poetry increased as the years passed, partly because the romantic British poets with the youthful Tennyson and Browning were increasingly studied, partly because the writer was more and more thought of as a propagandist in the impending civil conflict. But although the value of emotion was varyingly stated according to the belief of the theorist or critic, the great majority felt that knowledge was the matter of poetry, which, however transmuted by the poet's art, remained the major attribute of the creative writer.

THE CREATIVE IMAGINATION

Occupying a position connected with the poet's knowledge and his emotion was his imagination. Although there was some awareness that Samuel Johnson had written perceptively on this subject, the more recent pronouncements by Wordsworth and Coleridge naturally occupied a more prominent position in this late romantic age. Coleridge indeed had been ridiculed by the first *American Monthly Magazine*, as much for his poetry as for his poetic theory; his kindness of heart was sufficient to balance his softness of head. Richard Henry Dana the elder, however, who visited New York for extended periods, had been one of the first American proponents of the two Lake poets. He found in Coleridge's comments on Wordsworth as poet more "subtile analysis, and good taste" than in any book he could remember. His friend Bryant, who had become an admirer of Wordsworth's poetry a decade before he came to New York, was also an ardent Coleridgean. With others, these two gave New York a fairly good notion of the imagination as Coleridge had briefly analyzed it. Literary men as a whole quite naturally preferred Coleridge's treatment of this power to Wordsworth's; the latter had handled the subject only to the extent that he deemed necessary to introduce his classification of the poems in his edition of 1815, while Coleridge had approached the subject in its fundamental problems. Wordsworth on the imagination was briefly referred to in *Harper's* memorial after his death, in which the poet was praised for having shown the high moral function of the imagination. Otherwise, attention focused upon Coleridge.

In his third lecture before the Athenaeum, Bryant related the workings of the imagination to the poet's knowledge. Always alert to scientific advance, he spoke strongly against the romantic notion that the progress of knowledge was, as Poe was soon to write, dragging Diana from her car and generally ravaging the lands of poesy. On the contrary, Bryant declared, the imagination must have ideas on which to exercise itself. The more knowledge expands and the more provender the imagination finds, the more areas are opened for exploration. The traditional myths which science had exploded were in fact a restraint upon the imagination: professing to settle all questions, they left it scant room to roam. Each new acquisition of information is a springboard for an imaginative plunge into unknown waters. Nor was this, he asserted, mere speculative reasoning. In the present age, Britain was coupling an unprecedented preoccupation with scientific activities with her greatest surge of imaginative writing since the age of Elizabeth. Since these lectures remained unpublished until after Bryant's death, their direct influence upon New York thinking must remain an unsettled question. Bryant, however, was a power in the city, and his frequent speeches and constant newspaper statements repeated details of the lectures.

The poet was allowed considerable freedom in the exercise of his imagination, provided that he kept it within the control of reason. In 1829 George P. Morris reminded his contributors that genius without method, as Longinus had warned, lets the imagination run wild and often requires the checkrein of judgment. A year later, he tried nonetheless to preserve the poet's liberty of imagination: Frances Jeffrey, he asserted, was wrong in attempting to regulate imaginative works by established critical canons; to do so would "petrify the warmth and paralyze the energies of poets and poesy." In seeking a mean between regulation and license, he inclined slightly toward the latter without surrendering the duty of decent restraint. Like a plant in need of pruning, the imaginative power of genius, "unaided by study and labour, never produced anything truly great."

A degree of license should be conceded to the poet because his imaginative insight is deeper and clearer than that of an ordinary man. He stands above ordinary mortals in this respect, said the 1836 *American Monthly Magazine;* however strange the form in which his insights present themselves, men must endeavor to see with his eyes. The next year, the *New Yorker* admitted that the poet's revelation might tax human reason and invention; yet the mind of man must not stubbornly cling to the old and accepted but must look to the future in the expectation of new truths. Looking backward had provided a valuable perspective from which to view the future; it had been useful in plotting the best course for the imagination to pursue; it could not exert strong pressure upon the poet's insight nor foretell the advances of modern knowledge. These things the prophetic poet could and did perform. At times like the present, a later number of the *New-Yorker* admitted, the poetry of the age might be "the yearning of the spirit for the vast, the shadowy, the unattainable"—in other words, the romantically imaginative; but the poet must present his readers with some product of his emotion and imaginative insight.

Coleridge's brief analysis of the poetic imagination and fancy were frequently referred to or echoed in New York periodicals. It was, however, the secondary imagination which chiefly engaged their attention. They were willing to concede the existence of that primary imagination which relates to the divine nature, and they made some attempt, as will be shown in a later chapter, to dissect the fancy out from the imagination. But when the 1840 *New York Review* declared: "The sage and meditative imagination alone constitutes the inspiration of the greatest poets," the context clearly shows that the writer had in mind the secondary aspect of it. Walter Scott, he added, had wisely restricted his efforts to the description of a richly romantic period; he lacked that vision and faculty divine which fuses and that fancy which combines. A writer in the preceding volume had seen the artist as taking up nature and recasting her to image his thought, so that works of art are products of the imagination in its basic significance as a maker of objects that are new in nature.

Horace's shrewd mixture of artistic principle and common sense were suited, as frequent quotations and echoes show, to the mental habit of literary New York. In none of these is his influence more clearly shown than in his warning that philosopher and poet, though both concerned with ideas, treat them quite differently. The American writer should be poet rather than philosopher, it was generally agreed —a belief stemming from the immediate reaction against the cloudier German philosophers with their disciples Carlyle and Emerson. The 1838 *New York Review* opened this discussion with the statement that while the greatest poet no doubt possessed philosophic insights, a man could be a poet without these. In an article published two years later, it shifted its ground: since the poet illuminates facts by principles, from now on he must be a philosopher. W. A. Jones, reverting to Horace, asserted that poets are the "true masters and best expounders of the philosophers." If the poets devote long attention to speculation, the philosophers will injure their understanding—he no doubt had Coleridge's debacle in mind—which can be reinvigorated only through recourse to poetic practice of embodying truth instead of treating it abstractly.

A decade later, the 1848 *Knickerbocker* revived the discussion. Since truth and beauty are kindred manifestations of divine wisdom, the true poet and philosopher are co-workers in one great cause. In 1850, however, Tuckerman sharply corrected the fuzzy benevolence of the *Knickerbocker*. As John Crowe Ransom was to write ninety years later, he severed the poet's attitude from that of the philosopher or scientist. The poet is enthusiastic and delights to place himself in direct relation with whatever interests him; the philosopher, being merely curious, is satisfied to observe and become acquainted with the object. To him the primrose is just a primrose.

Endeavoring to settle this problem, the 1852 *Whig Review* listed among the important qualities of the younger American poet a practical vein of metaphysics—it did not resolve this paradox—but warned him away from its speculative side. The 1856 *Putnam's* agreed with the second part of this statement: since enthusiasm is the basic element in poetry, the poet will present clearly defined embodiments that have an air of actuality, not shadowy speculation and theory. A year later, another article in *Putnam's* would have the poets bridge the gap between the ideal and the actual—in other words, embody the ideal through the imaginative power. The philosopher should give place to the poet, who, as Horace had said, is his master.

THE AUTHOR AS PROPAGANDIST

Practical New Yorkers found a use for the creative artist as a propagandist. He must therefore be a patriot and a realist. The patriotic motif appeared from the start, some years before the concern with realism, and will be treated first.

America's own rampant nationalism was not only increased by the War of 1812, but was further augmented by echoes of the surge of nationalism that swept over Europe after the fall of Napoleon. Along with the rest of the nation, New Yorkers burned to justify the United States by proclaiming its virtues to readers both at home and abroad. For this propaganda the ready agent was the American author, at first the poet but then, as his craft gained prestige and popularity, the novelist also. American nationalism swayed American writing throughout the entire era; as late as 1852 the *New York Quarterly* placed second only to originality the author's fostering of qualities essential to his nation and age.

New York periodicals vehemently supported the demand that the author be a power for patriotism. The 1835 *Knickerbocker* summed up the position of preceding magazines: the author must be filled with patriotism and produce a distinctly American literature. Need for such infusion of spirit was sharply pointed by the 1838 *American Monthly Magazine*: in harmony with Emerson's demand a year earlier, it bitterly regretted that since 1800 every literary movement had originated on the other side of the Atlantic. The writer's warmth of feeling, or possibly his bias, let him ignore the contributions of Cooper to the novel, for Cooper's patriotism was at the time vehemently challenged. Four years later, the *Democratic Review,* that out-and-out apostle of democracy whether capitalized or in lower case, asserted that the spirits of literature and democracy were one. From its inception the broadest plank in this periodical's platform had been the demand that all human experience be reviewed in the light of the democratic principle. Author and scholar, it added, being the greatest patriots, add most to the national honor. The writer's duty was to "cheer us on, and go before like a trumpeter," not to sit like a fiddler, in the democratic march. The demagogic *Brother Jonathan*'s ideal writer was an iconoclast, who destroyed "those old landmarks which pride and fashion have set up, making impassable distinctions between the brethren of the Great Family"; he taught "to put down the high and bring up the low." At somewhat lower than the inflammatory temperature of these two periodicals, the *New World,* borrowing a Wordsworthian paradox, declared the true poet to be at once the child and the teacher of his age. In New York the majority were confident that the present age, as Whitman was soon to assert, belonged to America.

The poet could derive a modicum of protection from the pervasive patriotic mania by resort to the long-established theories of his craft, but no such precedent sheltered the novelist. Since the novel was a relatively new art-form, it was more freely ductile to the demands of propagandists than the poem. The rampant *Democratic Review* in 1843 praised Cornelius Mathews' *Poems on Man* for "a certain earnest spirit of Americanism," whereas other periodicals saw them for the trash they were. The novelist, however, was regularly expected to endorse American ideals while publicizing American life.

The most outspoken champion in New York of literary nationalism was for many years James Kirke Paulding. In his 1820 *Salmagundi* paper on nationalism he permitted the American novelist a choice; he might produce works that "appeal to national attachments, domestic habits, or those feelings which are the same yesterday, to-day, forever, and everywhere." He should be unmistakably American in daring to think and feel and express his feelings. Whether he wrote on the homely or the elevated level, he should dwell upon scenes and events that we recall with pride; he should record local peculiarities without sacrificing universality and in so doing pave the road to a genuine national literature. These subjects, he implied, would be American. Paulding's Americanism was reinforced by a virulent Anglophobia that mightily augmented his nationalistic feeling with the passing years. For three decades, however, there were New York periodicals that kept pace with him in demands for a distinctly American literature if not in his hatred of England.

The novelist's patriotic duty, the 1835 *Knickerbocker* insisted, was to produce a distinctively national literature. Although he need not confine himself to American materials, his works must be American in tone. This American tone, like too many other requisites of literature, it left in the limbo of undefined terms. Two years later, the *New-Yorker*, showing the influence of Mme de Staël and her fellows and anticipating Hippolyte Taine, saw the novelist as the product of his times, and by implication of his country also. In the United States, he could not help being a proponent of the democratic principle.

The determinism implicit in this view, so at variance with American romantic principles, was not noticed at this period. As to the novelist's handling of American materials, opinions varied. Although the 1841 *Knickerbocker* indicated the existence of pressures upon the novelist to write exclusively of America by urging that he ignore them, Duyckinck's scholarly *Literary World* in 1847, preferred that he write of "home subjects." In the same year the *Democratic Review*, its patriotic fires now banked, conceded that the novelist can demonstrate his patriotism and nationality by using "a due proportion of American themes." It was interested, however, chiefly in the American subjects, in treating which the author must "as from a faithful mirror, reflect the physical, moral, and intellectual aspects of the nation." By 1849 the *Literary World*, in an attempt to convert American nationalism into a more nearly literary criterion, defined Americanism in fiction as "rigorous straightforwardness of purpose and a practical energy, of which the principal ingredient is that rare quality in authorship, common sense." Far from narrowly national in outlook, it even permitted a French critic to use in its pages the term "Anglo-American literature";

but it showed no enthusiasm for such a hyphenation. Even the friends of Britain, and they were many in New York, wanted a separate American literature.

This American propaganda, as several of the preceding passages indicate, could be served best by the American author. New Yorkers saw him as the world's informer on not only the physical qualities of the new world, but also on American life in general. The familiar passage in praise of American scenery in Irving's *Sketch Book* is representative of numerous similar pronouncements, some of them apparently echoes of Vergil's glorification of Italy in his second *Georgic;* his apotheosis of rural life is also to be found in connection with these classical survivals. No other land, declared the 1835 *Mirror,* has local scenery and national recollections as inspiring to the artist in all media as are to be found in America; the arts should find here their most congenial habitation. It was, however, as inspiration and habitat that the artist was generally advised to use nature; descriptive poetry found little encouragement in comparison with treatment of American historical themes and pictures of everyday life.

It followed inevitably upon the acceptance of the author as a propagandist that he should represent America accurately. He should not, indeed, show the degree of objectivity that appeared in Cooper's frank criticism of Americans; they were as "raw" to the touch of adverse criticism as he had said they were. Propaganda, naturally, should tell the truth, but not necessarily the whole truth. The rudiments of commercial advertising were well known to New Yorkers.

In no respect was the novelist more free of traditional limitations than in his representation of people. Wordsworth had presented the claims of the common man for poetic consideration, but his poems found uphill going in the face of long-established habit. The novel was still malleable enough as an art-form to yield to the prevalent leveling tendency of American democracy. At first, indeed, in spite of Paulding's statement to the contrary, Americans feared that the classless American society was too drab for literary representation. Cooper had shared these fears and had doubted the success of *The Pioneers* on account of its large number of common characters; he was agreeably surprised by its reception. Five years later, he still recommended that the American novelist depict not American life but character in its universal qualities, although exactly what procedure he had in mind is open to question. In 1832, however, the *Mirror* deftly disarmed his objection. The author, as tradition agreed, should draw his agents from life; and since American life was alone well known to the American artist, he must obviously represent that. In 1840 the *Mirror* complained, "Our authors have a lamentable habit of running off to Europe to make novels." They should depict the life they know best.

THE AUTHOR AS REALIST

As works of art, novels should not present mere portraits, but must show agents who are true to nature. The 1837 *New York Review* praised Crabbe for having never violated for sickly sentiment the truth of life as he saw it. In the same year the *Knickerbocker* rated as the higher artist the man who invests the familiar with beauty, while it consigned to a far lower estate the former of unnatural or supernatural agents. The Wordsworthian undertone of this remark was repeatedly buttressed with Coleridge's theory of the fusing, creative imagination. In portraying the common man in America according to the tenets of Jacksonian democracy, the author had not yet arrived at the stage of realism.

In praising the poems of Crabbe, however, the 1837 *New York Review* had moved toward realism in art. In the 1840's, the *Democratic Review* took a further step in censuring what it considered Dickens' penchant for caricature: "his muse is *riant*, and oversteps the modesty of nature." The novelist was to represent life as he saw it, neither all virtuous nor all evil and grotesque. Here, however, a problem presented itself: should he portray both good and evil people realistically? As in other parts of the United States, this problem had presented itself point- edly to readers of Henry Fielding. There existed in life people who though attractive were not worthy of emulation, and moralists saw or fancied a danger in their depiction. The better magazines rallied gener- ally in support of the novelist's right to show men as they were. The 1847 *Democratic Review*'s likening the novelist to a faithful mirror of the nation indicates that the way was open for a realism that showed both good and bad agents, whether the writer of the article realized it or not.

Vigorous support for realism came from abroad in the popularity of Thackeray's *Vanity Fair*. Writing in 1848, the *Whig Review* retorted to adverse critics that he had been justified in portraying mostly dis- agreeable people since his tale required them. The author's purpose was to show people as they were, not as objects of emulation. Two years later, the *Literary World* regretted that American novelists did not portray people as actually as Thackeray did. Thackeray's first visit to the United States a year or two later, after *Pendennis* and *Henry Es- mond* had confirmed his reputation for realistic portrayal, was a tri-

umph in his various ports of call, but especially in New York, where
he got his most favorable reception and made many friends. This visit
enhanced the prestige of the newer representation of people as they
were. In 1855, *Putnam's* asked the American novelist to follow Thackeray's guidance in presenting so realistic a transcript of life as apparently
to be operating a camera lucida. In the same vein a year later, it dismissed Walter Scott as atypical, "an afterbirth of former centuries,"
and demanded of the novelist the life of the day depicted with genuine
feeling.

Reinforced by Thackeray's visit and example, novelists in the fifties
began to see clearly the realistic goal toward which they had been tend-
ing. To delineate real life, said the 1851 *Whig Review*, the novelist
must borrow from every other art. Far from merely recording data, he
must exercise the constructive faculty to saw and frame his lumber to
build his edifice. His work is as much an artistic creation as any great
drama. A year later, the same magazine warned the novelist not to deal
in shadows like Nathaniel Hawthorne, but in real, actual men; so doing,
he will feel and transmit a sense of "the strong pulse of nature throb-
bing beneath the turf he treads upon." The coming school of novelists,
the 1853 *Knickerbocker* accurately forecast, concentrates upon human
nature; and *Putnam's* a year later, spelling out the idea in more specific
detail, forecast that his new school would be vigorous and earnestly
veracious, in harmony with the more profoundly earnest spirit of the
age. The rank and file writers, catering to the popular market, continued
to write improbable romances, but for the significant thinkers the
proper subject of literary study was man, primarily in the United States
but also in the entire world. Considered as propaganda, the realistic
novel of American life in American settings was preferred to that dealing with foreign materials, and New Yorkers were well aware of such
values. Considered as literature, it was at once a reaction against the
pallid and improbable romances that were ground out by the presses
and a true representation of life.

M. H. Abrams has recently listed four elements of a work of art, with
one or another of which critics have at various times primarily busied
themselves. These are the artistic product, the artist, the universe or
"nature," and the audience. He classifies the romantic period as the
culmination of an interest in the artist which had been increasing since
the times of Hobbes and Locke. This classification applies also to the
New York literary public, but with one significant modification. Since
New Yorkers emphasized the artist's duties as patriot, propagandist,
and depicter of the real America, their concern with the artist was more

strongly bound up with the other three elements of art than was the case with their transatlantic romantic brethren. The effectiveness of the artist's work was of practical import to them. They demanded that he represent their segment of the universe and checked his performance in this respect. And they were conscious, at times almost morbidly so, of the audience upon whom this propaganda was to be exerted. This is not to say that they lacked men who added to these utilitarian views a considerable aesthetic consciousness and a strong sense of art-values— William A. Jones and Evert A. Duyckinck readily present themselves as competent art critics in literature—but the distinctive flavor of New York literary thinking about the artist, as in other matters, tasted strongly of politics and business.

WHAT IS POETRY?

Attempts to define poetry fared no better in New York than they have fared down through the ages. Since the wise men of Gotham had inherited the long tradition of Europe, they had ready-made ideas on the nature of poetry that made redefinition less pressing than in the case of the novel. They knew the classical concepts of poetry, somewhat warped to be sure from Renaissance, neoclassical, and current romantic interpretations. Bryant, for instance conceived of Aristotle's mimetic theory in terms of Lord Kames and Thomas Twining. They knew little about the Italian Renaissance, but had read extensively in Elizabethan and neoclassical theory that derived from it. They had some acquaintance with French classical theory and were beginning to read with interest German criticism since the time of Gotthold E. Lessing. Romantic thinking from England and the Continent was available to them; in addition to the British periodicals, some were reading magazines published in France. Without venturing many times to define poetry, they presented in their periodicals comments significant of the peculiar modifications that New York made in viewing the art.

Like other Americans of their day, New Yorkers read and composed a great deal of verse. Their leveling democratic principles led them to think of genius much as the eighteenth century had looked upon taste, as an innate quality of many men. That they were mistaken in their belief in genius as a relatively common characteristic, the quality of verse published in their magazines attests. Morris in his 1829 *Mirror* claimed the right to reject the bad and revise the passable before printing it; yet he had to admit the mediocrity of most contributions sent him. One of his bitterest comments was delivered in the 1830 *Mirror:* "A recent Boston work contained, we believe, the names of something like a hundred living American poets (heaven save the mark!) but we much doubt if a candid critic would not be sadly puzzled to single out from these, a dozen who stand the least chance of being read and admired in another generation." His list, beginning with Bryant and Halleck from New York, included only six who he thought would live, and the fact that Bryant alone of them is now remembered shows the undue optimism even of the skeptic. The new crop of poets, he added, possessed what he called genius, but "not properly cultured and restrained" by study and labor. Although other editors were seldom so outspoken in condemnation of American versifying as a whole, their agreement with Morris is evident.

However disappointing the actual product in the United States, there was general agreement that the new country must have its national poetry; and perhaps their dissatisfaction with their general ill success spurred American litterateurs to consider the more carefully the poetic art. Their random comments on the nature of poetry are helpful to show how New Yorkers regarded it.

At one extreme stood those who declared poetry to be indefinable. Such was the opinion of the 1837 *Knickerbocker.* Two years later, the *New York Review,* falling into the Platonic vein, asserted that poetry existed as an eternal idea to be partially discerned through the study of masterpieces and attending to one's responses to them. In the 1850's the *National Magazine* and the *Ladies' Repository,* concurring with Poe, saw poetry as being or building beauty. In such matters, where no practical or rational method of investigating the subject presented itself, New Yorkers were willing to yield room to the intuitive power, although Emerson's statements in "The Poet" were too visionary for most of them.

Other statements on the nature of poetry, although attempting to put it in a more understandable position, also lack definition. Bryant, while still actively engaged in practicing the art, spoke of poetry as the child of enthusiasm, begotten in moments of daemonic possession. The 1829 *Mirror* called it the language of the imagination. In 1837 the *New-Yorker* pessimistically placed it as the product of bygone, convulsive eras—a statement in which the 1847 *Knickerbocker* concurred. The two first statements though unobjectionable cast little light upon its nature; the third by its implied defeatism was repellent to patriots who demanded a national literature.

Admitting the unlikelihood of attaining full definition, some New York theorists nevertheless risked partial statements. Their practical common sense, refusing to yield to the mystical extremists among the romantic thinkers, insisted that there must be an art of poetry, a method of its working, and that therefore poetry lay within the area of rational investigation.

Bryant, whose significance for early American literary theory has been inadequately appreciated, made one of the earliest attempts at a partial definition. Speaking in 1826 before the New York Athenaeum, he took issue with Aristotle's concept of poetry as artistic imitation. Confusing the Platonic with the Aristotelian views of imitation, and confused by what he had read of the long commentary of the ages, he failed to grasp the fundamental part played by imitation in Aristotle's theory and overlooked the effects produced in imitation by differences in artistic media. He therefore classified the plastic arts alone as truly imitative—he was deeply concerned with their progress in New York—and placed poetry in a separate category as a suggestive art. His imperfect knowledge of Aristotle is indicated by his further statement, "ages ago the schools shook themselves loose from the fetters of Aristotle," an assertion that he would hardly have made if he had been thinking of the *Poetics* itself rather than of neoclassical perversions of its scholarly intent. The possibilities in poetry as a suggestive art occupied his attention in the greater part of his "Lectures on Poetry," and his penetrating remarks upon topics of importance to letters appear frequently in these pages.

Another early body of comment on the nature of poetry occurred between 1829 and 1832 in the *Mirror*, in unrelated but significant articles. Poetry was described as the product of severe toil by a person of cultivated, restrained genius and good sense. It was not morbid, not affectedly sentimental, not "namby-pamby madrigals of love"; nor was it merely whatever might occur to the mind of a man who has written poetry—a point that Richard P. Blackmur was to repeat a century later. It differed from philosophy in that it combined, whereas philosophy analyzed. As Sir Philip Sidney had shown, it stood above all other arts in its good effects. In fact, here as in other New York utterances on the art, the effects can be seen of the long combination of poetry with rhetoric whose beginnings appear in the first century A.D. in the work of Longinus. Bryant had in his lectures differentiated poetry from oratory solely in its metrical expression—a belief which no doubt helps to explain why he so readily shifted from poet to journalist and writer of editorials.

To these *disjecta membra* of poetic definition may be added two more. In 1837 the *Knickerbocker* noted the affinities of poetry to music in melody and consequent emotional effect—an idea implicit also in Poe's poetic theory. A year later, Jones described poetry as essentially democratic and, since he added democracy to the thirty-nine articles of his devout faith, on its highest level religious. Such isolated remarks, though hardly definitive, indicate the direction that New Yorkers' thought about poetry was taking. It was not merely a casual effusion, but a serious, thoughtful enterprise that could itself be rationally studied.

Some essays with a more carefully detailed definition now and then appeared. One of the earliest appeared in the 1830 *Mirror:* "Poetry is a description of animated or external nature, told in figurative, impassioned, yet natural language: rhyme is an attribute, not an essential of poetry." In this the emphasis upon the emotions of the poet, although applied to his language, is evident; and nature shares with man the subjective position. Nine years later, the *New York Review* resorted for definition to the proportional metaphor recommended by Aristotle: "Poetry fills in the world of thought the same place as flowers in the physical universe." The author, later Mrs. Julia Ward Howe, was concerned with the coincidence of poetic form with poetic content as well as with the poem's function to give aesthetic delight: translations of poems, she added, are "after all, but pressed flowers." In 1847, the *Knickerbocker*, roving beyond the poetry of words, defined poetry as "the language of the imagination, felt or uttered. It is not a thing of mere dactyls and spondees, but the outgush of a lofty genius, irrespective of the laws of versification." Whatever warms, cheers, or reassures the heart, "that object, be it what it may, is poetical." In these attempts at description if not true definition, two related views are apparent, both of them impatient of formal poetic restraint. First, whether they were aware of it or not, theorists were in accord with Plato's remark in the seventh book of the *Laws,* that lawmakers are in a sense tragic poets, for their devising of the state is also an imitation of the best and noblest life. New Yorkers believed with Emerson that America is a poem, and Whitman had only to pick up in 1855 an idea which he found in his New York and Concord reading. Secondly, these remarks again paralleled Emerson's opening the way for a poetry in which its soul, not conventional pattern, determined the bodily form of the poem. With these two influences at work upon him—and he expressed his debt to both—Whitman found little difficulty in breaking away from traditional versification when he decided he had new wine to put into his bottles.

A slightly later attempt at definition was indirectly the result of a charge by Lord Morpeth that American poets still worshiped at the shrine of Pope. Indignantly refuting his statement, the 1851 *Literary World* formulated an American concept of poetry that excluded nearly everything that the neoclassicist had taught while highlighting qualities that had been at the least objects of his deep suspicion. Poetry, the writer declared, is "the Art of giving expression to the subtlest effects of musical language, to the finest and noblest processes of the imagination, and the profoundest emotions of the heart." As in other attempts at definition of poetry, this assertion was more apologetic than objective. Americans, and especially New Yorkers, were less interested in abstract poetic theory than they were in the practice of the art and in its application to their peculiar problems. Poetry, to the New York reader and theorizer, was first an imaginative art, it is true. It was also —and more immediately significant in this sense—a means of furthering the development and advertisement of the United States by stating clearly the nature of American life, government, and aspirations. This was no time for theorizing about its nature. Moreover, the New Yorker generally reasoned that he was the heritor of British and earlier theorizing in this area; there seemed to be no profit in reworking fields already cropped. Wherever theory was inadequate or inapplicable to the new democracy, it should be modified or revised to fit the United States; otherwise, it was sound economy to use what was already available.

AIMS AND ENDS OF POETRY

Horace had mapped the path that poetry should follow: poets should instruct, or give pleasure, or preferably accomplish both ends together. This direction had stood the test of eighteen centuries; it allowed considerable flexibility in the proportions of the two ingredients, and New Yorkers saw no reason to depart from it. Its instruction should include the presentation of ideas and depictions of the United States, and the support of strong morals and true religion, thus benefiting the new country both at home and abroad. Overt didacticism, however, found little support. New York had been spared the dominance of that horde of moral and religious reformers ironically described by Emerson as flourishing in New England, and even religiously inclined journals doubted the efficacy of versified didacticism. There were of course moral and religious reformers aplenty in the city as elsewhere, but they dwelt in the fringe areas of public attention, representing on the whole obscurantist or nonartistic groups, and therefore need not hold our attention.

Poetry, Bryant declared in 1826, powerfully and delightfully excites thought. Generalizing what the *Literary Gazette,* of which he was a joint editor, had spelled out a year earlier, he claimed for poetry the right to inculcate such truths as are instinctively admitted by the mind —a doctrine that has recently been preached in elevating the religious ideas of Dante as better poetic material than those of John Milton. The 1838 *New York Review,* itself a quarterly with close religious affiliations, published an article by Evert Duyckinck which denied to the ultra-reformer the use of poetry as a medium of propaganda. Poetry deals with facts, the same magazine declared two years later, but it illuminates them by principles; Sidney had called it philosophy teaching by example. And the 1857 *Putnam's* closed the discussion for this period by assigning to poetry the function recently claimed for it by Allen Tate, of bridging the gap between the ideal and the actual. Whitman's statement in 1855 that it shows the relation between reality and men's souls had its concomitants in New York thought.

As for the moral effect of poetry, Bryant had said in 1826 that it powerfully moves us toward good moral conduct and enables us to discern good from evil. Its moral power lay in its capacity to move rather than in its capability to instruct. The 1837 *Knickerbocker,* in one of the rare aesthetic views of poetry in New York, admitted that such a moral effect was no doubt desirable but considered it hardly necessary. Three years later, the *New York Review,* which in 1838 had denied to reformers the use of poetry for their propaganda, would have a moral idea pervasive of the poem to provide it with a vital, unifying principle; but it denied that a literary work must show poetic justice in the outcome of its plot. In 1848, Charles Astor Bristed, no strait-laced moralist in belief or conduct, demanded that poetry occupy a mean position between defiance of accepted codes of morality and whole-hearted acceptance of them.

Although the term morals was commonly restricted to the terms of the Ten Commandments, implicit in the words of thinking men was its larger aspect denoted more accurately by the term mores. The Judaeo-Christian virtues received lip service by the most cosmopolitan, and reverence by the majority; yet the variability of mores in different cultures and different stages of a national culture was also recognized. Unrestricted, in contrast to New England, by a dominant Brahmin culture and a Puritan-conditioned populace, New York theorists felt less hesitation in objectively evaluating other than the traditional American mores; and this freedom naturally affected their literary practice.

Those religious journals which occupied the fringe areas of New York opinion and were organs of traditionally oriented sects naturally fulminated against works that seemed to them to be unorthodox or at variance with their several distinctive principles. The more literary journals, whether church-affiliated or not, treated sound religious doctrine as a desirable adjunct rather than an essential of poetry. The Episcopal *New York Review* in 1837 desired that poetry favorably affect sound religion and praised devout poets as diverse as George Herbert and Crabbe; it also spoke discriminatingly of Goethe, who conformed to neither criterion, and gave a friendly reception to a long article on Honoré de Balzac. Its articles written on specifically religious or theological subjects were kept separate from its literary discussions. Ten years later, the nonsectarian *Knickerbocker* in the same vein remarked casually that poetry was the better for giving Christian or moral uplift. The *Mirror* steadfastly resisted repeated attempts by religious groups at religious supervision. Its editor, though frankly professing Christian beliefs and interests, warned them to keep their hands off his literary periodical.

Concern with morals and religious faith is intimately bound up with the socio-political relations of poetry: whatever affects our sensibilities, Bryant had declared in 1826, is part of our moral education, and by influencing the individual produces significant effects upon society. However the members of the New York Athenaeum may have understood him, it seems inescapable that Bryant was thinking of morals in the broader sense of the mores of a society. *Arcturus* in 1840 countered with insistence that poetry also represent the society in which it is produced as well as serve its prophetic mission. The 1843 *Democratic Review* added that true poetry always conveys the most significant and striking features of its time. Six years earlier, in the first flush of its Jacksonian heat, it had trumpeted the assertion that poetry had always been the advocate of liberty; and it had by this time broadened the scope of poetry to all the definitive qualities of the right democratic society. In 1856 *Putnam's*, in less specific terms but still more inclusively, declared that poetry values its materials directly as they are favorable to man. Although some of these attitudes will receive more detailed treatment later, these comments serve to briefly indicate the position of poetry as a force active upon society.

New York litterateurs intertwined the instructive and pleasurable ends of poetry more closely than did their New England neighbors. Bryant had set the keynote in 1826 by coupling its aid to man's happiness and welfare with its relation to the intelligence, the imagination, and the passions. The children of this world in Gotham, wise in practical concerns, could hardly have separated these effects upon man as they saw him: not so much a rounded personality as an oblate spheroid like the earth he inhabited—somewhat depressed in elevation and broadened on the horizontal axis like Irving's Knickerbockers. In 1836 the traditionally minded Gulian Verplanck, shrewd in politics as in business, yet deeply concerned with literature as well, defended the Horatian tenet that poetry guides or pleases its readers; to him, however, the chief pleasure lay in public service—political, moral, or cultural. The breadth of his concern with letters included his composition of political satire, his editing of the works of Richard Sands, and in later years his editing of Shakespeare. The 1844 *Knickerbocker* fused the instructive with the enjoyable by asserting that descriptive poetry gives pleasure through investing its scenes with moral interest. Five years later, the *Literary World* took an opposed position: the poem *must* please; if it also gave instruction, so much the better. Between these extremes there were naturally many combinations of the two elements; and for a quarter-century after Bryant's statement to the New York Athenaeum, New York writers generally assumed that these two elements normally were combined in poetry.

During the final decade of the period, it is true, an interest in the more nearly aesthetic values of poetry found some expression. It is difficult to assess the sources of this movement at their proper value. New Yorkers were reading Ruskin, though with mixed reactions; his influence cannot be ignored. They were noticing the poems of Tennyson and Browning; and the elevation of Tennyson to the position of poet laureate in 1850 did not decrease their interest. Many knew the objective methods of Charles Sainte-Beuve in looking at literature; these at least weakened the force of didacticism and concern with the response of the audience to propaganda. At home, they had exhausted themselves in, or been bored by, the missionary antics of the "Young Americans" and their attempt to remake the world through letters. They had also been stirred, not always to friendly response, by the acid journalism of Poe, whose aesthetic emphasis was known to many editors and their readers.

The 1850's were not primarily concerned with poetry; yet some instances of the burgeoning aesthetic interest deserve mention. In a post-

mortem on Poe, the 1850 *Literary World* demanded that poetry paint
an idea; it should not attempt to demonstrate it. The *Whig Review* in
the same year, echoing Poe, stated as one object of poetry the begetting
and fostering of the perception of the beautiful. Continuing in Poe's
vaguely Platonic vein, it desired that poetry stir a divine discontent
with terrestrial things and a yearning for things above. If poetry is to
create a satisfactory product, it added, the ideal must be clothed in the
garb of the actual. Three years later, the *National Magazine* quoted
Poe's phrase in declaring that poetry does create beauty. Less clearly
and on a more popular level, the 1855 *Ladies' Repository*—which combined culture and piety in saccharine articles—followed Poe at somewhat greater distance: poetry builds something beautiful, and its true
mission is to exalt the mind. The editor was obviously dissatisfied with
Poe's affiliation of poetry to taste instead of to the moral sense.

New Yorkers were, however, not quite ready for a divorcement of
poetry from instruction or propaganda. In 1855, *Putnam's*—one of the
most influential magazines of the decade—firmly subordinated the
arousal of sublime feeling to the stirring of profound thought. This
position was established in a review of Tennyson's poetry. Admitting
that Tennyson was also "an exquisite singer," the writer set him apart
from other nineteenth-century prominent British poets; "his heart beats
with the time, and his sympathies are strong for the noblest human
aims." Shelley had the same tendency, but lacked the "strong English
common sense" that this New York mouthpiece naturally required of
poetry. "Of all these men, except, perhaps, Keats, Tennyson is the
purest poet or singer [pure poetry may be singing, but the writer does
not care for the pure product]: and it is remarkable that he should be
also the most earnest in thought. . . . His mind is essentially manly.
. . . He is not afraid to think more than to feel, and he expresses the
thought with an incredibly subtle precision." He does not preach because he thinks. "There is no twang of the sermon as in the prosy William Wordsworth; but the spirit, the thought, and the form, are all
entirely poetic." Wordsworth claimed that he felt the sober realities
of life, but "Tennyson makes us feel that he feels" them. A year later,
Putnam's repeated that the warmest and best English poetry expressed
the more natural feelings. With the sober realities of life looming ever
more imminent as the decade wore on to the election of Lincoln with
its consequences, New Yorkers were in no mood for the aesthetic approach to anything.

To sum up the predominant New York attitudes as to the purpose of
poetry: with the run-of-the-mine didactic concept of poetry, the liter-

ary opinions of Gotham had little sympathy; they refused to knuckle under to this sectarian-sponsored view, however much they felt its pressure. They did not, with Poe, go so far as to consider poetry only incidentally a teacher, nor were they in fact ready for the aesthetic approach to it. Poetry, they generally believed, expressed a sound fund of thought without demonstrating its proof; its instruction at best was pervasive and implicit, without sententious utterances or sermonizing; and its purpose was to purvey an elevated, universally human, intellectual combination of profit and pleasure that should be characteristic of the United States.

SUBJECTS AND MATERIALS

Nature

Although the earlier New York writers were well grounded in the polymorphous presentations of nature in the writings of the preceding century, they devoted little attention to abstract considerations of it. Their reception of Emerson's statements about nature was no more than lukewarm. In New York the term "nature" was bound up with the American scene and with the Wordsworthian nature revival. The Lake poet's enthusiasm for nature was not widely encouraged. Objects drawn from nature, the 1825 *Literary Gazette* admonished its readers, are not *ipso facto* poetical, nor are works of art necessarily unsuited for poetry. In fact, it continued, descriptions of nature are among the lesser poetical beauties. Twelve years later, the *New York Review* confirmed this position: the capacity to describe is only one of several poetic qualities. The belief that poetry is a description of animated or external nature, sandwiched between these two affirmations by the 1830 *Mirror*, was unacceptable to the New York literary thinkers. As the 1839 *Democratic Review* stated the position of the majority, nature provides external influences to which the poet must be delicately susceptible, but he writes what he has seen and thought in his mind. The *New York Review* in the same year repeated the Aristotelian-based idea that poetry presents creations like nature, and it added that they do not seem to be strange because they are compounded of nature and truth. Although Wordsworth had his admirers in the city, his approach to nature was generally misunderstood and consequently opposed. By the 1830's Bryant, his strongest proponent, had shifted his activities to journalism; and R. H. Dana, Sr., a Wordsworthian who made New York a second home, was never a compelling voice there. For the New Yorker, Wordsworth was too unworldly to attract much favorable attention.

Various poetic uses of nature found their advocates. Anticipating Emerson by a decade, Bryant had declared that poetry shows correspondences between the physical and moral worlds and can illustrate either by the other. Far from expressing a transcendental view, however, he seems rather to have been thinking in the vein of Sidney's contrast of poetry to history and philosophy, although he had seen more deeply also into Wordsworth's concept of nature than had his New York contemporaries. The 1844 *Knickerbocker*, attacking merely descriptive verse, declared that the best effect it could produce emotionally was to arouse the pleasure of recognition through awakened associations. Its scenes should be invested with moral interest if it were to be classed as true poetry, for interest comes less from the image than from the idea—a position more popular in the first half of nineteenth-century New York than in the corresponding period of twentieth-century America. With an admixture of Poe's doctrine, the 1850 *Whig Review* declared that true poetry idealizes natural objects which beget and foster the perception of the beautiful. Of this statement as of the preceding remarks, no New York critic of the period felt moved to work out those implications which have recently assumed greater importance.

Toward the end of the period, interest in nature poetry as a form declined among literary New Yorkers. *Putnam's* in 1856 classified the enthusiasm for nature so rife among readers as a mere poetic delusion, "little belonging to true poetry." The writer, who shared the view that poetry is at its best in primitive societies, added: "We mistake an acquired taste for a natural feeling. In the earliest poetry of nations, and even in the perfect classics, we do not find any of the passion for natural objects. . . . Matter was not at all spiritualized—it only received a mythologic dress, so to speak. But everything in nature was estimated as it was favorable or unfavorable to men." Although the writer did not say so, writers of verse were apparently attempting to aid readers to escape from the threatening immediate future by directing their attention to changeless natural objects. Along with other periodicals of the day, *Putnam's* asserted in true New York fashion not only that the proper study of mankind was man, but that literature had a practical value amid man's complex immediate problems.

Ideas

Our poetic themes, said the romantic writers, now include not only the mind but also the heart. For most New York thinkers, these two were separate concepts, although they must act in concert. Bryant's statement that poetry presents such ideas as are perceived without logical demonstration gives the clue to the general attitude, especially when combined with his comment that the poetic image finds its way to the heart when warmed by the passions. Strong feeling rarely offends against good taste; it may transgress established rules provided that it reach the heart. The presentation of the emotions was part of the business of poetry, yet the mind usually predominated; and *Arcturus* in 1840 declared that even the current poetry which no longer portrayed passion remained nonetheless "a tender companion and dear friend." When emotional poetry was shortly restored, the mind still retained its pre-eminent position for most New York literary men. Jones and Tuckerman spoke for the primacy of emotions as poetic material, and the 1856 *Putnam's* called poetry the language of enthusiasm. In general, however, theorists tried to keep emotions subsidiary to ideas. Without emotional appeal, poetry would fail of its purposes, but the poet was first and foremost a proclaimer of ideas.

The poet, as we have seen, could not be a madman. Although he needs the imaginative power, said the 1825 *Literary Gazette*, even this important faculty must not be exalted and developed to the detriment or disregard of the reason. A year later, Bryant listed the imagination as only one in a triad to which poetry should appeal; the others were the passions and the understanding. Poetry, he repeatedly affirmed, demands the highest intellectual faculties rationally employed. Throughout this romantic literary age, although the New York litterateurs continued the romantic revolt against the Age of Reason, they campaigned vigorously and constantly for the poetry of ideas; and as the Victorian age came upon them, they became as prone to what to John Crowe Ransom is the sin against the poetic holy ghost as the British themselves.

The reason and the intellect were elevated above several other qualities of poetry. The 1832 *Mirror* flatly rejected the eighteenth-century emphasis upon poetic finish: poetry consists in the thought, not in the trimmings. Evert Duyckinck in the 1840 *New York Review* declared that the future poetry must be philosophical, by which he meant that it should not only be speculative but investigative of the world and the social scene. It should, added the *Democratic Review* for 1845, foster serious views; it must be thoughtful and vigorous. *Putnam's* a decade later praised the contemporary British poets, especially Tennyson, for their high-minded seriousness, for daring to think as well as to feel. For most New Yorkers, poetry presented ideas made appealing by emotional treatment but not warped by it. Although Poe's assertion that it was doubtful if men had ever really thought before his age probably amused them, they saw their century as the age of thought. Without clinging to the previous Age of Reason, they would preserve its merits in the present emotional era.

Imagery

Few New Yorkers a century ago would have sympathized with the current emphasis on the poetic image. Poetry painted a picture, Bryant conventionally agreed; but the substitution of the image for the idea never occurred to him or his contemporaries. It was not mere superimposed ornament, he agreed with Coleridge, but an integral part of the poem. Paraphrase would have been to him as evil a perversion as it appears to Cleanth Brooks. Images, he said, in order to kindle the imagination, must be suggested by the matter of the poem, spontaneously generated in a mind warmed and filled by its subject. Under these circumstances they occur intuitively to the poet. Being spontaneous, they cannot be forced; emotion is the key to the storehouse of imagery.

A decade and more later, the *Knickerbocker* added that metaphors are to poetry what color is to painting. They must be laid on with the same nicety; too profusely mingled, they confuse the design of which they should be essential parts. Only a correct taste can determine their proper use. It agreed with Aristotle that the author proves his quality by judicious employment of figurative language, especially of metaphor. He must present an image distinct to the intellectual eye, a directive at variance with Poe's practice but in full harmony with the beliefs in New York.

A denigration of imagery occasionally appeared, a reaction probably against eighteenth-century usage. The 1839 *Mirror* classed coherence of metaphor below correct opinion, brilliant thought, or beauty of sentiment; to it imagery was of minor importance. It was apparently battling the employment of imagery recommended by those "rule-and-figure critics" Hugh Blair and Kames, against whom the defenders of imagery were likewise arrayed. However we admire lofty imagery, Tuckerman declared in 1850, it is the sentiment that touches us; expletives and strained metaphors cannot add to the sublime fact. Antipathy to imagery no doubt contributed to the 1851 *Literary World*'s sneer that Longfellow offered his readers "titbits of imagery, gathered from a thousand sources and prettily garnished with flowers." In 1853 *Putnam's* charged a fellow New Yorker, Herman Melville, with writing in a style plated with imagery: "he has a barbaric love of ornament, and does not mind how it is put on." Four years later it accused

him of having distorted the images in his mind before committing them
to paper, and thus spoiling their veracity and significance.

The period was in fact so devoted to the presentation of its ideas that
it made little progress in its thinking about the image beyond Bryant's
penetrating remarks in 1826. In this as in other literary matters, his defection to journalism must be considered a serious loss to letters. Although other writers occasionally adverted to the power of imagery,
they seem to have been actuated rather by distaste for obsolescent
theories of letters and by the need to make poetry palatable to the
populace than by constructive theory.

Beauty

The concept that poetry was the rhythmical creation of beauty, revived by Poe's death in 1849 and by the early volumes of Ruskin's
Modern Painters, briefly occupied the attention of the critics. Browning's poems with Renaissance cultural settings had also roused some
interest in the world of art. In spite of these influences, as well as the
less widely disseminated interest in German speculations, New York
writers showed little interest in discussing this abstraction. They generally accepted it as an element of poetry without attempting to examine it. Vague references to Platonic ideas do not indicate direct
acquaintance with his concept of beauty.

Beauty, said Bryant, is a quality whose presence distinguishes poetry
from prosaic writing; what is poetic not only excludes all that disgusts
but—and here Bryant by several years anticipated Poe—aspires after
superhuman beauty. But except for the early 1850's with their reaction
to Poe, only random remarks upon beauty in poetry occur. The 1825
Literary Gazette had found beauty to emanate from accurate delineation of character and profound knowledge of human nature. Twelve
years later the *Knickerbocker* advised the poet to focus his view upon
the beauty, delicacy, and force in the familiar and to avoid the unnatural. As a practical suggestion, it added that a beautiful sententious
thought is a sound mnemonic device. The 1845 *Democratic Review*
linked manly, serious, and beautiful views as effects produced by the
reading of poetry.

In addition to the aesthetic hints already noted, the 1850's ventured
a few remarks on poetry and beauty. One object of poetry, declared
the 1850 *Whig Review*, is to beget and foster the love of the beautiful.
The 1853 *National Magazine* accepted Poe's definition of poetry as the
only true statement of its nature; and the 1856 *Ladies' Repository* added

an echo of Keats: poetry is beauty, beauty is truth, and truth is eternal.
Every poet, it affirmed, must be able to *build* something beautiful and
true. But enquiries into the nature of beauty were not a major concern
of the New York litterateurs, who believed they had more pressing
problems to ponder than abstractions.

VERSE

For various reasons, New Yorkers exercised their pens far more extensively in discussing poetic techniques than upon problems of greater
literary scope. So far as poetic theory was concerned, they were on the
whole satisfied to adapt for American democratic use what they had
inherited from England. Since they were concerned to produce an
American as opposed to a European literature, and one that was democratic rather than monarchical or aristocratic, the details of this new
literature concerned them immediately. Although individual reaction
to the value of the courtly muses of Europe varied considerably, most
were agreed that the Western literature should be a legitimate offspring
of the Western world. They were accordingly alert to problems of
versification, diction, and that elusive thing called style.

Of these three requirements for the embodiment of poetry, versification troubled them the least. They accepted the conventions of prosody
but felt free to adapt them to their desires. In 1814, echoing Horace as
he frequently did, Verplanck had asked the American poet to produce
good verse that showed no concern with the hard labor needed to compose it. Verplanck, conservative in most things, was no innovator in
verse. Bryant, however, even before he had moved to New York had
defended the intermixture of trisyllabic feet in iambic verse. His ideas
were received with mixed feelings but no extended discussion by the
few who were moved to comment upon them. The *Mirror* through its
editor, Morris, complained bitterly of the slovenly versification of the
lyrics submitted to it and reserved the right to smooth out and otherwise improve those poems it was ready to print. A nice ear for harmony,
Morris said, was the gift of nature, and he was confident that he possessed it. In 1839, he counted a good ear for rhythm and taste in poetical
expression high on the list of the poet's requirements, but emphasized
their insignificance unless accompanied by higher gifts. "An unfortunate knack of tagging rhymes" had deluded many into thinking themselves poets. A decade later, Jones wrote that a fatal facility of turning
out verses must be enriched with a "curious felicity of expression" if
the poet's performance were to reach high quality; but to him as to
most critics other ingredients outweighed prosodic techniques or re-

quirements of expression. Poe's detailed analysis of meters in his reviews found few parallels in New York.

Let the verses be lame, provided these higher ingredients passed the critical test. According to the 1837 *Knickerbocker*, occasional false rhythms and inharmonious words are more than counterbalanced by other "abounding graces of language and diction, and by a pervading spirit of pure feeling, and moral and religious sentiment." As late as 1853, an admirer of Scott excused inferior verses in the *Lay of the Last Minstrel* on the ground that every word and expression showed complete propriety. The writer, as was frequently the case, neglected to define the term propriety; critics then as now were prone to an indeterminate, semiprofessional jargon. If, as most New York literary men agreed, ideas are the dominant requirement in poetry, then diction must express them clearly and attractively, whether verses limp or not.

In this connection, the admission of prosaic elements into the poem was hotly debated. Many thought that all lines containing nonpoetic expressions—again there was uncertainty as to what these were—should be pitilessly excised. With the increasing emphasis upon ideas, however, such purists fell into the background. An organic whole, according to the 1855 *Knickerbocker*, gives its vitality to its every part, and therefore normally nonpoetic expressions legitimately find their place in it. With this ingenious begging of the question, a problem which had vexed Dryden and Pope was summarily dismissed.

Under the circumstances just related, there were naturally no detailed studies of prosody. Romantic theorists had defended the use of novel verse-forms; the democratic feelings of the New Yorkers looked impatiently upon what seemed to them to be aristocratic restraints; and the transcendental doctrine that the soul makes the body which Emerson had been preaching was leaven working in at least the more radical thinkers. To men who felt so strongly that the new democracy had to express itself in new ways, the concept of democratic literature did not seem the hot ice and wondrous strange snow that it appears to be to us. Whitman's complete abandonment of traditional verse, viewed in the light of the circumstances, seems hardly surprising. Although his own generation refused to accept his innovations, they were a natural result of the forces at work, and the objections were motivated more by what seemed indecorous in content rather than in form.

DICTION

In the early years of the nineteenth century, New York critics were frequently concerned about the diction of American writers; with the passing decades interest in style supplanted to a great extent the discussions of words. For the most part, writers expressed much the same ideas whether they were discussing poetry or prose fiction; diction and style will accordingly be treated here for both literary forms.

Verplanck set the conservative pattern for early remarks on diction when he insisted that the author must always be in command of his linguistic medium. Words, he declared, are always to be employed in their true and received meanings, without the warping that critics of the next century were to approve. The poet must not yield to the pressure of the provincialisms in American speech, slovenly colloquialisms, or anomalous impurities. None of these convey the sense of the poet's true strength. Verplanck's standard, as one would expect of his precise nature and practical experience, was stricter than that advocated by most younger critics; yet his demand for purity and exactness of diction was frequently iterated.

Prior to the linguistic uproar attendant upon the appearance of Carlyle's essays in New York, the 1817 *American Monthly Magazine* had complained that extravagant language was then the sole passport to circulation among romance-hungry readers. Milton and Pope are no longer followed as models; they have been supplanted by a barbarous jargon with medieval overtones fathered by Walter Scott. Also on the conservative flank, the 1825 *New York Review* censured Cooper's use of common words in other than their accepted meanings and his tangled syntactical constructions. The 1829 *Mirror* likewise condemned an otherwise interesting work for its recurrent vulgarisms and inept syntax. In attacking "gew-gaw" English the 1834 *Knickerbocker* declared, "we are somewhat fastidious about good grammar and good English," for the lack of which no other merits could atone. To their credit be it said, the better monthlies and quarterlies in New York presented their articles in styles which, though sometimes ponderous, were as a rule couched in clear, attractive diction. For the poet, it was obvious, language was more important than prosody because errors in its use could deface or confuse the all-important meaning. As the *American Monthly Magazine* remarked in 1817 of Miss Maria Edgeworth's novels, utility had ever been their characteristic; they conveyed truth clearly and forcibly.

With the advent of Carlyle, Emerson, Bronson Alcott, and other lovers of the "literary Germanosities of the day," attacks upon abusers of diction doubled in violence. Emerson, although frequently reproved for his diction, was on the whole respected; Alcott was rejected as incomprehensible. When he complained that he could not find an organ

to express his views, one New York magazine suggested that he use a
hand organ. Carlyle bore the brunt of the attack as presumably the
greater enemy to sound expression. Objecting to the "windy verbosi-
ties" vented by him and other transcendental writers, the 1838 *Knickerbocker* besought them to learn propriety and terseness of diction and
avoid extravagance and affectation. A year later it condemned "their
interminable periods . . . and endless interlacings of diction; their
countermarchings and inversions of the component parts of sentences;
their pompous wordiness, and distension of periods." Of Carlyle's works,
Sartor Resartus alone found any favor: although filled with German
idioms, it was still on the whole comprehensible. Thomas Macaulay,
although in a different literary camp from Carlyle, was also considered
a dangerous model; his expression was suited to his copious information
but should be imitated only by those who could match his fund of
knowledge. The New Yorkers' desire for a practical medium of expression could not accept the cloudy ideas of German transcendentalism
nor the misty expression which they fostered.

The practical concern of reviewers and critics descended into details
of expression: dialect words, provincialisms, jargon, archaisms, and
foreign words. From Aristotle to Wordsworth, these had been advocated in moderation as proper embellishments of style; in New York
they were more severely scrutinized.

Dialect words came under heavy fire. If Scott's barbarous, unintelligible words are defensible, the 1822 *Niles' Weekly Register* opined, Cooper would be justified if he should use the Mohawk dialect in his forthcoming *The Pioneers.* The *American Monthly Magazine* a decade later
warned William Gilmore Simms to strip his work of provincial expressions: they were permissible only in dialogue and to be used spar-
ingly there. No author whose diction was vulgar could hope to survive.
If prose fiction received such linguistic scrutiny, one can imagine the
hedges built about the diction of poetry with its long tradition of expression. The 1837 *Knickerbocker* indicated something of this restric-
tive severity in refusing to countenance in prose or poetry words and
phrases that were not of long-established English literary usage and
adopted through the practice of the best authors. In an appreciation of
Fitz-Greene Halleck's poems the 1852 *Literary World* found their outstanding literary merits to include "their honest, straightforward adherence to the good old-fashioned standards of the language. They express genuine emotion in plain English, and they do not profess to
swell, and burst, and evaporate over an enormous surface of misty and
incomprehensible speculation." The 1856 *Ladies' Repository* asserted

the highest effort of genius consisted in making suitable language for poetic ideas, and came out rather strongly for English undefiled as their vehicle. The standards of style, however, remained as undefined almost as the concept of style itself. In this respect, as in so many others, literary men used tags and labels which had inadequately defined reference.

Jargon was less a problem than it is today because there were fewer professional and trade groups with their shoptalk and specialized terms. There is a slight indication that New Yorkers worried less about it than did their neighbors, as may be seen in the reaction to Cooper's sea-novels. The 1824 Philadelphia *Port Folio* regretted that he had filled *The Pilot* with marine jargon that could be understood only by sailors, and urged him to continue in the vein of Leatherstocking. The *United States Literary Gazette* in the same year declared *The Pilot* to be his best novel yet; and the *Mirror*, although finding fault with a few easily corrected obscure passages, praised his clarity above Scott's. The sea, it added, is Cooper's own element, and *The Pilot* a succession of beautiful sea-pictures that would do credit to any pen. If not the most free from faults, it is one of the most interesting novels written in America. It was not, surely, that New Yorkers were better acquainted than Philadelphians with the sea, but they were by virtue of their diverse concerns perhaps more tolerant of professional terminology.

New York reviewers and the more educated readers of course bowed to Horace's well-known sanction of revived words in poetic vocabulary. They contended correctly, however, that Horace had not countenanced the frequent insertion of such terms, with which romantic writers had interlarded their works. The *Mirror* for 1823 found fault with a minor poet for apparently trying to build his reputation upon the use of hard words, "some of which have long since become obsolete." Verplanck in 1834 found the archaisms of *Yamoyden* too frequent for his taste: its phrases and constructions were frequently not worth the reviving. The 1841 *Knickerbocker* felt that Emerson's vocabulary was often unjustifiably quaint; he brought back expressions unused since Shakespeare's day that were meaningless without a glossary. His thoughts would be effective if they were stripped of their "grotesque garb of motley language"—the term "motley" suggesting perhaps a slur also upon his thoughts. Browning's diction seemed to a writer in the 1849 *Literary World* to have merely substituted a new vocabulary for the old poetic diction, a new evil substituted for the old. Horace's purpose, to add only needed words to the active Latin vocabulary, was quite in harmony with the practical tastes of New York; superabundant ornament that confused the meaning was not.

Horace approved also of enriching the language by sparing use of words from foreign languages, slightly modified into Latin forms. Writers in the early nineteenth century, especially novelists, had introduced many foreign words into frequent use, a practice strongly disapproved by the 1823 *Mirror*. The poet must not use words that "seem to have been newly manufactured from the Greek, Latin, or French, and have never yet found their way into an English dictionary. This, of itself, is an unpardonable offence in any poem." The invasion of German terms was still some years in the future, a chiefly post–Civil War phenomenon; but the reaction against other foreign sources of words indicates rather clearly how it would have been opposed. The *Mirror* also inveighed against the insertion into English poems of Greek verses in Greek characters, which threw headlong into the mud the reader who had been galloping along with the English dactyls.

By 1835, the *Mirror* noted, novelists were liberally seasoning the dialogue of fashionable novels with foreign words and phrases. Ironically taking the novelist's point of view, it remarked: "All precedent is in favour of a very copious introduction of French and Italian to express what, to the apprehension of ordinary people, might be expressed quite as well in English." The stupidly pedantic parson, moreover, who is standard equipment of such novels, must spout Latin tags. If the novelist has a nodding acquaintance with these tongues, all he need do is to translate the most commonplace remarks into the appropriate language for the speaker, and he has created dialogue. Two years later, the *Knickerbocker* declared that the American speech was rich enough to need no admixture of French phrases. Foreign terms neither clarified nor beautified the expression; to New York theorists they were simply superfluities to be discarded or veils to be ripped off.

Words, in fine, were symbols designed to express ideas clearly and persuasively. Whether in prose or poetry—the problem for the two differed only in detail—fidelity to the idea held paramount importance. All else should be employed only to render the idea attractive without concealing or distorting it. The underlying theory was less organic, as a rule, than practical, as a few comments from the magazines will show. The 1824 *Atlantic Magazine* ruled against the current tendency of lighter compositions to pack their expression with needless allusions: such practice laid an unsound alien basis for the nascent American literature. Willis' blank verse, the *American Monthly Magazine* forcefully declared, expressed but few ideas. Perhaps it was not the "d——d unintelligible irredeemable nonsense" that another reviewer had called it; it was nontheless a mere facile stringing of mellifluous words. Where meaning is present, said the 1839 *Democratic Review,* truly delicate and refined diction rules out all turgidness.

Carlyle again provided the target for the critics in his style. He uses language to conceal his thoughts, charged the 1839 *Mirror:* like an ancient oracle, he is full of mysticism, obscurity, and humbug. The 1843 *Knickerbocker* brought similar charges against its favorite whipping boy, Cornelius Mathews. The Centurion, as he was ironically nicknamed, was little better than Carlyle. He seemed to "fire away with the high-soundingest words he can get, whereby his meaning looms larger than it is, like a fishing-boat in a fog. . . . Where there is such a ground-swell of language, there can be no great depth of ideas." The 1848 *Whig Review* chimed in: it was a common device of small poets to make sound supply the place of sense instead of echoing it. Even great power over language can, said Jones, degenerate into mere verbosity; this fault had spoiled the fine talent of Thomas Moore. Melville also, according to the 1853 *Putnam's,* had been betrayed by his barbaric love of ornament and subjection to round, luscious words.

These excesses in diction were uniformly ascribed to the undisciplined virility of the adolescent nation; they were a sign of vibrant health, that needed only a minimum of restraint and proper guidance. For such vigor, it was at first thought, Wordsworth's advocacy of ordinary speech for poetic expression provided too feeble a medium; the 1825 *Atlantic Magazine* condemned it as utterly unworthy of his own work and mind. The conventional recommendation of training through books and nature naturally found frequent expression. The 1829 *Mirror* found American authors ambitious of literary fame but averse to the prerequisite study. The poet must read, and any man without access to good books should not even attempt to write. To look upon nature is all very well for him, but nature cannot teach him to make poems as books can. Without going overboard in claims for abundant American geniuses, the editor believed firmly in the future of soundly prepared American authors.

Somewhat surprisingly, since it commanded the services of competent literary scholars, the 1840 *New York Review*—an organ of the Protestant Episcopal Church—showed a preference for poetic training through nature. The Bible, it affirmed was "the best safeguard for the purity of different languages—the standard by which the lawfulness and good taste of words and phrases are to be tested." But nature is "the other chief companion and teacher of men. . . . It is here that errors are rebuked, and excesses discountenanced." Disagreeing with

the editor of the *Mirror*, the writer declared that even the poet instructed solely by nature has merit. "Uncharitable criticism has
stigmatized the rural doctrines of his rhymes, from negative rather than
positive charges. But there is often a great deal of strength and meaning in his couplets." It happens often that men who are masters of
a scholarly technique belittle it in comparison with what they have
not, out of sheer familiarity. In New York, too, writers who descanted
upon the training offered the poet by nature might start out by valuing
instruction in expression, but soon they shifted from attention to form
to concentration upon content. In a new country where libraries were
scarce and inadequate, to require the writer to know books was to
severely restrict the number of authors and indirectly to condemn the
democratic trust in the common man's competency. In literary matters
the editor of the *Mirror* showed a practical knowledge of the craft
that many lacked or overlooked.

New York theorists were apparently untroubled by the fact that
American authors wrote in the same language as the British. Walter
Channing of Harvard had written in the 1815 *North American Review*
that a nation without its peculiar language could hardly produce a
truly national literature, but no parallel fear was expressed in New
York. Partly no doubt as the result of their polyglot mixture of citizens,
New York theorists found less cramping the linguistic ties with
England. Along with the rest of the country, they held the belief
that whatever British literature had existed before the Revolution was
American by inheritance. They also consistently played down the
periodic outbursts of anti-British sentiment; these were bad for business, and business ties helped to cement other relations with the mother
country.

Literary style, it was agreed, was as Horace had said improved by
revision. Turgid American style, declared the 1830 *Mirror*, must be
refined by pruning the redundant, clarifying the obscure, weighing
and condensing the expression of every thought. "Casual warmth of
language" does not produce literature. In 1835 it handled gently the
shortcomings of a posthumously published book: the author had not
lived to revise it. William Gilmore Simms, according to the 1836
American Monthly Magazine, "must labor, must study, must revise.
He must not write one half so *much* in bulk, one half so *rapidly* in
time." Propriety and terse diction, agreed the 1838 *Knickerbocker*,
are not natural endowments, but are won only through practice. Although much of this sounds like parroting of traditional, conventional

clichés, it was genuine belief; it expressed views at variance with the current opinion that longed for an immediate and abundant American literature.

In their desire for carefully executed works, New Yorkers were careful to allow the author freedom of expression. His language must clearly and attractively express what he has in mind, but "we have no patience," declared the 1837 *American Monthly Magazine,* "with that miserable spirit, which loves to dabble in grammatical hypercriticisms." Tuckerman complained in 1851 that the philologist was narrowing "the original authority and laws of language." Its natural simplicity had been arbitrarily complicated; its natural principles had been made dry formulas; the importance of details had been exaggerated; and the whole subject had assumed the abstractness of theory. The same complicated approach which was already throttling the study of the classical languages, Tuckerman found at work on English. He attacked not only the arid codification of style which derived from the textbooks of the Scottish rhetoricians, but he opposed also the tendency toward "school-marm English" with its stringent provisions that seemed to be the inevitable concomitant of general popular instruction. Although the decorous Tuckerman could hardly have approved the message of Whitman, the latter's praise of flexible American speech would have seemed to him just. In their concessions to authors on linguistic matters, New York critics opened the way for Howells' plea to authors to write as "Americanly" as they could.

STYLE

Of the elements of style simplicity was the most frequently enjoined upon the writer. Emphasis was placed not so much upon its positive sense as upon the avoidance of superfluity. The 1824 *Atlantic Magazine* labeled American style ornate, overloaded, obviously artificial, and dissolute in the root and derived senses of that term—a shaky foundation for the American literary edifice. The 1837 *Knickerbocker,* transferring a Horatian phrase from a tantalizing redheaded flirt, begged that style be *simplex munditiis*—a baffling phrase rendered by the writer as "of a simple elegance of expression." Hawthorne's style, "at once simple and graceful," provided his American instance.

The demand for simplicity frequently recurred. The 1847 *Literary World* found in it the basic strength of Bryant's poetry; and five years later it scolded Melville for having abandoned this quality so evident in his early work. "Why does he give us incoherencies of thought, in infelicities of language?" The 1856 *Putnam's* closed the account by asserting that simplicity is not mere ease of reading but that unity of concept and expression found only in the greatest works of art. Such repeated admonitions were needed in a literary arena where writers felt obligated to flex their muscles in order to impress readers with their abundant materials and exuberant power to handle them.

Simplicity makes mandatory other important qualities: statements must accurately express the facts or sentiments conveyed, for example. The 1829 *Mirror* had noted that American writers were enfeebling their work by exaggeration. Eight years later the *Knickerbocker* came out in like vein for just sentiments, which it ranked with good sense, sound knowledge, and faithful conformity to those nebulous standards truth and nature. In both prose and verse, insisted the 1849 *Democratic Review*, "to be possessed of ideas is the first great requisite; the next, to express them as clearly and correctly as possible." Concord writers, by common consent, were defective in both. In 1854, *Putnam's* ventured the doubtful assertion that readers no longer desired extravagant sentiment, but preferred the natural in thought and feeling. Although these critics might have hesitated to state with Aristotle and Emerson that half the man is his expression—the sentiment of the times forbade such elevation of form—they clearly felt its necessity.

The short early reign of rhetorician and rule-maker ended in New York with the 1830's; the 1840 *Knickerbocker* angrily proclaimed, "there is no such thing as establishing *a rule* for writing." Certain generalizations were, however, widely accepted in a spirit like that of Henry James four decades later. The style of a work, it was agreed, should be uniform throughout. The 1839 *Democratic Review*—no friend to the patrician attitude of Halleck—protested against his "unnatural blending of the bold and strong with the frail and feeble," which Byron's *Don Juan* had evidently taught him. The unlucky Melville was here again condemned. *Holden's Dollar Magazine* in 1850, while conceding to an author the right to choose his style—the reviewer apparently did not subscribe to Georges de Buffon's dictum that the style is the man—called *Redburn* a hodgepodge of romance, narrative, and satire. To the *Literary World, Moby Dick* was "a most remarkable sea-dish—an intellectual chowder of romance, philosophy, natural history, fine writing, good feelings, bad sayings" mingled with satire and strained through an allegory. The 1853 *Putnam's* fervently wished that he would revert to the clear narrative and simple style of *Typee*.

The traditional admonition to study sound models was greeted with clearly defined reservations. The 1829 *Mirror* spoke for the majority: of course an author will be familiar with the acknowledged masters of English composition. Plato's concept of the artist as copier of copies was accepted as a dreadful warning. Edward Young's echoing of Longinus was known but on the whole ignored. Faulty imitation of what were considered undesirable models occupied the reviewers' attention.

The most viciously attacked apes of other men's style were the writers like Carlyle and Emerson who were charged with imitating German literary expression. These two, who in turn were followed by young writers, were held up as "somewhat formidable conspirators against clear style" by the 1838 *Knickerbocker*. Three years later it reproved Emerson for imitating "the German-English style of Thomas Carlyle, which whoso handleth, not being expert therewith, useth an edged tool, and will assuredly be wounded thereby." Ideas were meant to be expressed, not concealed, and his followers were earnestly advised to eschew his obfuscation of thought. Emerson usually fared better than most of his fellow-transcendentalists: at least he had ideas and sometimes expressed them properly. His militant Americanism atoned for his stylistic sins, although the gospel of transcendentalism made few converts in Gotham.

The attack upon use of alien literary models was most vigorously pressed, as one would expect, by the *Democratic Review*. Since its flourishing years coincided with periods in which Anglo-American relations were politically and economically strained, its militant democracy was augmented by the general anti-British sentiment of the times. Its position was clearly stated in 1849, although the attitude expressed had obtained for more than a decade: "there must be less worship of British models, less imitation of English writers, and less deference to English criticism"—a principle it frequently documented in detail. Four years later Parke Godwin, Bryant's liberally minded son-in-law, spiritedly defended American authors from this charge: at their best they do not ape British models. In fact, it was racially well-nigh impossible that they should do so. In the United States, he informed his readers, the melting pot had blended with the earnest northern character the volatile and graceful variety of the south which the Briton notoriously lacked; New York had not forgotten Mme de Staël's comments on British life and letters. The American combination showed a "fresh, buoyant, genial enthusiasm" that was unique in the world. The common ruck of writers might ape the British authors, it was admitted; but many agreed with Godwin that our ablest writers were becoming more and more distinctly American in outlook and therefore in style.

However democratic speakers might proclaim the natural powers of the common man, the influential journals were agreed that good style was the result of careful revision. The 1835 *Mirror*, in fact, considered style and revision to be almost synonymous. It wrote approvingly of that "rich colouring of style by which asperities of diction are smoothed, involved periods cleared of their incumbrances, and the subject like the style irradiated with all the lights and brilliancy that industrious polish and patient thought can bestow upon it." Even the *Democratic Review*, for all its campaign for literature for the people, advised a minor poet in 1842: "let him labor—write, rewrite, condense, polish, and above all freely blot and burn." The young intellectuals who so fervently preached the democratic gospel a la Andrew Jackson could not jump off their shadows and escape the very principles which the preceding century had overemphasized. Finished style was less important than the idea, and it had aristocratic associations which they abhorred; but they could not ignore it.

Stimulated by the vogue of Hazlitt in New York, and probably reinforced later by the vivid presence of Thackeray, New York writers regularly listed gusto or zest among the elements of a good style. The principle was hardly new, but a normal outgrowth among vigorous people of the traditional Horatian demand that the author feel deeply what he portrays. Zest, said the 1837 *Knickerbocker*, could go far to atone for the Americans' "overweening fondness for superabundant finery in style." Some used it as a counterweight for the faults so vehemently condemned in Carlyle's writing. Jones based his condemnation of Thomas Moore's poetry upon his lack of this virtue, and two years later, in 1851, Tuckerman iterated its essentiality in good style. Perhaps another cause for the emphasis upon gusto was the haunting fear that our writers somehow lacked it. At any rate, toward the end of the fifties Evert Duyckinck, for all his patriotic support of American letters, wrote regretfully of the pallid products of American poets who lacked zest and spirit.

Upon the spirited quality of American letters, in fact, New Yorkers changed their opinion as the decades passed. The 1835 *American Monthly Magazine* had praised the "spirited, easy, and graceful" style of Longfellow's *Outre-Mer*—a combination of epithets surprising to its later readers. By 1842, the *New World* wished that Longfellow would add to his quiet elegance vigor and boldness. Lowell in 1848 admonished readers of *A Fable for Critics*, which was published in New York, to "remember that elegance also is force" in their strictures upon Longfellow; he singled out the New Yorker Cornelius Mathews along with Poe as forgetful of this equation. His plea was ineffectual. The 1851 *Literary World* classified Longfellow as "a dainty embroidered poet, quaint, happy, benevolent—for the boudoir and well-gloved fingers, not for this 'working-day' world." Three years later a reviewer was in like manner to find fault with Lowell himself for the incrustation of mannerism and affectation that hid the author's enormous capacity for enjoying the vigor of life and expressing human feeling. Longfellow was only the major target for attack. American poetry as a whole, mourned the 1855 *National Magazine*, suffers from pretty conceits, fanciful similitudes, and a feminine daintiness. A year later, the *United States Magazine* summed up the general demand for that zest so woefully deficient in American writing: "Our literature is growing fine rather than forceful, more elegant than original. . . . We are tired of the whole school of mosaic workers like Longfellow. . . . The very soul of man nauseates at all this weakness, and dulness, and incompleteness." Whitman, to be sure, had somewhat surprisingly in view of this chorus of his contemporary New Yorkers, written as early as 1846 in praise of Longfellow: "the country is not half just to this eloquent writer; an honor and glory as he is to the American name—and deserving to stand on the same platform with Bryant and Wordsworth." The apostle of vigor and the "working-day world" saw in Longfellow a quality that his New York fellow-democrats overlooked in their demand for forceful literature of the common man.

The emphasis placed by New York critics upon simplicity, just expression, proper study of good models, revision, and zest, and their frequent recurrence to these topics, indicate that they found such qualities lacking in the writing of their contemporaries. This deficiency worried them deeply. As the century advanced toward the Civil War, they came around to Buffon's position that the style is the man. If American writing showed scant signs of these necessary stylistic ingredients, what were the prospects for an American literature? Their facing of this problem was supplanted by 1860 with the greater danger to the prospects for the nation itself, but traces of their perturbation showed themselves clearly in remarks such as those just quoted.

THREE

THE ART AND
PRACTICE OF FICTION

Fiction flourished in New York from the early years of the nine-teenth century. By 1812 James Kirke Paulding had begun a long career as a novelist. A decade later came James Fenimore Cooper. Lesser writers of fiction were also numerous. Prior to 1835, however, interested persons were for the most part too busy in the practice of the art to give it much theoretical attention. Novel-writing was a modern addition to the various literary arts. For some time it was doubtfully received as not perhaps wholly reputable and hardly to be dignified with a theory. As in many activities in which there was no long-established, cramping tradition, New Yorkers were inclined to put the practice before the precept and to theorize on a *fait accompli,* looking for explanations of what had been accomplished rather than guiding principles for its performance. By 1835, however, prescriptions for the novel began to appear. In that year the *American Monthly Magazine,* in a review of William Gilmore Simms's *The Yemassee,* described the novel as being all things to all readers. It should include a dash of poetry for the cultivated and intellectual; a strong infusion of excitement, bustle, and interest to hold the attention of rank-and-file readers; a soupçon of metaphysics for the self-imagined philos-opher; the whole to be seasoned with well-considered situations, lively dialogue, and strongly outlined characters. If he had added a carefully wrought out moral for the innocent young female reader, this reviewer would have pretty well covered the ground then assigned to the novel.

In another important matter, this reviewer of *The Yemassee* conformed to the current view of fiction: he divided the field between the novel and the romance in prose. The novel proper, he said, deals with customs and gives body to the spirit of the times it treats, in which process it may satirize the follies of mankind. Like many men of his time, his definition indicates his interest in Fielding's *Tom Jones.* The romance mingles truth with fiction on a historical theme, lightly coloring and poetically shading the serious events of history and instructing while seemingly bent only upon pleasing. Although not necessarily dealing with the past, it generally does so. The adding of a didactic role to the romance indicates rather clearly that it was aimed at the young and impressionable, mostly feminine character.

The novel was by far the more respectable of the two varieties. In 1840, for example, the well-informed and literarily competent *New York Review* described the modern novel as derived from the old romance of chivalry with the latter's absurd extravagances checked by common sense and filled with "the sincere pathos of the Saxon school." It possesses affinities with epic, comedy, tragedy, and history, but its agents are limited to beings of ordinary human prowess acting in scenes representative of actual life. This description, to be sure, tallies with the description of the novel just cited, but the placing of its origin in the romance indicates that all reputable fiction was subsumed under the term novel.

It was not until 1850 that New York critics got around to serious attempts to define the novel-romance. In that year the *Whig Review,* still preserving the distinction between the two varieties of prose fiction, went into considerable detail to indicate their nature and purpose. "A novel," it declared, "is a picture of society, a delineation of manners, increased in interest and effect by the aid of plot and incident." The New Yorkers' concern for American propaganda appears in the values assigned to accurate picture and plot. The novel, the writer continued, epitomizes philosophy in dramatic, popular form. It elucidates morals through more ductile examples than the stubborn and often paradoxical events of history. It instructs through amusing, on the one hand making knowledge more familiar to the wise, on the other luring the careless or ignorant into the temple of learning. Little was said about its plot. A romance is a panorama of outward life and, like John Banvard's and other popular pictorial panoramas, it depicts other scenes and times than ours. Its purposes are less serious or well defined than those of the novel, and it frequently restricts itself to the surface of events or character. Its plots, too, may be mere aggregations of incidents. The philosophical content of the romance may be nil, and such instruction as it sees fit to offer affects only the externals of life. It differentiates by using high light and deep shadow rather than delicate shading. Finally, it need give little or no inkling of the author's thought. The *Whig Review* naturally belittled the romance as a form pleasing chiefly the *Democratic Review*'s idol, the common man. Besides dividing the instructive purpose between novel and romance instead of relating it to the latter, this definition proceeds beyond that given in 1835 in its greater concern with realistic depiction and omission of satirical emphasis in the novel. The addition of didactic intent to the novel was no doubt due to the Victorian sentiment in America as well as to the impending national crisis, while the shift toward realism, although it had other causes to be discussed later, owed something to the vogue of Thackeray, soon to be reinforced by his American lecture-tour.

It remained for the 1854 *Putnam's* to present the most systematic treatment of prose fiction of any New York periodical. In "Novels: Their Meaning and Mission," William Swinton resolved the novel and romance on a Coleridgean basis. The Romance, he wrote, is the product of the Fancy, the Novel of the Imagination; an idea adumbrated in earlier discussions but never quite attained. The Romance is consequently a combination of "wonderful deeds and darings; outreisms and bizarreries"; the Novel is an Art-creation, "not an accretion of circumstances and particulars from without but an inly [*sic*] production of the mind in its highest imagining or poetic moods." Swinton concurred with Coleridge that the imagination and the fancy always coexist in prose fiction, but the novel fuses its elements while the romance is satisfied to combine fixities and definites. He proceeded to subdivide the two types. The romance he analyzed into the apologue, the extravaganza, and the sentimental romance. The species of the novel were the "historico-descriptive," the analytic, and the novel of men and manners. Such analysis of the new forms of literature was only now possible, he insisted: the notable advance in fiction during the preceding quarter-century had opened the way for it. Since the novel was now an art-form, it should be composed, read, and judged by artistic principles. With this assertion he indicated that the time was now at hand for the novel to be rated on the same level as poetry, and he declared war on the New Yorkers' preconception of its chief value as propaganda. He did not, however, win the campaign; and in any case he wrote too late to seriously affect the prewar thinking of New York litterateurs.

This novel-romance dichotomy, although established in theory by the writers on prose fiction, was not consistently observed by reviewers and commentators on current fiction. The term novel embraced the two. In the details which follow concerning the art and practice of fiction, it is rarely possible to discover whether the distinction was active in the writer's mind, and it was generally the case that the term novel denoted prose fiction as a whole.

THE END OF THE NOVEL

The end, purpose, or effect of the novel was a topic hotly argued throughout the entire period, increasing in significance as prose fiction gained in literary stature. In early years, as the 1824 *Minerva* slightingly remarked, novels were works "possessing little inherent utility, and written only for the recreation of the passing moment"; no one would think of their pleasing, as Horace had said of poetry, when read ten times over. The few survivors among them owed their longevity to their admirably developed representations of human nature and their rare style of writing—in other words, to essentially poetic properties which they had conveyed to their own use. The Reverend James G. Brooks, who wrote most of *Minerva*'s reviews, approved of those novels which he noticed if by implication or explicitly they pointed out the faults of the present age or, as in the case of Catherine Sedgwick's *Redwood*, drew "the lines of purity and piety with beautiful touches" while depicting "the harsh features of vice, the smooth visage of hypocrisy, and the brutal face of moral degradation, with equal sternness and truth." In short Brooks would have the novelist write in the same vein that received his approbation in poetry. He, and others like him, had no premonition that a new art-form was developing.

Defenders of the new fiction were soon to appear. The 1831 *Mirror* stoutly supported its freedom and dignity. A novel justified its existence without emphasizing a moral principle or warmly depicting human nature, provided it possessed acute—not necessarily deep—observation of life, a keen sense of the ridiculous, and kindly satire of minor human foibles. To be sure, its position was more defensible if it contained more depth; but such witty, "easy graceful trifling" characterizes a work of art. It may not be imaginative, the writer admitted; it is perhaps only fanciful, yet it is lifelike. Subsequent reviewers and commentators in the thirties contented themselves with less vigorous support of the lighter novel. The 1839 *Knickerbocker*, for example, mildly defended the novel that sought only to entertain on the ground that readers desired nothing more of the novel; and as late as 1847 the *Columbian* flatly stated that the business of the novelist was simply to tell a good story. But the novel was more strongly supported on what were believed to be its higher levels.

The proper way of telling a story, however it might be stated, required that it have some degree of meaning. The 1834 *American Monthly Magazine* urged the novelist to entertain rather than merely to enlighten his readers, but in so stating it admitted serious purpose to fiction. Three years later it bluntly stated that good fiction must convey meaning, significance. The cudgels were taken up and vigorously swung by the *Democratic Review;* the Young Americans saw in fiction a vehicle to carry the gospel of democracy. Their blatant propagandizing by fiction was, however, soon attacked. In 1847 the *Columbian* denied to the novelist any right to make his work a mere channel for political or other homilies—a prohibition echoed naturally by the *Democratic Review*'s archopponent the *Whig Review*. Its meaning should be implicit rather than overt.

A like objection was advanced against the tendency, especially noted in the religious press, to inculcate through fiction the principles of sound morality or orthodox theology. Such explicit didacticism was on the whole less welcome in New York than down east. Even the pious *Minerva* in 1824 condemned morally or religiously aimed novels; they generally failed in their intent. Often their authors lacked literary capacity. Not infrequently they were written by cranks or special pleaders whose moral conceptions were questionable or impracticable, and their religious tenets smacked of sectarian dogma rather than Christian doctrine. Using nearly identical arguments, William A. Jones twenty years later delivered another volley against religiously inspired novels. Although he was himself devoutly religious, Jones disapproved of weak literary efforts to inculcate religious faith, and he implied strongly that such efforts could not be other than weak, being misdirected. The 1838 *Mirror*, a nonsectarian weekly edited by a man of strong religious convictions, flatly declared that the novelist must not put forth theological propaganda disguised as a novel. A year later it attacked the centuries-old insertion of the sententious utterance into literature: however it might be backed by great literary theorists, it was nonetheless boring to readers.

On the other hand, the novel must not pander to evil. The 1830 *Mirror* forbade the novelist to make rogues attractive and honest men dull. So strongly did it feel that in 1834 it vigorously championed poetic justice, demanding that virtue be shown, however, as its own reward and vice its own punishment instead of the traditional social or pecuniary emoluments attached by writers to virtuous conduct. Fielding was a better teacher than Samuel Richardson. The 1840 *New York Review* feared that the portrayal of superhumanly depraved or abnormally guilty persons might stir readers' evil passions as well as be bad art. In this it echoed the commonly accepted position as stated in the 1839 *Knickerbocker:* the novelist must not pander to evil passions or keep the mind of the reader in tumult, fever, or sensuality. Such writing fills the brothels with inmates as well as patrons; our young women must be protected. On the other hand, it continued, "scenes of evil import" were admissible to the novel when contrasted with the happier scenes of normal life and provided that poetic justice was evenly administered. As another writer declared, there was no place in literature for deliberately pornographic writing; works that were merely "venomous, venereous, and vendible" were proscribed by all right-thinking men. While keeping an eye on the moral effect, the best reviewers kept in mind that the work was to be judged primarily by literary principles. The charge brought by the 1846 *New York Evangelist* against Melville's unflattering picture of missionaries in *Typee* was countered by *Holden's Dollar Magazine*'s retort in 1850 that orthodoxy and moral purity were no makeweights for bad writing.

Implicit in the foregoing remarks was the general belief that the well-written novel conveyed instruction without obtruding it. As the 1831 *Mirror* put it, properly made fiction influences manners and morals through its keen discrimination and sagacious observation of life. Three years later it cited a specific value: by acquainting the embryo statesman and warrior with the private life of an age, the novel could supplement his study of that age in history by bringing it to life for him. The 1837 *Knickerbocker* amplified this idea in asserting that historical fiction pictures the actual living men and women of those periods which history treats. When the novelist added moral or didactic strains—a fault attributed by many male reviewers particularly to female novelists—they were overstepping their bounds and marring their work.

One of the especially interesting treatments of the moral and didactic in fiction appeared in the 1840 *New York Review*, a quarterly with one foot in the religious, the other in the secular world. In reading Walter Scott's novels, the writer asserted, only materialistic, utilitarian minds inquire after their good or bad moral effect. Such genuinely imaginative work contains an "enlarged moral" quite beyond their grasp. They cannot see that by showing all kinds and conditions of men in many times and places, Scott shows the "common human heartedness of mankind." He thereby teaches the reader to recognize similarity instead of looking for differences in men. Novels, he concluded, are not written to inculcate philosophical truths, but through their presenting men in action these truths become evident. Although, as the 1852 *Whig Review* proclaimed, a work of art should favor progress and make the world better, along with other enlightened critics of these latter years it sharply severed art from propaganda. As mentioned before, however, this severance came too late to affect the major trends of the period.

The preference for profitable pleasure as the end of literature, advocated from Roman times through those of Samuel Johnson, still constituted an ideal often held up before New York writers. In the novel, however, the pleasurable ends generally dominated the instructive. As early as 1822, the conservative yet daring Cooper had observed that a good story "best animates our solitude, refreshes our weariness, and beguiles our care"; as a secondary effect, he added, it interests our curiosity, increases our knowledge, corrects our false opinions, and through its poetic justice it illustrates the "obvious system of Providence"—obvious at any rate to as single-minded a man as Cooper. The novelist benefits his readers, Cooper continued, either by delighting their imagination and transporting the mind from its limited existence, or—to Cooper a higher aim than mere escape or variety—by showing the nature common to man, his conditions and his fortunes. Cooper's statement neatly sandwiched the moral-instructive function of fiction between two slabs of enjoyment, and he did not find its flavor in the filler.

By 1835 the *American Monthly Magazine* had expanded the purveying of enjoyment into a patriotic effort: the novelist's task, it declared, is to provide nationwide pleasure. Since all men now read, he must insert matter to please all, whether poetic, exciting, metaphysical, or dramatic. The pleasure provided must covertly instruct through giving a body to the spirit of the times, but his immediate end must be entertainment. Fifteen years later, the 1850 *Whig Review* showed the effect of the greater seriousness with which the author's function was coming to be regarded. It would have readers rise from the reading of a novel strengthened in intellect and exalted in sentiment, with a better knowledge of the world and the ways of man. Noun and adjective had changed places in the statement of the novel's purpose, so that now it was pleasurable profit. So it remained for the rest of the decade.

THE TREND TOWARD REALISM

Romantic principles, it must be admitted, still ruled most of the literary world; in New York, however, novelists and theorists moved steadily toward a greater realism. Theorists generally preceded the novelists in this progress, although it is not always easy to determine exactly what they meant in their statements. Truth to nature or fidelity to the American scene, terms frequently found in their essays or reviews, are as likely to be echoes of Wordsworth's precept that the poet should keep his eye steadfastly on his subject yet throw over it a veil or coloring of the imagination; and the term nature was still as troublesome for the definer as ever.

One of the earliest to consider this problem, James Kirke Paulding, had insisted in 1818 that the novel's characters and events should be such as every generation shows. On its face this declaration could mean simply that they should display universal characteristics. Paulding's consistent practice, however, strongly implies that these words have realistic overtones. Four years later, in *A Sketch of Old England*, he praised far above Walter Scott the eighteenth-century novelists Fielding, Tobias G. Smollett, and Oliver Goldsmith. "Each of these writers, without going against the 'modesty of nature' by extravagant or incongruous events, or boisterous, uncontrolled passion, has produced works, that appeal far more powerfully to the heart and the imagination, than the dashing succession of characters and events that only hang together by a chain of improbabilities, or by the thread of history, exhibited in the works of the Great Unknown. . . . The characters delineated by Miss Edgeworth, are admirable for their nature and probability." So strong was his feeling for real characters in everyday life that he even overcame his chronic hostility to Scott long enough to praise these qualities in *The Heart of Midlothian*. Paulding was at that time almost the only novelist to hold realistic principles with consistency.

Paulding repeatedly demanded that the novel treat of probable and natural events and agents and that it display wide knowledge of the world coupled with a sense of reality. In 1830 he attacked the typical romantic historical novel as a badly organized work from a writer with a mere smattering of historical knowledge. It possessed "a mighty hero, and a very little heroine" and was quite deficient in reality. Until its agents should become actual men and women and the events such as might probably occur in their lives, Paulding saw no excuse for the existence of such a novel. His reality, to be sure, cannot be fully equated with realism, but it travels the road toward that destination.

The two succeeding decades produced several converts to Paulding's doctrine. The 1831 *Mirror* complimented him for the naturalness of incident in his *Koningsmarke*. Cooper's *The Pioneers* had early received like praise for its realistic lowly agents, to the considerable relief of its author, whose letters had disclosed his trepidation about their propriety. The *Mirror*'s reviewer suspected him of having depicted actual inhabitants whom he had known in Cooperstown. Bryant's *United States Review and Literary Gazette* in 1826 severely censured a fantastic American historical novel for "setting all reality at defiance" in posing a situation in history which every reader knew had never occurred. Reversing Aristotle's famous truism, the reviewer declared that we will not believe an event possible which we know has not happened. A year later, it demanded that novels present real, not heroically conceived agents. The 1837 *Mirror* in like vein decried the "default of exactness" in novels. Even poetic licence, it declared, is a mere figment of the brain, "in short, a falsehood." Other periodicals reiterated the demand for their concept of realism.

When writers scored event or agent for unnaturalness, at first these strictures were as much a revulsion from romantic excess as a positive demand for realism. Current romances were charged with having disregarded probability and with having concentrated upon sensational agents and events until moderately sober-minded readers could hardly stomach them. Although Howells' definition of realism as the truthful treatment of material would have sounded acceptable to many New York theorists in the thirties, they were hardly ready for his practice of realism. What they had in mind at first was more credible situations and persons in the novel than current writers were offering. Full-fledged theories of realism did not in New York precede its practice, but the demands made by the New York writers and critics were more than mere straws in the wind that was blowing in that direction.

The later 1830's witnessed further progress toward realism. Reaction against extravagant romantic practice was then reinforced by the demands of flaming New York Young Americans for a democratic literature which, being of and for the people, should represent the American in all his presumed actual glory; the picture, they proclaimed, required no retouching. The *Democratic Review* in every issue thundered its gospel and demands and found support for its assertions, although on a less inflamed patriotic level, from other magazines. The

1839 *Corsair* insisted that pictures of American character and society be drawn in strict accord with the facts. In the same year, the *New York Review* came out against the addition of fictitious qualities to historical personages in fiction and warned against presentation of a caricature as a type. The *Mirror* elevated the tale of real life above the historical novel and bade the novelist to *take* materials as he found them, not to *make* them. Recurring to the subject in 1840, the *New York Review* envisioned the true novel as showing ordinary, not heroic prowess in its agents. The rising young litterateur Henry T. Tuckerman in 1841 rebuked readers who preferred the startling in fiction and the peculiar in character; the true and original are alone possessions for all time. In such pronouncements literary principle outweighed patriotic designs, although the latter also were present.

Arcturus, Evert Duyckinck's new organ, also championed the new trend toward realism. Genius, it declared, finds in common things more than common men find, and imagination reveals itself more clearly in full awareness of reality than in putting together exaggerations. A first-rate author should depict the present because it is greater than the past and should deal with ordinary life because it is infinitely diversified to the seeing eye in both character and incident. Duyckinck indignantly denied the often adduced charge of previous decades that all American life exists on a dead level of monotony. In these statements he was undoubtedly drawing heavily on Wordsworth's practice, but he was equally swayed by the patriotic fervor of times that demanded a democratic American literature without delay. He furnished a bridge from Wordsworth to Whitman of which the latter took full advantage.

The antiromantic attack, with its patriotic support, developed rapidly. In 1841 the *New York Review* branded plots developed with Gothic machinery as obviously inferior to those drawn from ordinary life. Although it still desired a seasoning of idealization in the agents of the novel, it added as Aristotle had done for the drama that they should also be true to life. Two years later the New York *Mirror* charged popular novelists with blasphemously deforming the human character which God had made in His own image. In 1851 *Holden's Dollar Magazine* would have American novelists depict American life with daguerreotype fidelity. The new photographic process quickly furnished several of these incipient realistic theorists with analogies: the daguerreotype or camera lucida appear frequently as analogies of the course the novel should take.

That ideal character mentioned as desirable by the *New York Review* was not to be confused with perfect humanity. It is naturalness, Tuckerman wrote in 1851, rather than perfection that gives agents a hold on their beholders. Venturing a glance into the future, the 1853 *Knickerbocker* shrewdly prophesied that the coming school of novel-writing would portray human nature more accurately; and at the same time the *New York Quarterly* asked for more novels of American daily life, for they would constitute an original American literature. The 1854 *Putnam's*, surveying the field of the novel, found it to include both the real and the ideal. The new novelists, it added, were vigorous and veracious, for "the world's 'Idea' now is the *true*." *Putnam's* was suffering the usual trouble with literary labels. Although its truth cannot be equated with realism, it verges upon what post–Civil War novelists were to attempt in the name of realism.

Both the term and the object it denotes appear full-fledged in Parke Godwin's 1855 review of Thackeray's *The Newcomes:*

> It is this remarkable realism which gives his books their aspect of an actual transcript of the life of society. Everybody, on reading them, is quite convinced that the author has seen what he sets forth, and some even suppose that his own agency in the business is little more than that of the *camera lucida* which reflects the picture. . . . Almost every person . . . is in the habit of looking at the world and its ways with his eyes, and Thackeray does no more; but there is something so sharp, so penetrating, so luminous in his look, that when he sees the thing he sees the whole of it—inside as well as out—and that not only with his eyes, but with his brain and heart.

The impending Civil War was to preempt the attention of men like Godwin, and humanitarian and patriotic activities inevitably delayed for a few years their profound attention to the arts of fiction. Such understanding of Thackeray's effects and methods demonstrates, however, that men who felt as he did had gone across the threshold into the house of realism.

THE NOVEL'S AGENTS

New York theories of fiction advanced by slight degrees from early scattered remarks about characters and characterization to formulated theories concerning the agents. Traditional criticism of narrative as found in epic and heroic poetry had concerned itself chiefly with other matters, and in this as in other matters poetic theory attached itself to the comparatively new art of prose fiction. Only haphazard remarks appeared at first, as the new art and its imagined or real requirements in the new country obtruded themselves into the tradition. New Yorkers cannot, it must be remembered, be classified as traditionalists in attitude; yet tradition contains a lot of common sense and proven practice, which men of their cast of mind would appreciate. It could not, however, bind them to the impractical or to what they considered un-American.

In 1818, the same year in which we have noted Paulding's plea that characters be such as every generation shows, the *American Monthly Magazine* was still repeating the dramatic direction that the novel's agents be set in vivid contrast, an idea repeated in 1824 by the more constructively conservative *Minerva*. A year later, the *United States Literary Gazette* concurred as to the desirability of varied agents and added that the United States now afforded character in ample variety. This retort to those who felt that democracy set people on a dead, monotonous level was now fairly often heard. At about the same time, the *New York Review* required that characters be fully developed, not merely outlined, and a later number of the *United States Literary Gazette* insisted that they be clearly individualized without at the same time being made peculiar. The *Mirror* for 1830 reminded readers —who never seem to learn this obvious truth—that the faults present in the agents of a novel cannot be ascribed to its author, an idea which the 1841 *Knickerbocker* felt constrained to repeat. Such scattered remarks, which represent the periodical comment of the period on the agents, indicate the lack of organized thinking about them.

The popular historically based romance provided an opening for more theorizing by its very deficiencies in art. The 1834 *Mirror* desired the teller of historical tales to form his agents out of qualities existing in ordinary private citizens, not from incredible or heroic elements. The *Knickerbocker* saw in the well-written historical tale a supplement to the record in history, in that it portrayed personages of former times as actual, living and breathing men and women; the student could with their aid relive the page of history. The general run of such compositions, however, was beneath the notice of the serious reviewer, except to point a warning or raise a literary laugh at their ineptness. It was too often turned out, as it is today, in response to the demand for excitement according to the tastes of readers with little literary interest or appreciative power. It was seldom even meant to be a work of art. The ridiculously cheap publishing of novels engineered by Park Benjamin and the callous spirit behind his throat-cutting tactics afford a dark commentary on the literary market for trash.

Although the puritanical wing of literary comment stood generally on the defensive in New York, in the field of the novel it was both vocal and influential: vocal because easily scandalized and influential because it acted upon a major segment of the market for novels. Largely to meet this biased, often anti-intellectual view, literary theorists and reviewers had to discuss to an undue degree the morals of the agents, often on what to them must have appeared a painfully obvious level. The 1830 *Mirror*, besides pointing out that the novelist is a plastic artist, not an autobiographer, explained that human nature, if accurately portrayed, will be depicted with evil as well as good traits. Evil indeed must not be gratuitously introduced, but must serve the purposes of the tale. The 1839 *Knickerbocker* would have agents drawn so as to clearly indicate which are proper moral tendencies. Such remarks show the force of the moral pressure exerted upon the press. Read by a man of letters, these could have been construed as salutary hints for portrayal of men as they are. No man of sound culture cares for the obscene or pornographic; brilliance and dullness are not exclusive accompaniments of either virtue or vice; and proper moral tendencies in general accord with proper social adjustment. To the moralist, these statements would sound the salutary didactic note he sought. Their expression, however, would hardly have been necessary without such puritanical pressures.

Reinforced by the success of Thackeray's novels in New York—*Vanity Fair*, that novel without a hero, had just captured readers' interest—the 1848 *Whig Review* returned to the defense of presenting undesirable agents. The end of a story, it affirmed, may well justify the introduction of many disagreeable characters; even *Vanity Fair*, in which the term disagreeable is the mildest censure applicable to many persons, is justifiable as literature. The novelist who writes such a story cannot achieve success in depicting such life unless he contains within himself a norm by which to assess his agents; and his tale must convey to the reader the regulative principle by which they are evaluated. Naturalness in the characters interests us, not perfection, Tuckerman wrote in 1851. Victorian and Puritan attitudes were strong in combination during the 1850's; they did not, however, force the periodicals to knuckle under to all their demands.

The trend toward realism exerted a directing pressure also upon the portrayal of the persons in the novel. The 1827 *United States Review* had without reservation found Scott's agents to be real persons. Although it made no distinction, it evidently had in mind his lowly characters. It advised the American novelist to discard representation of the noble classes; he should rather picture his own countrymen as Scott had so brilliantly done. As corollary advice the 1834 *Mirror* pointedly remarked that the American novelist knew Americans better than foreign nobility. Lowness, however, was a term that the American knew better than to apply to his fellow-citizens; he reserved it for persons of doubtful morality. The *American Monthly Magazine* and the *Knickerbocker* in their campaign for the full American picture came out against an undue percentage of low persons in the novel; they should be of some degree of refinement and moral stature. Although the 1839 *Corsair* spoke out with piratical violence for depiction of Americans in strict accord with the facts, William Leggett could hardly have wished the entire range of American persons to be shown. In their rage at Dickens' charges of American vulgarity, theorists skillfully equipped their preferred novelist with slightly rose-tinted spectacles before permitting him to study the American scene. These roseate tints were furnished through the courtesy of the American dream and the conviction of manifest destiny.

The 1848 *Democratic Review* declared that novels of high life had now become passé in the United States. Acceptable representation of the nobility emphasized their weaknesses and so elevated nature's noblemen. Literature had gone over to the people, it claimed—a claim to which a poll of leading American authors gave considerable support. A decade later *Putnam's* condemned the introduction of noblemen into novels as lay figures: unless they contributed something to the action, let them be replaced by agents who advance the plot or at least illustrate a principle. However the general American reader viewed such entertainment—and fiction-hucksters crowded agents of noble birth into their trash—the consensus of the better periodicals indicated that serious readers were ready to welcome such agents as Howells was soon to create.

Here and there appeared a few scattered remarks on the art of proper characterization. The 1829 *Mirror* would have agents created like Scott's, not anatomized like Edward Bulwer-Lytton's; ten years later it repeated that inventory description of a heroine was a bore. She must be a flesh-and-blood representation, not a mere assemblage of physical and emotional components. The 1850 *Whig Review*, echoing Aristotle, desired that the novelist enter plastically into his agents, and a year later added that he must show discriminating insight into character. For American fiction, it was repeatedly affirmed, the outstanding example of such plastic creativity was Cooper's Leatherstocking. Only Cooper's most venomous enemies decried this embodiment; to many it atoned for his lack of other literary qualities. An author has scored a towering success, said the 1842 *New York Review*, when he has created a personage who will exist for ages to come. Leatherstocking, declared the

1860 *National Quarterly Review,* was probably the outstanding character in all fiction. Although most New York journals frowned upon such literary chauvinism, the city was proud to claim Leatherstocking as her own, however her citizens might belabor his creator.

Another criterion of character bearing the Aristotelian stamp is the demand, frequently iterated by New York periodicals, that the agents of the novel be not merely typical, but individualized. Persons with only the common humain traits are incompletely formed, asserted the 1840 *Knickerbocker;* and it added later that while a novel may interest without clearly individualized agents, it is not good art. Characters, the *Democratic Review* concurred, are not types; they are people with ideas and feelings of their own. They must rouse in readers, added *Holden's Dollar Magazine* in 1850, an affinity which can be maintained only if they are made consistent in character throughout. Hawthorne's inability to create flesh-and-blood people seemed to the 1852 *Whig Review* to be an unhealthy taint in his otherwise fine work.

Cooper's preface to the Leatherstocking Tales, written in 1850, is as complete a statement on this problem as any made during this period. He saw his principal agent as a creation suited to the environment in which he dwelt, a combination of the highest principles of civilized life that could harmonize with these virtues. But this being, he added, must possess *vraisemblance,* so as to be "a reasonable picture of human nature," by which in this statement he meant a credible human being. Recent theorists who philosophize that Cooper deliberately created an American mythical character severely strain the evidence of Cooper's mature statement. As for the degree to which he believed that such agents can be decorously individualized, he delivered a pronouncement in his opinion of the proper method of representing the Indians. His own picture of them was true, he declared, but presented "the *beau ideal* of their characters to the reader." They could not be shown in all their squalid realism without offense to the reader's taste. Such a searching demand for realism would in fact, he asserted, deprive the world even of Homer. How much further in realism Cooper might have seen fit to proceed, if unrestrained by the decorum of the times—or perhaps of his wife—it is unimportant to speculate.

Reviewers and theorists regularly proclaimed the supremacy of the novel that focused attention upon the character of its agents, a feeling of very early origin in New York. Interest comes from character, the 1823 New York *Mirror* had declared; it added, however, that a good plot helps. In the view of the 1841 *New York Review,* the highest efforts of the imagination are put forth to create character; a year later it added that the creation of a genuine person is proof of the author's success. Writers in the magazines regularly subscribed to the Renaissance dictum of Castelvetro: the greater the difficulty overcome, the greater the poet; here it was applied to the making of the agents. And the 1859 *Harper's* closed the era by stating unequivocally that the novel which delineates character is higher than that which merely tells a story. This grading was in quality, however, not in popularity, for *Harper's* added plaintively that only thoughtful readers prefer it to that which surprises by unexpected events. As Howells and James painfully discovered in following decades, discriminating insight into character was not a passport to popularity with the mass of readers. The dream of the Young Americans so often stated as truth in the *Democratic Review*, of a great "literature for the people," remained unrealized as the period came to an end, and still remains a dream.

AMERICA AS MATERIAL FOR FICTION

Increasing confidence in the literary qualities of American materials marked the period between the two wars. At first, indeed, many doubted that the United States could be made into literature; objections were advanced to its scenery, its aboriginal people and its transplanted Europeans, and its social and political institutions, as being all unsuitable for imaginative representation. In 1818, John Bristed included in his survey, *The Resources of the American People*, a chapter "On the Literature of the United States," in which he scouted the likelihood of an American fiction for decades to come. There were few American novels, he wrote, and none good. In his opinion the situation was for the time at least irremediable. The events of American history were too recent and well known to permit their imaginative, fictional embellishment. As for our most distinctive feature, the Indians, "a novel describing these miserable barbarians, their squaws and papooses, would not be very interesting to the present race of American readers." Nor was life among white Americans—he showed no knowledge of Negro life—sufficiently varied to afford interesting situations; equalitarian society existed perforce on a humdrum, debased social level. What the more distant future might offer, Bristed forbore to prophesy, but he saw the present, so far as fiction was concerned, as an arid, sterile desert.

Such a jeremiad from a foreign-born observer did not represent the rampant majority, who seldom purchased American books but resented any slur upon the feasibility of their being written. True, admitted the 1823 *Mirror*, there were few American novels. The aspirant to novel-writing should cultivate this unworked field. His novel, the *Mirror* asserted, would be American whether written on an American subject or not. One should recall that in 1823 Cooper had published only *The Spy*, although *The Pioneers* and *The Pilot* were soon to appear; and Paulding was then producing his first novel, *Koningsmarke*. All three treated American subjects, as the *Mirror* in fact preferred. Cooper's earlier *Precaution*, with its English setting and agents, had encountered a mixed reaction, only in part indeed from its foreign scene; but Cooper himself evidently realized that he would do better to write of scenes that he knew. *The Pioneers* and *The Last of the Mohicans*, as well as *The Pilot* with its American theme, were with few exceptions hailed as genuinely American fiction; and Paulding's early labors in the American field also met with general approval. Within a decade of Bristed's pessimistic report, the *United States Review and Literary Gazette* declared the fitness for fiction of American materials to have been firmly established. Walter Scott's example in exploiting his native Scotland, it noted, had already stimulated some American novelists to treat the early history of their country, a practice which the reviewer hoped would prove contagious.

It was freely conceded by theorists that American materials must be carefully selected and circumspectly handled. The literary desire for the mists of romanticism here jarred against the patriotic longing to present an accurate picture of the United States to a censorious world. The 1834 *Mirror*'s demand that the novelist present familiar scenes, characters, and incidents was countered by the *Knickerbocker*'s warning five years later against the fatal pitfall of excessive description. For suitable incidents and characters, the novelist would much more safely revert to the American revolutionary times, as William Gilmore Simms was soon to advocate in the South; a certain romantic distance attached to events now a normal life-span in the past. Age alone, the 1840 *Mirror* retorted, cannot make materials suitable for fiction: tales of Pilgrim and early Dutch times are a safe venture, while Indian legend, though older and mistier, is not. The *Knickerbocker* expanded the area open to American fiction by annexing the adventures of Columbus and whatever of European events impinged upon American life or history. Local American life also afforded a fresh and fertile field which the *Knickerbocker* believed to be susceptible of piquant and picturesque treatment. And in 1841 the *New York Review* sweepingly conceded to the novelist the privilege of depicting with poetic license our American history as already of the usable past.

American theorists, in fact, slightly modifying the much-abused Horatian tag, consistently declared *ut pictura novella*. The successful

American novel, *Holden's Dollar Magazine* declared in 1849, interestingly worked details from life or history into a well-executed picture. Such a picture was imaginative—mere fancy was unequal to it—with softness of imagery and striking views of men. In the latter years of our period, the terms picture, picturesque, depict, and American scene crop up with inescapable frequency in the reviews. American materials stood in such high esteem that Bryant could declare that, as in Cooper's *The Prairie*, its scenes and agents alone were sufficient to ensure the novel's greatness.

America, it was agreed by the vocal majority, could furnish all the raw materials for the novel. European influence was welcome for what it might contribute to the general effect, and novelists like Dickens and Thackeray were held up as models for study, but Europe must not try to dictate literary practice. As in political problems, the 1841 *Democratic Review* proclaimed, readers should expect from the American West bolder and manlier actions of the mind in both action and writing than the more derivative Atlantic seaboard could provide. The West was not hampered by British trammels and could therefore more freely and truthfully paint the real American picture. Since the novel was a literary form whose development in large part postdated the independence of the United States, American writers enjoyed greater independence in framing it than in writing in any more traditional genre whose shaping had been effected in Europe. Theorists varied in their degree of friendliness to transatlantic impact, but as a whole they supported the novelist's liberty to write unrestrained by traditional bonds.

PLOT VERSUS CHARACTERIZATION IN THE NOVEL

The shift of emphasis in literary theory and practice from plot to delineation of agents has already been mentioned. Walter Scott and his imitators, as George Edward Woodberry has remarked, broke with the time-honored principle of the primacy of plot, a principle which had been deduced with mistaken emphasis from Aristotle's *Poetics*. Aristotle's argument, which had to do with the drama, can hardly be gainsayed for that literary genre: action is the *sine qua non* in the theater; something must happen on the stage, and agents display their character through what they do as well as through what they say. The Greek play lacked a printed program to guide its beholders, and when written down it lacked stage directions or author's marginal glosses such as the modern playwright furnishes to his readers. Although the story of a tragedy was generally known in its outlines and the denouement was anticipated, the complication and resolution of the play allowed the dramatist considerable latitude of detail in elaborating his plot. Aristotle can hardly be confuted in his assertion that plot is the very soul of Greek drama.

At the same time, it is becoming increasingly apparent to students of Greek drama and the *Poetics* that the agents of the Greek tragedy were framed with much greater complexity than scholars formerly recognized. Aristotle's reiteration of the importance of plot misled them into minimizing the importance of the agents. Far from portrayal of character being classed by Aristotle as a weak second in importance to the action, it is now apparent that he saw it as vitally significant, as running almost in double harness with the plot. Whether some contemporary situation in the drama or in some other area made him write more copiously of plot than of agents, or whether it simply was of more interest to him, Aristotle almost certainly saw the vital necessity of proper representation of the agents in the drama.

The somewhat careless assumption of Renaissance scholars that what Aristotle had deduced from Greek tragedies as their valuable characteristics should be set up as the law of all drama was also extended to the newer literary form, the novel. The obvious chances for exposition offered by the novel that are not present in the drama were ignored, as were the differences in actual presentation. Principles which had been mandatory when the action occurred on the stage were sometimes inoperative in the novel. With the advent of prose fiction, which is closer in some respects to the epic, the center of the problem shifted. Aristotle had treated the epic cursorily, chiefly to distinguish it from the drama and not for itself; his comments on the epic are accordingly not particularly helpful to the novelist.

In a novel, obviously, the prime necessity of physical action or speech disappears. Besides the dialogue, the author has at his disposal descriptive and expository comment to gloss the action and speech, and he may analyze a situation to his heart's content, if at times beyond his reader's full satisfaction. Doubtless Poe went too far in claiming that capital tales can be written with no plot at all. In "The Masque of the Red Death," his experiment in that direction, he cheated by suggesting to his readers in his setting the spritely action of Boccaccio's *Decameron*. He did, however, indicate some of the other matters that enter into a tale: attitudes of the agents, descriptive detail, and the total effect. When one adds to these considerations the intense nineteenth-century interest in man and in social problems—which latter incidentally were lacking in Poe's work—the upsurge of concern with portrayal of the agents is more readily understood. Aristotle was not applicable to the

novel in the degree that he related to the drama; however details of his
discussion of plot and agents were still operative in the new genre.

New York of course had her theorists and reviewers who clung to
the old authority of Aristotle over literature. The usually conventional
Minerva declared in 1824 that American readers demand plot and incidents above all else; the writer was, however, belittling the value of
style, not of the agents. Ten years later, Verplanck in his memoir of
R. C. Sands asserted that the elements of prime importance were plot,
style, diction, and knowledge; character was not mentioned. In this
same year, however, the *American Monthly Magazine*, evidently conceding a primary place to characterization, remarked that plot can
carry a story when the characters lack depth; plot was a makeweight
for deficiency in the agents. The contemporary *Mirror* paired consistent plot and characterization as twin sources of success for the
novelist. In 1835 the *American Monthly Magazine* veered to the traditional side in warning writers that success comes from "the key-stone
of the art, the well-adjusted plot, the clear arrangement of the characters, the *lucidus ordo* of old Horace." Characters were to this reviewer
ancillary to the action, pawns in the game; although they were needed
to win the contest, tactics were all-important. His conventionality reappeared in his demand that the author form his plot before beginning to
write in order that the emotion mount gradually to the catastrophe,
which every event and all the characters subserve—common-sense remarks which bear the age-long stamp. In spite of such forcible statements, however, plot was forced to yield the first place to characterization. By 1840, plot had sunk to a position among several desiderata for
the novel; and in 1852 Bryant could assert that although a novel should
be well constructed, it could give pleasure without good organization
—a statement strongly implied earlier in reviews of tales by John Neal.

The displacement of plot by character was strongly implied for another reason in the 1826 *United States Review and Literary Gazette*.
The novel has progressed, the writer conceded, from mere unity of hero
to unity of action; it has shed the loosely hung episodes of the pica-
resque tale. In so doing, however, it has fallen into the opposite error
of excessive organization. Incidents too artfully dovetailed, he warned,
bore many readers with their creakingly obvious mechanism. They
seem to be contrived, unnatural. This periodical, deepening the same
furrow, declared that casual connection in the plot may be intricately
elaborated only to serve some specific and important end. To say all
that can be said, the 1831 *Mirror* noted, causes dullness; life is not all
demonstrable cause and effect. Although it was still a far cry to the

liberty of stream-of-consciousness, readers were increasingly desirous of truth to actual life in the novel.

No one, of course, championed the abandonment of the orderly plot for crass casualty. The overwhelming majority believed in an ordered universe, which the novelist should accept as a working premise. Cause and effect ruled the universe, and hence the novel. Throughout the forty-five years of the period, writers were expected to follow this principle of design in the universe. Paulding had observed in 1818 that motives, actions, and passions in the novel properly arise only out of natural, possible circumstances. In 1826 the *United States Review and Literary Gazette* applied this belief in Coleridgean phrase to the desired effect of the novel, "that illusion, that momentary belief of the reader, from which every tale must derive its power of interesting." Even when a romance is based upon the wildest superstition, the 1833 *Mirror* observed, the author must make his most impossible agents do only such things as are consistent with their natures—a reminiscence perhaps of Aristotle's demand that agents must at least be consistently inconsistent. Three years later, the *American Monthly Magazine* reminded writers that a narrative must show connection of episodes and progressive interest; and the *Knickerbocker* reiterated the advice that novelists plan ahead, for incidents without plan do not make a plot.

Similar comments appear in many other periodicals. Agreeing with the 1839 *Knickerbocker,* which echoed Richard Hurd's demand that episodes spread from some focal point, theorists pretty generally demanded some sort of unified action; yet both *Arcturus* and the *New York Review* in 1841 repeated the earlier warning issued against the elaborately contrived plot: readers like a story they can logically or credibly follow, but they also enjoy exercising their own wits to fill some gaps. As the *Whig Review* in 1852 succinctly summed up the matter, events should "be probable and harmonious . . . ; actions should justly follow purpose; and . . . nothing should be introduced which does not bear directly on the story. . . . He [the novelist] must possess a copious share of the analytical faculty, which disjoins, and unravels, and separates causes and effects, and discovers the true connection between purpose and event."

In harmony with their rational views, New York literary men early threw into the discard the Gothic plot to make room for the more plausible action. The 1837 *American Monthly Magazine* sternly rebuked readers who demand that everything be expressed in hyperbole —impossible incidents, nerve-wracking suspense, and outrages upon common sense. The *Mirror* two years later ordered the novelist to take events from life, not to make them, whether his theme lie in the present or in the past; persons and events must be credible. So eager was the *Mirror* for the author to achieve credibility that a year later it forgot the parallel need to effect an illusion of actuality: it advocated the insertion of footnotes or appendices to support the actuality of episodes in historical tales, as Walter Scott had done. The appetite of the lower-level reading public for sensational "penny-dreadfuls" was a constant thorn in the flesh of the better journals.

The proponents of plot and the more numerous advocates of characterization fought, as might be expected, an indecisive battle. Plot, though demoted, was not driven from the field. In the early 1850's *Harper's* expressed the consensus of the theorists that the novel which delineated character was unquestionably of a higher class than that which merely narrated events, and that characterization was at least as important an ingredient as the formation of the plot.

FOUR

NEW YORKERS'
CONCEPTS OF
LITERARY CRITICISM

However reluctant they might be to admit it, New Yorkers at the end of the War of 1812 were still bound by many provincial ties to England; among these bonds was their heritage of critical theory. Such a mental habit was more binding even than politics and survived long after the government had severed from the parent stock. In the new society, moreover, practical problems necessarily took precedence over artistic theory. Like other Americans, New Yorkers were concerned to develop a national literature with all possible speed; consequently, they preferred to comment upon American literary products rather than to begin with principles. They no doubt realized, moreover, that their theoretical problem would be to adapt the time-tested principles of criticism to American needs, not to start anew; although America had the protagonists of simon-pure American criticism in other areas, they did not appear in New York in any number until the fourth decade.

Bryant's "Lectures on Poetry," delivered in 1826 before the New York Athenaeum but unpublished until 1884, provide one of the earliest statements dealing with the nature of criticism. Bryant was then a newcomer to the city who had won reputation as a poet in New England; he was joint editor of the *United States Review and Literary Gazette*, whose short life was far from commensurate with its quality.

Looking upon criticism as a satellite shot off from the art of poetry, he conceived of criticism primarily from the poet's point of view. Critics, he told his audience, "speculate upon what the poets have written, . . . define the elements and investigate the principles of art, and fix the degrees of estimation in which its [poetry's] several productions should be held." Although he was well read in "Johnson deep and Addison refined," he was also a fervid disciple of Wordsworth and Coleridge in both their creative and their critical methods. For him, the critic postdates the poet; he does not legislate the art, but speculatively and analytically investigates it.

Twelve years after Bryant had delivered his lectures, the *New York Review* published George Allen's "Reproductive Criticism," one of the most ambitious attempts to describe the art during the entire period. Allen added to the knowledge of the English romantic movement a considerable acquaintance with German thought; his essay was a review of works by Friedrich Schlegel and Heinrich Heine. Criticism, according to Allen, is simply a guide to the study of art or creative genius and their products. Critical treatises are then guidebooks of travel in the domains of art. Criticism, as T. S. Eliot was to repeat, is not an autotelic art; treatises spring into being whenever there appear sufficient specimens of art to warrant them, and especially when art becomes a subject of extensive study. In a sense, their production is governed by the economic principle of supply and demand. And since they take their angle of approach from the prevailing intellectual tendency of the age, the country, or the individual who composes them, they are written from varying points of view. Allen's essay was one of the major attempts by an American to make his countrymen aware of contemporary Franco-German thinking about criticism.

The 1843 *New World* noted two critical approaches to the art, the analytic and the synthetic. When employing the former the critic expresses his conclusion with the bases upon which he has established it. Only a profound scholar can be entrusted with such critical work; a sciolist can at best only abuse it. In the latter, opinion is asserted without supporting evidence; the writer had in mind such intuitive procedures as those practiced in Concord. It is a questionable activity because assertions are validated only by the reputation of the man who makes the declaration; New Yorkers were skeptical of modern prophetic utterance. Such utterance leads astray crowds of enthusiastic readers who have not learned to prove all things and hold fast that which is good. "Synthetic" appears to be a term unfortunately chosen for the second class; "subjective" is perhaps a better term. To this writer, true criticism is a rational activity, untinged with transcendentalism.

E. W. Johnson reverted in the 1845 *Whig Review* to the concept of criticism as a police action. His attitude, however, is less a throwback to tradition than a reaction against the fear of the rampant posture by Young America toward literature—and concurrently criticism—of, by, and for the people that had been fostered by the *Whig Review*'s archfoe, the *Democratic Review*. The business of criticism, Johnson wrote, is chiefly conservative: to check the growth of ill taste in the reader and writer who lack inspiration; it does not seek to teach those who write with genuine power. It should "guard a mature literature from direct corruption, rather than . . . infuse life and strength into one just forming itself. Genius teaches it, not it genius." It may at the same time inspire a young literature by holding up before it literary works that are noble models while sternly warning young writers against the peril of servile imitation. The function of criticism as the handmaid of literature is here strictly delimited in view of the exigencies of the contemporary situation.

A second description of criticism worthy of mention with Allen's, by S. A. Allibone, appeared in *Putnam's* for 1853. The task of the critic, Allibone wrote, is "to refine the taste, to elevate the style, to improve the morals"—here to be broadly interpreted as mores. In performing its task in the republic of letters it beareth not the sword in vain. The details of his account are less forbidding than this grim opening might lead one to anticipate. He starts by separating criticism from reviewing. The critic treats of literature in general, theoretically; the reviewer examines specific literary works. Although the two are related and need not be completely divorced, they are nonetheless dissimilar activities. This distinction, needless to say, was almost completely ignored in general practice. Criticism proper, he added, is a liberal art: it teaches men how to approve or condemn and exalts the human mind by displaying to it correct sentiments, pure models, and sound views that have stood the test of time. Although traditional, Allibone is still not legislative in his attitude, and he evidently feels that the United States stands in great need of such stern literary training.

One more definition that should be considered here is that in the contemporary Webster's dictionary, which lumped criticism and reviewing together with emphasis upon the latter: criticism is "the art of judging with propriety of a literary performance, or any production of the fine arts." *Emerson's Magazine*, in approving of this definition in

1858, added bitterly that its practitioners honored the statement more in the breach than the observance; if they bore the sword of justice, they all too seldom slew. Both the preceding diatribes stem from exasperation, not from critical attitude.

These statements are usefully descriptive, no doubt, but lack the precision of cool judicial scholarship. From them, however, one may conclude that literary criticism was on the whole considered a legitimate, respectable, and beneficial literary activity, to be employed either as an aid to the better appreciation of literature or as a fence for keeping out pretenders to that function. It was in theory allowed no legislative powers, although it might execute in both senses of the word. It was an expression less of edicts than of directions to guide the literary prospector. It was instructive in method, and it prepared readers to judge for themselves. In actual practice it did sometimes tend to legislate. The aristocratic minority, distrusting the *profanum vulgus* as incompetent to judge, naturally felt obligated to think for the mass of readers. The democratic proponents of literature for the people, in their eagerness to establish this novel body of writing, too often let their speculation and exposition drift into near-dictatorial statement. The general tendency, however, held steadfastly to the liberal concept of criticism. The course of debate on this matter merits recording.

Rather than legislating, said George Morris in the 1832 *Mirror*, criticism should be argumentative and present all sides of the literary problem under examination. In accord with his principle, he opened his columns to opinion at variance with his own. In reviewing a poem, he would qualify his judgment with the phrase, "as I understand it"; he declined to express a bald approval or censure. His concession was unfortunately nearly unique. A year later the "Introduction" to the first volume of the *Knickerbocker* promised to furnish to its readers criticism "unbiassed by any feeling of national prejudice, and consideration of personal popularity, by the partiality of private circles, or the favor of general society." This statement accurately listed the pitfalls of the American review. Whether the *Knickerbocker* would have escaped them under the editorship that published this platform will never be known. Lewis Gaylord Clark, who within a few months took over its direction, was far from being the man to live up to its prescriptions. While Charles Fenno Hoffman's liberal editorship still flavored its pages, however, a brief enlightened openmindedness remained in evidence. In a later number of the first volume, an article "by an Emeritus Professor" asserted the critic's first care to be the evaluation of the author's material, the second to be to discover where he had gotten it if it did have any value. If it proved to be worthless or derivative but still ornamental, he should credit the writer as a skillful artisan although withholding from him the higher rank of author. A year later, the *Knickerbocker* declared that America's best reviews did not "permit their pages to be made the conduits of private bile and individual spleen. They judge with justice, and in kindness they condemn." Its policy at its best, however, did not include a generosity equal to Morris'; and under Clark, though skillfully edited, it quite lost its first tolerance.

In 1835 Morris fired another round of his benevolent barrage. This time his target was the Scottish quarterlies, which he lashed for their permitting political or literary bias to color their decisions. The critic's task, he bluntly insisted, was not to punish refractory authors but to correct and guide them into better literary paths. The true critic is never a malignant abuser of writers; he should "enlighten the public mind, and brace it up fully with sound literature, that each may become the judge of what he reads." The herculean task of inculcating a modicum of critical taste throughout the whole democracy did not intimidate him. The critic's activity required, he added, the duty to defend the worthy writer; the literary air was polluted by buzzards seeking the carrion of author's corpses.

Opinion seesawed between rigorous chastisement and kindly correction. Excepting Melville in a fit of enthusiasm, no reputable reviewer reverted to the view chastised in 1818 by Bryant, that an American author be praised merely because he was American and his work not decidedly bad. The 1838 *New-Yorker* envisaged the critic as now administering the rod, now the pat somewhat higher on the back, but always to benefit the writer. Later, it warned the creative artist not to develop the critic's inquiring, analytic faculties: his should be a believing mind, not skeptical. He should let the critic hold the scales of judgment. More sternly, the contemporary *American Monthly Magazine* held out for severe judgment: harsh criticism had never in the past deterred the writer from practice of his art, and it conveyed sound benefit. The reviews were still pronouncing upon the functions of an art which they had not seriously undertaken to define.

By 1839 the *New York Review* realized that the air must be cleared through more accurate definition of criticism. The popular notion of what constitutes poetry, it wrote, is vague and confused; although poetry is probably at bottom indefinable, the critic should at least be able to present its salient characteristics. By so doing he would soon be able to define his own purposes. Allen and others in the same quarterly made a start, as already noted, in their belief that the critic should attempt to share the author's feeling; his judgment would gain thereby in clarity as well as in sympathy. Irving in the *Knickerbocker* somewhat petulantly reinforced this demand, although actuated more by personal fear than by knowledge of German theory. Unsympathetic, harsh comment may prune too closely the sprouts of American literature and so paralyze the author as to make him fearful of yielding to his feelings or to the promptings of his imagination, while it may frighten the reader from attempting to judge for himself.

The 1840 *New York Review* warned the reader to recognize his own powers and limitations in forming his judgment of a work. There are so many kinds of literary excellence, and he should not fear to admire qualities in a book that fail to appeal to others. He should likewise not condemn a book because it fails to appeal to him; the *New York Review* had practically adopted Morris' qualification of two decades earlier in advising the reader to append to his conclusions the clause, "as I understand it." A later number branded Kames's *Elements of Criticism*, which had been molding British and American attitudes for three generations, as hopelessly narrow and outdated.

Although the New York critics were not to succeed in composing a satisfactory definition of their art, their battles over the proper critical attitude help us to picture their inchoate concepts of its nature. They continued during the 1840's to worry the problem. *Arcturus*, a short-lived but brilliant review that Evert Duyckinck edited, late in 1840 expressed its hope in its "Prologue" that young writers would not fearfully see it as emulating its mythological prototype in hunting victims across the literary firmament. They had better, nonetheless, mind their literary manners. "We fervently trust . . . that no unshriven back, or harsh tongue, will tempt us to wield the executive thong." Duyckinck did review his subjects on the whole with kindly impartiality. In fact *Arcturus* wryly remarked in 1841, since criticism itself aspires to be counted as an art, it must itself submit to judgment. The 1844 *Columbian*, thinking in the same line, revived the authors' complaint of the early 1800's in demanding that critics surrender their long-treasured refuge in anonymity. Critics had drawn their first canons from the genius of authors; they should pay this debt by judging with candor and fairness and should, like the authors, assume personal responsibility for their utterances. Just as authors had been driven from their hiding-places to bear the onus of their works, so the critic should no longer pretend that his judgment was part of the collective voice of the periodical in which it was printed. Although reviewers have never been entirely dislodged from their anonymity, by the 1850's there was a noticeable increase in the number of signed articles on literary subjects.

The benefits for the United States of a properly developed criticism came in also for consideration, although no unanimity of opinion as to what constituted its propriety was established. Jones, writing in the 1844 *Democratic Review*, declared that a pure, just criticism would prove to be as salutary an influence upon the public as an accepted high moral standard of personal conduct. The *New World* agreed with the 1845 *Broadway Journal*'s assertion that "honest criticism has no more evil in it than the scalpel of the surgeon"—and such an analogy, with the employment a year later of anaesthetics in surgery, served soon to diminish the pain of criticism too. At the time, however, the *Broadway Journal* was probably considering with alarm the feverish symptoms of the *Democratic Review*, which might well spread a politically minded, biased, critical contagion analogous to that which had infected British reviews. The 1848 *Literary World*, if one may continue the infectious analogy, preferred to emphasize the preventive medical aspects of criticism. It should seek the good and ward off the evil, and so build up the resistance of the reading public by keeping it aware of good literature wherever it appears.

By 1849 legislative criticism had lost its battle. In that year, the *Literary World*, defending Wordsworth's performance in *The Excursion*, declared that such a poem is *sui generis*, obeying the laws of its own nature. The organic concept of literature had by this time become firmly entrenched in the thinking of liberal New York literati. The *Literary World* appealed for support to Goethe's twofold critical query, recently brought to New York's attention by Margaret Fuller of the *Tribune*, which runs also throughout much of the decade's criticism: What did the author intend to do? and how well did he succeed in doing it? The art of poetic criticism was still in its infancy, the writer added. Coleridge had indeed provided a noble specimen in his critique of Wordsworth's theories and performance, but his fragmentary analysis of the imagination must be completed before we can find the fundamental laws determining the merit of a work of art.

The *Literary World*'s statement that poetic criticism was still in its infancy was expanded by the 1850 *Whig Review* to include all of literary criticism. It is, the writer declared, a difficult performance. It may enlighten and delight; it may also be so abused as to mislead and offend. Its duty to the reader obliges it to annihilate what is worthless; its obligation to the writer requires it to foster whatever of promise he shows. A year later Tuckerman attacked the often repeated belief that interpretation requires powers inferior to those needed for creation. Only men of profound thought can bring to bear the concentrated attention requisite to examination of works of genius. And where would these works of genius stand in popular estimation without the constant services of the intellectual go-between who interprets them? Modern criticism, he added in the vein of Allen twelve years earlier, shows in its best performance the activity of a striking intelligence, by whose aid it explores and illuminates the work under review and often casts new light upon the subject. Whether the creative or the critical intellect occupies the higher level is a fruitless question; in literary criticism they function as a team.

Not that traditional critical methods and the aids they had designed were entirely scrapped in the new era. New Yorkers as a whole, however enthusiasts like the Young Americans might cry out to make all things new, were cannily conservative of whatever could be salvaged out of the old machinery; they knew that a system that had held sway for centuries probably possessed elements of worth. Even during the final decade of the period traditional criteria cropped up. *Holden's Dollar Magazine* in 1851, for example, found fault with Melville because he had so confused the literary genera in *Moby Dick* as to render it extremely difficult to interpret. It was permissible to mark out a new literary course, as Wordsworth had done in *The Excursion*, provided that the product justified the innovation, but wanton disregard of tradition was not praised. One finds the unities also occasionally invoked as if still binding. The 1856 *Democratic Review*, however, probably expressed the majority opinion when it threw out as of little benefit to critical understanding the minute organization of poetry into classes and subclasses: the poet understands his art better than the critic. New Yorkers were nearly ready for James Huneker's assertion a half-century later: "there are no schools of art; there are only artists."

Swinton's brilliant apologia for novels in the 1854 *Putnam's* refused to admit the traditional principles to be binding upon the new art-form. First, he commented bitterly on the bad odor attaching to the novel among the unco guid: "Nothing is more easy or gratuitous than the vituperative condemnation and contempt that have so often been lavished on novels and novel-writing. . . . The guardian makes it a point to keep his ward as carefully from a novel as from the measles, and would as lief that she should dose herself with ratsbane as devour a romance." The world's idea is now the true, he continued; the realm of criticism has been turned upside down. The new movement has "swept away the 'old drowsy shop'" of Aristotelian logic and ontology, and erected—or, at least, laid the foundation of—that splendid fabric among whose master builders are the German philosophers who have subverted the ancient systems. Swinton does not, indeed, discard the Aristotelian conception of the creative artist, which he claims for the novelist equally with the poet; but the minute legislation which the three preceding centuries had built upon the *Poetics* he wholeheartedly rejects.

The old oracles of criticism were not, however, wholly dumb, and their loss of prestige was sometimes regretted. The 1856 *Putnam's*, for example, maintained that they still existed although their utterances were drowned out amidst the new conventional criticisms of the time, which were expressed doubtfully in "the labyrinth of indecision of the modern muses and the modern critics." To the few surviving conservatives, their age seemed to be as skeptical as Dryden's had been but without Dryden's good sense, and they looked upon its openmindedness as uncertainty and lack of direction. They were answered in 1857 by Jones, that adherence to any one system breeds intolerance: "systems are invariably one-sided and exclusive, exhibiting in general but a partial view of the question. . . . Truth lies between the extremes of opposite theories"—a position defended by Aristotle himself. The battle over regulative versus organic attitudes of criticism was brought to an abrupt end by the diversion of men's minds to the Civil War, but the regulative critic had been by that time thoroughly routed in New York. No well-defined critical theories had been formulated and no method wholly adopted. The way was open, nonetheless, for new approaches to his material by the author and for corresponding critical freedom of judgment on the part of critic and reviewer.

Among the varied criteria employed by New York critics in estimating literature, a nationalist or patriotic yardstick was perhaps the most flamboyantly used. Discussion of this criterion belongs, however, to the subsequent discussion of criticism and the American literary scene. The more specifically literary standards treated here include the moral qualities or effects of the work, its appeal to popular taste, and its emotional appeal.

THE MORAL YARDSTICK

The nationwide social and religious background made inevitable judgment of literature by its moral content or effect. As the period advanced, the effect of literature upon morals came more and more to the fore. Although morals can be taken in the broader sense of mores, and were so construed, the term regularly carried with it the sense of personal conduct; and although the better reviews usually strove to effect a distinction between the morally didactic and the socially representative, they never lost their awareness of the narrower sense of the term in their concern over the broader. Sectarian periodicals, with which we are but slightly concerned here, as one would expect emphasized matters of personal morality in their so-called literary judgments.

The degree of concern with literary treatment of personal morality varied somewhat in different parts of the country. New York was on the whole less strait-laced than New England or the South. It had its piously moral publications, to be sure, but these did not set the tone of criticism in Gotham. The literary magazines tended to equate decency in conduct with good taste, which did not rigidly interpret the Decalogue though adhering to its intent. And while they professed to be staunch supporters of sound morals as well as sound religion, they declined to submit to sectarian dictation on either head.

During the early years of this period, the reviews generally agreed with the 1817 *American Monthly Magazine* in preferring profound moral reflection to factitious sentiment. During these years, little separation was made between morals and Christian doctrine. As for the novel, Paulding had written in 1823 in praising Cooper's *The Pioneers* that it should omit vulgar, vicious scenes. Vulgarity he defined, differing slightly from Cooper in this respect, as bad conduct on any social level; and he included both mores and personal morality. Sound moral principles must not, however, be attacked: the 1824 *Atlantic Magazine* stated as its policy that it would ignore worthless books except for innocent merriment at their expense, for the exposure of quackery, or "to repel all attacks upon morality, or correct principle, when there is talent enough developed to render them dangerous." Its practice indicates that the final purpose occupied the editors' attention more often than the others.

The pious *Minerva* was more concerned with establishing sound principles: the novelist should "further the great and eternal interests of virtue" while at the same time including nothing to offend the most delicate conscience. Somewhat surprisingly, the author is adjured also to furnish "a faithful and spirited delineation of human character"—the truth but not the whole truth, it would seem. The editor, the Reverend James Brooks, had literary concerns beyond those delimited by his cloth. Very few novels written to give moral or religious instruction satisfied him: the authors were incompetent litterateurs; the morality of their works was either questionable or beyond mortal attainment; or their point of view was narrowly sectarian. When they were not dull and didactic, they were ignorant or self-sufficient; they lacked invention and knowledge of the world. Brooks's literary enthusiasms were, however, colored by his religious concerns. Byron by his death "in the cause of freedom and our religion" atoned for his and his poems' moral lapses. Jonathan Swift, on the other hand, met no such leniency. His prose is generally "unamiable and repulsive," and only the most depraved taste can enjoy "his obscene and disgusting attempts at poetry." A cleric had no excuse such as might be advanced for Byron: "if ever mortal was actuated by the malevolence of a demon, it was the Dean of St. Patrick's."

The morals-mores combination produced other responses in these early years. The 1828 *Critic* looked askance at Hawthorne's innocuous *Fanshawe* on the ground that it presented too many bad characters, a defect the more reprehensible since its unknown author was obviously a scholar and gentleman of sensibility. It twice refused to say a good word for Bulwer-Lytton's *Pelham* in spite of its wide popularity: its undoubted literary merits deserved no praise when they were employed to make vice alluring. The reviewer incidentally regretted the necessity to mention it at all: his testimony would "induce many to peruse it with an augmentation of interest." The 1832 *Mirror*, taking a less moralistic line, asked its readers to bear in mind that seeming indecencies in Francis Beaumont's plays, as in Fielding's novels, had not appeared improper to their less scrupulous times. Applying the same principle five years later, it inveighed against the dumping of trashy European novels upon American markets. Forecasting Howells' attitude fifty years later, the *Mirror* insisted that, however these might represent accepted practice abroad, they in no way conformed to American mores. A year earlier, trying to set bounds to the moral criterion of literature, the *Mirror* had declared that a great deal of nonsense had been written about the moral defects of Bulwer's novels; these denunciations had obscured their just claims as works of a gifted, cultivated mind. More in keeping with current attitudes in America toward Bulwer, the *Knickerbocker* commended him for having omitted from *The Last Days of Pompeii* those specimens of an immoral tendency so censurable in his earlier works. Literary men, although aware of a distinction between moral and literary standards, had in New York not progressed so far in this matter as had their contemporaries in Concord.

Developing the position taken by the 1836 *Mirror*, Samuel Ward in the 1837 *New York Review* tackled the problem posed by the novels of Balzac. Adopting a restriction that would have infuriated the new *Democratic Review*, he would have them removed from the open shelves of libraries. They should not be offered to the public beside the works of Shakespeare and Scott. On the other hand, he would not proscribe them from the literary world. Balzac's novels, he argued, present a life governed by a morality other than that of America; it is consequently unjust to judge them by moral standards alien to their world. In moral outlook indeed they cannot serve as models for American writers, but they possess solid merits that the student cannot overlook. Any novelist who depicts the whole range of human nature must include many unsavory characters. "If vice is to be portrayed"—and Ward never doubted that it should be—"it can hardly be a question, which is most perilous to morals,—to have it veiled in the attire of virtue, or exposed, as in ours [Balzac's] in all its naked deformities." Without going so far expressly as Ward had gone, the 1845 *Broadway Journal* declared that American life must be represented as human life, and Americans as human beings. The article left the reader to finish the statement, confident that readers knew that no man is perfect. Thackeray's novels, as we have seen, drove the wedge deeper into the tough log of American prudery.

In the eyes of many New York magazines the besetting sin of popular literature was its pandering to the general desire for excitement. Although the 1833 *Mirror* optimistically maintained that American fiction had abandoned "star-gazing, building castles in the air, and wild theory" for scenes and tales which show man his duty to Man and to God, its hope that readers would accept a more serious literature was neither supported by the event nor in harmony with the spirit of the times. Ward noted in the 1839 *New York Review* that "the highly wrought fiction and the wild drama accord well now with our existence of increasing excitement. . . . But we are, unhappily, prone to judge all productions of the mind by the touchstone of their effect upon sensations habituated to unnatural excitement; and to measure by dynamical rules, things which should be considered under conditions of repose." Such unduly exhilarated senses, he feared, boded ill for the reception of his friend Longfellow's *Hyperion*. (It is amusing to find Sam Ward, the *bon vivant* and adventurer, protesting against sensational works; but his literary taste, if not his conduct, was irreproachable.) The *Knickerbocker* too deplored this unhealthy heat which must become "a hot-bed of impetuous and irrational feeling, reaching a precocious and unhealthy growth, and going through society corrupted and corrupting." How could a representative national literature that would show the fundamental health of the country sprout and grow amid such abnormal emotional disturbances? And how could a sound moral nature be developed in America for future writers to present?

Anticipating Henry James by some thirty-five years, the 1849 *Literary World* stood among the first to offer a solution to what was actually a twofold problem. It was willing to criticize Wordsworth's *The Excursion* on moral grounds because it felt that the author had invited such a standard of judgment. At the same time, this writer noted, employment of a moral criterion was not judgment of "its poetry, strictly so called." Twofold criticism of the poem was indeed warranted. The author's avowed intent of moral instruction invited application of the former criterion, while the fact that the work was a poem justified the use of the latter; but these were distinct approaches. Such clear-sighted dichotomy in criticism was however rare in theory and still more rare in practice.

Approximating a concept held early in the century but in a kindlier vein, the 1857 *Putnam's* pictured the critic not as the watchdog of society but as the wary paterfamilias. "His duty to them requires him to examine very particularly into the purposes and intents of each new aspirant to the familiarities of the arm-chair and the study-lamp." Seduction of the guileless young reader by the possibly misguiding novel had replaced as the prime danger erroneous instruction of the more mature. Hoping to dam literary evil at its fountainhead, *Putnam's* added paternal advice to the ambitious novice in letters. The bite of the earlier critic had nonetheless been almost muzzled. He had once guarded the threshold like the Roman watchdog, and the suppliant author had feared his fangs like the Roman client attending his patron. Unlike the Roman father, this later critic exercised no power of life and death, and the way lay open for that friendly alliance of author with critic or editor which Howells was soon to champion.

DEMOCRATIC CRITICISM

For many thinkers the democratic ideal had critical implications. Although it had been noted earlier, after the Jacksonian era had taken form the connections between democracy and literature were for several years drawn more tightly. The proponents of this union somewhat paradoxically included men of highly cultivated taste, whose love affair with democracy in its proletarian extension induced them to believe in public opinion and popular choice as literary criteria of excellence. This alliance becomes less astounding, however, when one reflects that the United States then felt obliged to prove itself to the world in both literature and government; it is hardly surprising that theorists should have applied the same principle to both activities.

At first, indeed, the democratic idea in relation to literature was rather patronizingly presented. In the opinion of the 1823 *Mirror*, able poets write acceptably for the higher class of readers who can appreciate literary niceties; at the same time, they improve the minds and happiness of middle- and lower-class audiences. Whether the lesser quality of readers were equated with lower social classes, the writer tactfully omitted to state. He was evidently a Jeffersonian at heart, for he declared that poets, who form a nation's character more than prose-writers, should take Virgil's example seriously to heart. In agrarian America it was peculiarly appropriate that they teach the rising generation the advantages of rural and agricultural life as the fit setting for the gentleman and author. The *Mirror* was evidently not yet ready to conceive of a literature of, by, or for the people, whether in prose or in verse. A year later the *Mirror* condescendingly ascribed Cooper's early popularity as a novelist to an aberration of popular taste from which the country would soon recover. Cooper pretended to no "delicacy and elevation of sentiment, elegance of style, or . . . literary refinement." Persons of a regulated taste could never greatly admire such work; they would perhaps keep it in some dusty corner of their libraries, to be dusted off and read for pastime when nothing better had come to hand.

Regulated taste, however, could not long control New York reading or thinking on literature; the admirers of Addison and Pope were no longer in the literary saddle. The 1825 *New York Literary Gazette* was already declaring that no amount of literary talent could successfully array itself against opinions and principles which the majority accepted and believed to be bound up with the safety of society. Later, as Jacksonian democracy triumphed in letters, this sentiment controlled; the voice of the people should be the voice of letters. (Democracy, it should be parenthetically noted, still drew the color line. Following the footsteps of an earlier Boston periodical which condemned Cooper for needlessly sacrificing Cora and Uncas in *The Last of the Mohicans*— since Uncas was an Indian anyhow, Cora in spite of her mixed blood might have been allowed to live and marry him—later New York magazines branded Desdemona a strumpet for having married the Negro Othello.) Popular opinion, editors recognized, was a force no writer could ignore.

Equally hostile at first was reaction to authorship by the common man. The 1834 *Mirror* lamented: "The pestilence of poetry or verse-making rages past endurance. For one author of any pretensions, we have ten hundred of none. . . . Numerous are the fountains of inspiration, or inspissation in this author-ridden land—great the fecundity of scribblers." Verse-making was not a concomitant of suffrage, Morris declared. He published much of the verse submitted to him chiefly because it kept open an outlet for such true poems as might appear; but he felt obliged to testify to the meager merit of most of the poems submitted to him, and he reserved the right to edit according to his own taste such verse as he admitted to his columns. Although readable poems occasionally appeared in various periodicals, the poetic level was low even for magazine verse, and Morris probably differed from other editors chiefly in the frank admission of his feelings.

One foreboding of the growing popular voice in literature which did not escape those editors who read their subscription lists was the increasing circulation of periodicals west of the Alleghanies. Books in surprising numbers also found their way across the mountains. The 1835 *Mirror* remarked that the western folk in spite of their pioneering labors not only took the time to read books but supported periodicals printed in their own areas as well as subscribing to many from the east. Democratic leveling, it was generally conceded, was most noticeably at work in the new western states, and their demand for books and periodicals provided a market that no publisher could afford to slight.

In 1834 the *Knickerbocker*, which had always an eye single to its own best interests, capitulated to the power of popular literary judgment. "We take the *public* to be the umpire in letters; and we look upon any opinions which clash with a verdict from that source, as of very little value indeed." Such canny yielding to the Jacksonian spirit of the age was the conclusion to a shrewd assessment of the public situation and was not made without reservations. In 1835, although still accepting the democratic voice as divine, a writer in the *Knickerbocker* declared the critic's function to be "to enlighten the public mind, and brace it up fully with sound literature, that each may become the judge of what he reads." Although the power of the people in literary decisions was admitted, its capacity was still in the optative mood. A few pages later, another writer found that the public taste, manners, and morals had suffered grievously from a surfeit of Scott, Victor Hugo, and Bulwer-Lytton. Readers among the masses had developed "a respect for the license of barbarous ages," for outlaws and freebooters, of which they must be purged. The critic, the *American Monthly Magazine* chimed in, found the education of popular taste a difficult task indeed. He could not begin by ignoring the reading habits already developed; since all men now read, he could hardly expect the author to run counter to their tastes in reading. The writer apparently deplored these preferences, but was in a quandary how to improve them.

Perhaps the most significant summary of the relation of criticism to

American literature made in New York up to that time, Edward Sherman Gould's address in 1836 to the Mercantile Association, was quickly published in the *Mirror* and soon copied out into other magazines over the country. Under the title, "American Criticism on American Authors," Gould included not only the critical opinion of writers but the attitudes of periodical editors toward the American literary effort. Although he commended the attainments made by American authors, he felt that their improvement had failed to keep abreast of American progress in other endeavors, and he sought for the causes that had delayed their achievement. The seven items which he discussed, and which individually were often brought up in periodicals, were these. First, an editor who receives a complimentary book from an author feels bound in common courtesy to refrain from adverse comment or review. Secondly, the overworked editor sometimes receives a prepared review of the book from a friend of the author (Whitman even wrote reviews of his *Leaves of Grass* in later years) which he prints in order to save himself the labor of reading the book. Thirdly, editors who are concerned with fostering the national literature sincerely hesitate to blight what may be "native genius" by treating its product with the severity it merits. Fourthly, the editor may be apprehensive of public hostility to his magazine if it condemns an American book. Although it is the editor's critical duty to direct the public taste rather than to be governed by it, he has to consider fearfully any threat to his subscription list; and he may feel, though incorrectly, that fearless expression of opinion can make him enemies. Fifthly, editors feel a constraint about expressing adverse opinions of works by living authors, whom they may meet and sometimes personally respect. They sacrifice the welfare of American letters to salve some writer's feelings with a value-less emollient of panegyric. Sixthly, the editor understandably feels grateful to authors who are themselves contributors to his periodical. One can hardly condemn a work by an author when he has already given him the accolade of printing his works in his columns. Authors who contribute to periodicals do often earnestly desire to further the cause of periodical literature, and it would seem like biting the hand that feeds you to respond with harsh words to their efforts. Finally, "the production of sound and genuine criticism, like that of genuine poetry, requires much more labour, much more study, and much more talent, than that of its spurious substitute." The majority of so-called critics look upon their work as drudgery and are hacks who desire merely to turn out the requisite amount of copy. Inducements to criticize are few and are more often on the side of error and corruption than on the side of justice. "As a general rule (for there are honourable exceptions), they whose business it is to *do* criticism, seem really not to be aware of the dignity and importance of their vocation, nor of the capabilities of the style of writing belonging to it."

Gould's analysis of the current state of criticism found support in other periodicals. The 1837 *New-Yorker* advocated a constant, stern criticism as "the only present corrective of the hot-bed growth" of books that were sprouting from the unguided, uncontrolled popular presses. Other writers in the same periodical, tackling the problem from another side, tried to assess the impression of an age upon the literature it produces. One felt that while poetry comes from an individual mind, it is molded by its times; he felt that the age was more effective upon the poet than was the poet upon his age: "Genius may make an era, but it more commonly is developed by it." The critic must accordingly place a part of the responsibility for the work upon the poet's social environment. Another challenged the primitivistic notion that the rudest states of society foster the boldest, most original writing. In his view the author made the age. "A few minds give tone and character to the literature of each successive age, and with these few it is a matter of little importance whether the general mind be in a sound and healthful condition." In one volume of the *New-Yorker*, then, the two sides of the debate on responsibility for the nature of a work were presented, with the added injunction from a third writer that whatever the product stemmed from, it must be rigidly inspected by the critic. This injunction demanded no authoritarian judgment, but it was still too severe for the taste of the majority and seemed moreover to be based on literary principles which were for a time forced to yield to other bases for judgment.

The eight-year ascendancy of Jacksonian democracy was now ready to bear fruit in a triumph for the popular judgment. The most widely known expression of its victory is Emerson's "The American Scholar," which was echoed on violently democratic grounds in the trumpetings of Orestes Brownson. The *Democratic Review* was an equally vocal mouthpiece of the new democratic concept; its files contain the most vigorous and articulate championing of the common man produced in New York. Its manifesto asserted: "the vital principle of an American national literature must be democracy." This new democracy makes mandatory the rewriting of all history and the reconsideration of all political science and moral truth; all old subjects of thought and all others that may arise in relation to human existence must be reexamined in the light of this new concept. Literature as the medium of expression for the new gospel obviously participated in the universal alteration.

The democratic evangel appeared in other New York periodicals as well. The politic *Knickerbocker* immediately supported the dogma and in so doing sounded the keynote of New York's habitual atttitude toward the arts. Since the enjoyment of freedom favors the dignity and intelligence of men, the aristocratic assumption that literature and the fine arts suffer under free institutions is palpably absurd. The elegant and ornamental, however, must never be given precedence over the useful arts; yet "a competent skill in literature and the fine arts is a just source of national pride." The same virtues that preserve liberty foster "the pure and rational refinements of a wholesome, natural, manly taste." Our rational freedom and liberal diffusion of property and intelligence, it concluded, make a climate more favorable to cultivation of an independent literature than all the patronage ever lavished by royalty.

Such extreme democratic reviews, as they appeared to more conservative New Yorkers, were not long uncontested. The open-minded but moderate *New York Review*, founded in the same year with the *Democratic Review*, declared that the popular notion of what constitutes poetry needed more definition. The contemporary *Corsair* warned its readers that the undiscriminating appetite for trashy British novels seemed to support adverse British reflections upon our popular literary taste. Taking up this admonition, the *New York Review* found highly wrought and seasoned European fiction to be exactly suited to the restless American populace, which refuses to take time for thoughtful judgment of literary values. Such reviews looked with alarm upon the headlong course taken by the *Democratic Review*. The latter periodical had, however, caught the fancy of the young liberals; Whitman in later years said that it had possessed "a profounder quality of talent than any since," and it had support of more orthodox liberals such as Bryant, Hawthorne, and Lowell.

But deference to popular literary taste, it seemed to many literary men, had been carried too far. The *Knickerbocker*, as usual with its ear to the ground to catch the vibration of sentiment, by 1839 had abandoned its temporary support of the Young Americans. It published an article by Washington Irving that embodied a plea for more considered judgment of literature than the people seemed to him likely or competent to make. Irving complained that such criticism as the United States was producing was crude and hasty, written principally to support the sales of books—in which charge he had Poe's vigorous seconding—and hence so oppressive of individual judgment that readers actually feared to express or even to form opinions of their own. The author who pleases the great crowd of readers must, Irving conceded, demonstrate a variety of skills, yet the reader must form sounder personal judgments as a palliative to commercialized noticing of books. Apprehensive himself of the fickleness of popular preference, Irving feared that no author or reader could feel secure when so many long-established literary altars were being overthrown and so many household deities dashed to the ground. Irving himself, it may be mentioned in passing, had some reason for apprehension; the mention of his literary career in the thirties and forties, though frequent, partook regularly of epitaphic eulogy and seldom bothered to criticize his works.

Irving's complaint of subsidized reviews found frequent repetition during the pre–Civil War period, as indeed throughout the century. The best comfort that the usually optimistic *Mirror* could salvage from the literary wreck which it feared to be impending in the United States was the morose reflection that, bad though American reviewing was, it was only one-half as depraved as that practiced in Britain: the latter puff and then, having administered the kiss of Judas, they assassinate; we merely puff.

In three thoughtful articles the 1840 *New York Review* attempted to throw some light upon the condition of criticism and to offer suggestions for its improvement. In one article the current "modes of critical judgment—the writer declines to call them laws"—were defended as just and impartial. The *New York Review*'s known hostility to the excesses of the Young Americans obviously precluded any support of their evangel. The writer accepted the hypothesis that there could be many distinct species of literary excellence, and he particularly approved examination of the author's life and personality as illuminating his works. Such an emphasis indicates the writer's agreement with the *New York Review*'s recent championship of the new German literary thinking as one source of improvement for American critical practice.

German theory reappeared in the second article. The writer assailed the ruling passion of the American reader, an itch for novelty that, as Irving had lamented, made him an iconoclast: "It claims the right to doubt the wisdom of the past, and set aside the authority of experience." It sees the mind as a mere sponge that soaks up learning without labor and needs no discipline: "Thinking is useless, observation all-sufficient. . . . It substitutes blocks for books, turns universities into work-shops, and discards all knowledge but that which presents itself in a visible and tangible shape." The plague of visual aids had already struck from kindergarten to college. Germany, the writer added, has resisted these Anglo-American educational trends—which the twentieth-century educator may recognize with some redness of face. The true critical position, the writer concluded, is as always somewhere between the extremes of dogmatic traditionalism and irresponsible worship of mutability.

In the third article, Evert Duyckinck threw out Kames's *Elements of Criticism*, which had passed through several American printings and had been standard precept in matters of judgment. Our literary salvation, he wrote, depends upon the appearance of a great American poet, for the poet, the sole interpreter of his age, can alone deliver us from our vagaries in letters. In this mediating position the *New York Review* found supporters.

Among these cohorts was naturally the *Knickerbocker*, eager to leap upon the bandwagon, but carefully hedging its bets. Approaching the problem obliquely in an essay on the criticism of painting, it placed the critic of art in the same relation to his readers that the preacher occupies in the field of religion; and in those days, it must be remembered, the preacher was to many Americans the voice of authority. Probably fearful that it had leaned too far to the right, in a subsequent utterance its shifted its position: "The people are the only true tribunal. They separate, with the hand of a refiner, the dross from the gold. By them genius is preserved, and pretensions discarded." It is true, this article conceded, that the nation has not widely cultivated the taste for poetry and prefers to await the accolade of a critic as ennobling what it reads; but it can judge if it once sets its mind to do so. Popular judgment, it maintained, existed *in posse*, not yet *in esse;* and in so doing it deftly kept a foot in either camp by supporting an unassailable assertion—incontrovertible because it did not deal with ascertainable facts.

In the fifth decade defection from the democratic ranks was frequent. William Alfred Jones, who had led the van of the *Democratic Review*, had tempered considerably his claims for the validity of popular judgment. Criticism, he wrote in the 1841 *Arcturus*, is an art and therefore has its rules; it is a practice to be learned, not merely observed. Most critics lack standards, partly from defective training, partly from lack of instinctive feeling for the beauties of literature. Reason and taste are both active in criticizing, and neither is the common possession of all men in effective amount. In a revulsion that went beyond Jones's position, the *New World* longed for a return to the elegant simplicity of the *Spectator* and the majestic periods of the *Rambler*.

The *Democratic Review* had itself noticeably cooled off from its earlier fervor, but had still a volley to discharge. In 1843 it admitted that cheap reprints of novels had dealt the deathblow to criticism as it had been practiced. Everyone could now read novels, and the excerpts with which critics had formerly filled their columns had become superfluous. Until some other filler for the quarterlies' pages could be devised, critics would be at a loss, and popular reaction to novels would remain paramount. Although this volley was directed at opponents of the Democratic dogma and although the *Democratic Review* had itself abandoned the excerpt in its relatively brief articles, it admitted that even its discussions had declined in influence under the wave of cheap reprints. As is the case today, cheap duplication of books multiplied copies of worthless books far in excess of the better, and both radical and conservative were alive to the danger to popular taste in these reprints.

Many thoughtful people saw the state of criticism as worsening in the forties. The 1844 *Columbian* charged that professed critics were not merely venal or biased, but were ignorant of the very sources upon which critical practice must be based. Instead of studying Aristotle, Horace, Quintilian, Longinus, Erasmus, or Dryden, they consulted— if indeed they read at all—the *Edinburgh* and *Quarterly* reviews or the *London Literary Gazette* and so gained views ignorant of and hostile to American letters. Many simply ran down their prey by instinct, as a badly trained pointer scents and courses any game it meets. Those readers, moreover, who did consult the reviews demanded sensationalism in them as in their fiction. As Jones mourned in the *Democratic Review*, "a flat reviewer, however accurate and true, must fail . . . while a clever conjecture passes for more than an acknowledged truth, which wants the stimulus of novelty." Although Jones's immediate target was Macaulay, his stricture applied equally to American reviewing. The *New World* noted that politics was beginning to add its stain to the desired clarity of literary judgment. Politics "draws a film over the eyes of criticism," a film long-darkening British vision but hitherto not an American critical weakness. And finally, the critic's voice carried no weight since he did not sign his reviews; his judgment was in the eyes of the 1844 *Columbian* "the *ipse dixit* of an anonymous nobody." Suffering such a list of ailments, it was feared that American criticism was doomed to permanent ill-health.

In an attempt to sound the bottom of the critical morass, the 1845 *Broadway Journal* noted an unfortunate connection between the weakness of popular taste and the strength of popular desire for the instantaneous creation of a national literature. Americans were still prone to ascribe high quality to whatever work an American had produced. This rampant nationalism darkened counsel by its measuring an American work against another American work instead of against some predetermined or universal standard. In their haste to create an American literature by fiat, the people had snatched a few "terrified Tompkinses" from their secure obscurity in the poet's corner of newspapers and set them "upon the bald top of our American Parnassus" where they became the targets for the merited scorn of the foreign press. Obstinately using these nonentities as yardsticks to measure subsequent American performance, the ignorant populace sought ruthlessly to exterminate all that progress which might proceed from originality and independent judgment. Until the public should realize that the best literature is not merely national but "that which is the same under all languages and under all skies," the country could not achieve a truly national literature, which, as Goethe had shown, is paradoxically the more national the more nearly it approximates the universal. Duyckinck agreed in the *Whig Review* to the spirit of this diatribe: "A sudden *cacoethes laudandi* seemed to have seized the press and thrown it into paroxysms of admiration" for American writing.

Continuing in the same vein, W. A. Jones declared that Americans needed to learn the facts of their literary situation. Using as his springboard Margaret Fuller's *Papers on Literature and Art*, Jones in the 1846 *Democratic Review* agreed with her that Americans were strong enough to be told the truth, that their literature assayed for the most part as low-grade ore; and he shared her confidence in American ability to work richer mines that stood ready to be opened. He approved also her statement that American literature should be an expression of "the original, naturally developed life of the country" in high and elevated forms that would rank with the best in the world; and like her in this also, he made no effort to dictate what these forms should be. The *Literary World* a year later cordially seconded his remarks. Americans, it declared, should rid themselves of that bombastic nationalism which made ridiculous literary pretensions and by so doing clear the decks for efficient action. Duyckinck added in the same number that our criticism was unjust, unreliable, and insincere; morally and intellectually it lacked soundness. "Much of it is paltry and shallow, more is spurious and mercenary. . . . Criticism absolutely just, we hardly have at all." Americans must no longer follow such blind guides if they would find the way to a national literature.

Low-grade criticism, being cheap and easy to produce, was as always stubborn in relinquishing its place. In 1849 Jones repeated his complaint that judicious reviewing sounded tame and insipid to "those who love the slashing style, who consider abuse, satire, and presumption, boldness; who vote ribaldry, wit; and give the palm of copious, manly eloquence to coarse, declamatory invective." The world's coarse thumb, he reminded readers, lacks the delicate touch to test poets and works of art. *Holden's Dollar Magazine* charged that Americans, "bolder if not wiser than our fathers," overthrew and tomahawked the idols they were incompetent to judge.

Tuckerman urged in 1850 a renewed study of established literary masterpieces in the hope of discovering the sources of their popularity and durability. At present, he wrote, "the passion for novelty seeks for such unlicensed indulgence" that such studies are needed to renew the taste for the simple in art. Hazlitt was Tuckerman's pattern. The *Literary World* preferred that such a study should take Coleridge as its master; he "always gave the principle with the fact, and spoke from the center." His marginal notations on his favorite authors like John Donne "are capable of setting up, and have set up, a race of critics." The note of appreciative and constructive rather than minatory and destructive criticism appeared also in vigorous objections to Poe's frequent use of the hatchet upon luckless contemporary writers.

Loud-mouthed patriots who demanded a one-hundred–per cent American literature were attacked with far less than Longfellow's urbane irony in *Kavanagh*. People who deplored foreign influence upon American literature and art, charged the 1852 *Whig Review*, were guilty of "shallow cant and ignorant gossip. . . . Art submits to no such limitations." A national school of art derives from the practice of the nation's artists collectively; it is the sum total of their efforts. Where they studied, or what were their subjects, are matters irrelevant to the quality of nationality. Such art-criticism was readily transferred to literary matters by numerous informed reviewers and critics.

Advocates of a national literature that was also universal met at times with vituperative attack. George N. Sanders, for example, in the *Democratic Review* for 1852 lumped together the *North American Review* and the appreciative essays of William A. Jones as the principal exponents of "fogydom" in the United States. Such widely inclusive concepts of American literature were "English black draughts from an American bottle. Young America does not require such pap. . . . We do not want such a disgusting and sickening literature. The American constitution will not be strengthened by swallowing such emetics" as Jones's decoctions from Lamb and Hazlitt, which are "incubi"—in his rage Sanders magnificently mingled his metaphors—"upon American republicanism which must be rooted out and deadened."

Less rabid but still vigorous contenders for a distinctly natural poetry also appeared, who would let popular taste be its criterion. The 1853 *New York Quarterly* rebuked reviewers who had condemned Longfellow's "A Psalm of Life" and the average American's delight in it. Its popularity had its source not in a depraved popular taste, but in the enjoyment of what the author had successfully undertaken to do; the poem presented no unknown quantity but something readers could recognize pleasurably, "what they know, and believe, and feel."

The efforts of these nationalists were skillfully countered by *Putnam's* in a defense of Lowell's European concerns. "Lowell is a truly American poet," the writer averred. "Those patriotic sticklers for an ultra-national literature, who show their nationality by constant allusions to the Alleghanies and the Mississippi, may not find in him what they desire. Here is a man who is willing to recognize the existence of other national objects, yet infuses into his writings the spirit of our times and our institutions, so unmistakably, that no one could be deceived as to his birth-place."

By the sixth decade, the belief in criticism as an art requiring special aptitude and training had perceptibly gained ground; on this the majority of better periodicals were agreed. Some proponents of the popular voice in criticism were still vocal. The 1856 *Harper's* asked: "Is it criticism of a picture when Jones says he does not like it? or when Jenkins says he does? . . . Is it criticism of a poem for Smith to say that it is not what he expected? Yet if it seems foolish in the individual case, it is not in the general. Art addresses itself to everybody." This writer sees the artist as a middleman between nature and the public, and he hears the voice of the people as the voice of God. The public is the recipient; its reaction is the only one of value. He did not rule out the service to the populace of the trained critic, but such a function was apparently only ancillary. And *Putnam's* once went so far as to doubt the value of professional literary guidance: efforts by critics to clarify and evaluate literature, having generally darkened counsel, now offered little hope of profit from future exertions. R. H. Stoddard in the *National Magazine* accused critics of possessing no clearer poetical knowledge or critical skill than the populace they had undertaken to instruct. When guides are blind, he concluded, their following must seek its own way.

In spite of attack criticism retained its place, however ill-defined that place might be. Demands were made, however, that it improve its methods. The time has come in America, declared the 1857 *Putnam's,* when serious critics must try artists by the true laws of art. Patriotic reviewers, practicing only "the delicious criticism of sympathy," might be preferable to the exponents of "starveling ill-will" who constituted the bulk of British criticism. Good will, however, is no equivalent for objective evaluation; it is at bottom patronizing, of no use to writer or reader. The *Knickerbocker* pointed up a like situation in dividing reviewers into those who wrote *up* an author's work and those who wrote it *down;* specimens of any intermediate criticism were as rare as they were desirable. The 1858 *Emerson's Magazine* described by implication its ideal critic in condemning the reviewing cliques: these were often the mere mouthpieces of someone's "partiality, cowardice, spite, or bile."

It is evident that some clearing of underbrush was in train preparatory to the establishment of better-defined critical principles, when the imminence of the civil conflict diverted men's minds to more pressing problems. When the crisis had passed, new critical forces made it impossible to resume where the war had put an end to speculation.

FIVE

FORCES AT WORK IN NEW YORK CRITICISM

Although they were practicing admittedly an undefined art, New York critics and reviewers were little hampered by this deficiency. Freedom of speech in criticism belonged to the press, and all but the most intransigent became restive at the slightest hint of prescription. From the revolutionary Young Americans to the extreme right critical wing, expression was free, although extreme conservatism found small audience; and the several stages were frequently at war among themselves. Amid so many warring parties, such pulling and hauling could not come to rest in equilibrium. In a new country unsettled as to its immediate purposes, in a city of varied and frequently changing population, and in an age itself characterized by change, it is not surprising that the attainment of an established canon of criticism should have been as difficult to accomplish as were other goals of man's concern.

New York litterateurs were notable for the unrestraint with which they waged their critical battles. Of the leading periodicals the greater number held that critical activity required trained, competent practitioners; yet nearly all realized that the new democracy granted freedom to all individuals to exercise judgment upon what they read. In the varied attempts to reconcile discordant attitudes, the trained critic occupied degrees of prestige ranging from a nearly authoritarian position to one in which he was hardly more than a consultant. He might supplement the reader's opinion and, if he received a hearing, might modify it; he could not seriously expect to direct it. Although he might express himself in the pages of a periodical affiliated with some political or religious party, this connection would help him little in New York, where the vigorously sectarian periodicals in particular carried far less weight than elsewhere. Whig readers might lament, as Clarence Day's father did later, that God had made so many damned fools and Democrats; but only the most violently partisan among the literary men considered of prime importance the political connection of the *Whig Review* or *Democratic Review*. Except during the flurry caused by the early violence of the *Democratic Review*, the opinions on letters advanced by a magazine so connected were seldom ascribed to its politics; it was their literary or critical theories that were of interest to literary circles rather than their political theories.

EMOTION AND CRITICISM

As might reasonably be presumed of an age in which various aspects of romanticism constituted powerful forces, the emotional appeal exerted by literature occupied a large space in the critical scene. With the prevailing interest in the didactic, this appeal seemed of outstanding significance to the supporters of popular judgment; trained critics, although conceding its importance, held certain reservations. Many of these inveighed against the baneful effect of emotional appeal upon sound judgment. The normal New Yorker moreover possessed a considerable amount of that unemotional hardheadedness so necessary for the pursuit of the dominant mercantile interests of the city. The 1829 *Mirror* spoke for them in demanding that the reviewer exercise rational moderation in judging. Enthusiastic approval was indeed superior to excessive condemnation in fostering a young literature, yet it was a danger to the development of just criticism. The reader of Bulwer's *Devereux*, for example, must delay his final judgment of it until the emotions aroused by reading it shall have had time to level off: "while these emotions are present, all capacity to judge is gone." Popular judgment of Bulwer, the *American Monthly Magazine* sadly admitted, is totally unreliable; the heart of man everywhere responds so vehemently to his call that it is ink wasted to point out his errors and sophistries.

The 1831 *Mirror* warned its readers that partisan emotions vitiated the pronouncements of British magazines, especially the quarterlies. These attack or support the author's literary or political position instead of soberly considering his work. The *Quarterly*'s praise of Mrs.

Frances Trollope's anti-American book was attacked as an instance of
their bias by the *American Monthly Magazine*. After noting its errors,
this magazine acidly added that once one had properly discounted the
violent prejudices of British quarterlies, he would hardly find elsewhere fairer reviews. What was left after this discount was effected,
the writer forbore to indicate.

In the ensuing decade critical speculation became engrossed in the
part played by sympathy in judging. Sympathy came, however, to
mean less emotional judgment of a book than the reconstruction of the
author's emotional state when he was writing. George Allen's "Reproductive Criticism" in the 1838 *New York Review*—the most detailed
expression of the German-derived attitude—required the critic to enter
into the poet's self and relive his experience in creating the work under
review. The critic cannot evaluate the work until he has appreciated
the author's spirit. The principle, although with a somewhat different
reference, had been enunciated long before in Pope's "Essay on Criticism," but here it was tied to the Schlegels and Heine. This attitude was
supported in the 1846 *Democratic Review* by Jones. The critic, he
wrote, equals the poet in enthusiasm though not in invention, imagination, or fancy—the task performed by these three creative powers has
been undertaken before the critic appears upon the scene. Uncontrolled
emotional expression is objectionable in both poet and critic. Like the
poet—one is reminded of Ruskin's *Modern Painters*—the critic must
combine genuine feeling with objective, equal justice; he should react
with full sympathy to the situation but keep the eyes of his judgment
firmly fixed upon his subject. In the 1848 *Whig Review* George Peck
reiterated this principle with even greater emphasis. The author himself, he declared, should evaluate and control the emotional expression
of his agents; failure to do so adequately was a fatal defect in *Wuthering Heights*.

Poe's death brought about a revival of interest in the effects of emotional bias upon criticism. The *Knickerbocker* of 1850, following a
course mapped by the late Margaret Fuller, assailed him as a critical
hatchet man who gloried in slaughter. Although he showed acute and
ingenious insights into some phases of literary art, Poe nonetheless produced critiques that were for the most part "carping and utterly worthless . . . ; he was so much the creature of kindly or malicious prejudice." Poe's "Literati" papers, brief sketches of notable figures in the
New York literary world, were also assailed as generally unfair; when
they did not damn with tongue-in-cheek praise they puffed with adulation. It was implied that Poe had blackmailed his subjects in some

cases, while in others he had rid himself of his spite at those whom he envied or who had failed to serve his personal ends. In this instance, Poe evidently was the occasion of as emotionally biased criticism as he had been charged with inflicting; pot and kettle were alike smirched.

Reading of the German writers already mentioned—Goethe, the Schlegels, and Heine—and of Coleridge, Carlyle, and Hazlitt, had given added impetus to a sentiment of sympathy with the author's emotional state while writing. Tuckerman during the fifties became a prominent advocate of this concern. He was careful to discriminate this attitude from the vapid emotionalism of those who accepted a dreamy emotional response as the sole criterion of judgment; the imagination must never become so emancipated as to own no rational direction.

Tuckerman's ideal critic found embodiment in Hazlitt. His capacities united the sensitive, the imaginative, and the purely intellectual. A genuine relish for good literature gave him insights into the nature and processes of genius impossible to one who lacked this gusto. His judgments were indeed not infallible, but his "fearless and sympathetic reflection . . . is an immense advance upon the prescriptive and technical course once in vogue." Hazlitt ushered in a new era of criticism by emphasizing hitherto ignored components of the critical art. "Knowledge is only a part of the critic's preparation. . . . To realize how needful is a just enlistment of the sympathies, as well as a calm exercise of judgment based on knowledge, in the highest criticism, we must remember that works of real genius appeal to the soul—to the entire consciousness; and if the intellect and the memory alone respond, it is obvious that the criticism is incomplete. . . . Common sense and the sense of beauty are totally different endowments; and when one usurps the office of the other, the effect is pitiable. Both are indispensable to the true critic." His best performance requires also that he appreciate widely divergent kinds of literature and respond to their dissimilar qualities. To some critics, such ideas were tarred with the transcendental brush, but Tuckerman's vigorous support of what George Allen had dubbed "reproductive criticism" was no isolated phenomenon in the later literary circles of pre–Civil War Gotham.

ORIGINALITY

A second force, traditional yet with added American coloring, was the New Yorkers' concern for originality in literature. For Americans generally the term touched a sore spot in their sensoria; slurring foreign comment on American imitativeness irritated those raw American nerves upon which Cooper remarked pointedly in his *Gleanings in*

Europe. New Yorkers on the whole were less deferential to transatlantic example and opinion than were their compatriots to the south
and the northeast. For one thing, their populace and its spokesmen were
less homogeneously British in origin than was the case elsewhere in the
country. Their first settlers, who still added their flavor to the bouquet
of the city, had been Dutch, not English, and among their older literary
leaders the Dutch were prominent in Paulding, Gulian Verplanck, and
the Duyckincks. Other leaders in literary circles were Irish and other
immigrants whose heritage was in some instances actively anti-British.
No doubt also their ready access to the western hinterland and their
wideflung commercial concerns by land as well as by sea kept them
from being submerged by any foreign flood of precedent from Britain.

One of New York's first literary spokesmen, James K. Paulding, was
his life long violently hostile to English influences of any sort. In 1820
he had inveighed against the dumb following of bad British models
and avoidance of American resources that was characteristic of our
nascent fiction. The situation appeared to him full of ridiculous con-
tradictions: "We were born rich, and yet have all our lives subsisted
by borrowing. Hence it has continually occurred, that those who might
have gone before had they chosen a new path, have been content to
come last, merely by following the old track." These were as bold
words as you shall hear of a summer's day, and accordingly they were
indignantly brushed aside. For the defense, the 1821 *Literary and Scientific Repository* complimented Eastburn and Sands because their *Yamoyden* so strongly reminded readers of Scott's poems; it was credita-
ble to have followed so good a pattern. Paulding's parallel attack upon
critics who echoed British opinion four years later received Bryant's
support. American reviewers must not, Bryant wrote, wait for the
British quarterlies before they dared to commit themselves to praise or
blame of any work. Even *Minerva,* conservative in many of its attitudes, bluntly declined to accept submissively the prescriptions or conclusions of old-line critics. Although the tide was beginning to turn for
both creative literature and criticism, no clear statement defending
American originality had yet appeared in print.

Bryant's lectures in 1826 before the New York Athenaeum are the
locus classicus for American claim to originality. The young poet-
editor's traditional training had been buttressed by appreciative reading of the romantic writers. Steeped in the tradition of "Johnson deep
and Addison refined," he asserted that America must learn the accepted
modes of poetic composition, the degrees to which the examples and
labors of others may be applied to strengthen the artist's own vigor. He

recommended, counter to the American tendency, that no single poet or class of poets be held up as a model. By studying the beauties of all poets the aspirant would escape the inevitable narrowness resultant from the following of any single guide. With such discipline the poet —and incidentally the critic, who was equally Bryant's concern—could formulate a literary standard higher than any poet has attained, which he should apply as his yardstick of perfection.

But, Bryant continued, the American litterateur's eyes should focus upon original views, not upon patterns; these latter he should employ as aids and checks merely. "Ages ago," he declaimed with more eloquence than accuracy, "the schools shook themselves loose from the fetters of Aristotle. He now no more delivers the oracles of philosophy than the priests of Apollo deliver the oracles of religion. Why should the chains of authority be worn any longer by the heart and the imagination than by the reason?" Whether he failed to realize that those very schools had forged the fetters and foisted them off upon Aristotle or was merely accepting the careless information of the average romantic man of letters, Bryant's plea for originality was vigorously advanced. His reasoning from his premises was sound. An age that is habitually imitative is less likely to produce possessions for all time than is an age which tries to represent what its own eyes have seen. The errors of originality, he added, soon pass from memory, while its merits stand. Tame, frigid taste can employ itself only in servilely copying another's work. In practice as well as precept, Bryant showed the virtue of originality and of the values derivable from sound models.

The 1832 *Mirror* spelled out some of Bryant's ideas. American literary apprentices should concentrate their study upon the ancient classics as the foundation for a superstructure of study in the postclassical development of those continental literatures from which British and American authors alike can derive great value. Two years later, it added Bryant's plea for firsthand observation of nature: inept American authorlings were stupidly transplanting European flora and fauna into American poetry; trite similes made of British objects assailed the reader's eye from every American page. The 1835 *Knickerbocker* neatly clinched this admonition: "the surest way of securing the contempt of any man, is to become his abject imitator"; even successful copying sets an author merely in competition with a baboon aping a man.

The new nation's writers faced a stiff task in winning for it literary originality. The 1838 *Knickerbocker* mentioned the powerful spell cast by the sharing of a common language with British authors—a dan-

ger which, British critics ironically contended, did not exist. Walter
Channing in the *North American Review* had two decades earlier pessimistically called it an insurmountable barrier to national literature. The
New York magazine declared that Americans could bypass this barrier
by developing a national character more distinct from that of Britain
than was at present the case. This would probably be a process involv-
ing several generations, but upon its completion the language would
no longer constitute a hindrance. Americans could, however, in the
meantime act far more independently than they were acting. To recognize the presence of a defect is fortunately to take the first step toward
rectifying it, and regardless of temporary inconvenience or awkward-
ness this step should at once be taken. Intentionally original American
poetry might for a time be inferior to that cast in the British mold, yet
it would surely prove better for the nation's literature to strike out for
itself than to play the sedulous ape. The *Knickerbocker* was more concerned with the establishment of an independent attitude than with
the formulation of means for its attainment. It did not prescribe the
abandonment of any traditional forms, although such an idea was in
the air and soon to find expression, notably in Whitman's *Leaves of
Grass*. Even Whitman, however, was not yet ready in 1838 to take
such a daring step.

Evert Duyckinck in the 1840 *New York Review* soberly pointed
out the risk that American zeal for originality might mistake novelty
for the genuine article. In spite of his fear, however, he was ready to
venture into the byways of the Muses. "A land without its original authors, is like a man without the faculty of speech, who is thrust aside
and overlooked in every company." In *Arcturus* a year later he declared originality to be the prime element in true literary success. It
might lie temporarily unnoticed while novelty—a totally different
quality—seized the public favor; but such an error would not be long
undetected by the public. The 1844 *Columbian* felt less sanguine: the
utter ignorance of contemporary critics concerning literary canons
rendered them incapable of pointing out true originality if they should
encounter it. Jones reminded readers of the *Democratic Review* that
critics might easily derive proper canons from the practice of Hazlitt,
who trusted his own reactions and refused to rely upon time-honored
but time-worn codes of judgment. New York literary men in general
sided on this matter with Duyckinck and Jones in demanding that the
literary and critical leading-strings be untied. For a similar declaration
three years previously, Emerson had been branded by some of his

hearers as a stargazer; influential New Yorkers were now ready to risk the venture.

Given a strong, great, free nation, "the softer arts will follow and shape a proper and peculiar literature for the people." With these words the 1845 *Whig Review* reminded its readers to put first things first; Americans should first attend to their national development. Literature as the expression of nationality would develop with the nation itself, and when the nation was a new, well-formed entity its literature would attain also to originality. Neither the *Whig Review* nor its contemporaries were clear as to what American nationality was to be, although they agreed that we had not yet attained to it. Until America should have reached this far-off goal, the critic's contribution to a national literature lay chiefly, the *Whig Review* stated, in preparing readers and writers for literature by inspiring in both "a manly spirit and love of noble models, so far as models are wanted," while at the same time warding off "any casual tendency to merely imitative efforts." It recognized two possible sources of original literature: from "a race either not derivative from another since its refinement has reached the point of literary cultivation; or one which, if secondary, has, in new seats, under a new body of influences, formed for itself a fresh and complete identity of its own." The prior alternative certainly did not apply to the United States, nor, the writer lamented, could we conform to the latter until we should have developed our language into a quite different dialect from that of England. It would be better if we could have an entirely separate language, but under the circumstances we could hope only for a distinct dialect.

The *Whig Review*'s revival of the linguistic problem was swallowed up in the growing conviction that the content of the literary work was of more concern than the medium in which it was conveyed. In the 1846 *Democratic Review*, Jones approved heartily of Margaret Fuller's description of the desirable American literature. "By American literature, she understands a literature which shall be an expression of the original, naturally developed life of the country, in such high and elevated forms, as to rank with the literature of the world. *It must be genuine, and it must be elevated.*" Jones agreed with the *Whig Review* that the United States was unready for a national literature: the quarries must first be opened before the marble for the structure could be fashioned. Neither Jones nor Margaret Fuller worried over the shared language with England, nor did either express concern that the elevated literary forms would presumably also be traditional.

Under Evert Duyckinck's moderate editorship, the *Literary World* was likewise indisposed to concern because America and Britain had much in common. Basically, he wrote in 1847, the two countries shared many characteristics; they differed essentially, however, in outlook and in stage of development. Politically the United States was far in advance of Britain; in literature it trailed. In spite of this literary lag, Duyckinck reminded Americans, Britain has consistently recommended that the United States should think for itself; it should regard American life as materials for an original literature and not write in servile copying of others. The inferior British journals that adopted a depreciating tone toward American letters were negligible. Such incisive, well-meant advice, he proceeded, should be heeded in the United States. Our reviews in particular should have voices of their own, not be mere echoes, and should judge American authors without reference to transatlantic opinion. They might even, Duyckinck hinted in a subsequent article, more competently judge recent and contemporary British writing than could the British. Thousands of miles distant and free of British national biases, they could more dispassionately examine the British product upon a new and in some respects superior basis; distance in space gave Americans a perspective comparable to that which passage of time gave the British in viewing their earlier authors.

Before Americans could perform worthy critical service for either their own or British writers, Duyckinck warned, American criticism would have to purge itself of its baser practitioners so as to gain honesty and depth. Repeatedly he analyzed the state of American criticism, pointing out its ignorance, malice, and venality and praying for a thorough housecleaning to rid the literary scene of its quacks. Although Duyckinck, who had traveled widely, expressed opinions on the whole more Anglophile in tenor than were held by the majority, his known moderation and honesty were extremely influential in the city's literary circles; and the majority of serious thinkers undoubtedly preferred to chauvinist ravings his cautious optimism and readiness to accept whatever good Britain could offer. Occasional vituperative attacks upon American subservience to Britain appeared, as when the *Democratic Review* spitefully declared that we were too bound by British patterns to give even a Milton or a Shakespeare freedom to write should they appear in our Western world. The better journals, although they tolerated no assumption of British superiority in any field, were ordinarily friendly toward Britain. Here once more the commercial concerns of the New Yorkers, which entered into the marrow of their thinking, no doubt contributed to their lack of belligerence toward Britain when compared with the Boston and the Concord circles.

A continental note was injected into the discussion when the 1849 *Literary World* published an article on American letters by the distinguished French scholar Philarete Chasles. Chasles argued from the premise that nations, like human beings, show the characteristics of childhood, maturity, and senescence. A nation begins its existence by imitating others; originality comes late in the course of national development and cannot be had for the asking. How then, he inquired, could Americans be justly condemned for lack of a quality it was impossible for them to possess? Originality belongs to ripe minds. The article, which was undoubtedly printed for its stimulative value, naturally made no converts in a nation that felt it was already a giant. Americans might indeed have progressed a shorter distance than had other older nations with several centuries of history behind them, as Parke Godwin admitted in the 1853 *Putnam's;* in seventy short years, with all the other demands made upon their powers since their founding, there were obvious limits to their possible achievement. He conceded that some of the imitativeness of youth was still evident, but declared that it would soon be outgrown. America could agree that she was still in her youth; she rejected the charge that she had not outgrown her childhood.

New Yorkers concluded, with Godwin, that it was better to be young and vigorous than effete and exhausted. They were, on the whole, ready to learn from other nations, but not to be patronized; and they were convinced that they had the potential, if not the actuality, for a truly original national literature.

AMERICA AS LITERARY MATERIAL

In the early nineteenth century those Americans who were concerned with literary originality faced also the question whether American materials were proper for literary representation. Early New York periodicals were among the first to defend their use. In an appreciation of Eastburn and Sands's *Yamoyden* the 1821 *Literary and Scientific Repository* declared that writers who have attained any degree of success in making our matter-of-fact history romantically interesting deserve well of all who remember with pleasure the striking features of the work. Such a restrained approbation moderated considerably the fiery assertion of James K. Paulding three years earlier that Americans had no need to follow British authors in any way; with all his reservations he was nonetheless on the side of those who would use American materials if possible. The 1824 *Atlantic Magazine,* closely following in Paulding's footsteps, categorically declared that the American writer should "devote his abilities and apply his acquirements to subjects of domestic interest; exclusively so, so far as opportunities admit." He should possess a liberal knowledge of past and present world history, but to write of foreign matters is tantamount to imitating foreign writers. The 1823 *Mirror* had already praised Paulding's *Koningsmarke* for its American subject. Like Cooper's *Lionel Lincoln*, which it later reviewed, *Koningsmarke* would have profited from careful revision; but the *Mirror* joined the 1825 *New York Review* in its decision that Cooper's many literary faults were more than balanced by his having provided a view of a critical period of American history that readers enjoyed for its reminder of their fathers' hardihood. New Yorkers did not seriously trouble themselves, as William Gilmore Simms did later, with calculations of the number of years of aging needed by an event before it became seasoned romantic material.

Cooper became the focus of the debate over the propriety of American events and personages as literary material. Upon the appearance of his *The Pioneers* several newspapers and periodicals commented favorably—more favorably, Cooper admitted, than he had dared hope —on the faithful portrayal of American scene and character in that novel. The 1825 *Minerva*, no admirer of Cooper as a rule, found no fault with his choice of subjects; it objected that he was unable worthily to display the beauties of his materials. When the 1826 *New York Review* wrote of *The Last of the Mohicans* that it had proved beyond dispute the suitability of American history and manners for literary representation, the question was settled for most New Yorkers.

As time passed, their confidence in American materials rapidly increased, with parallel decrease in the weight attached to foreign opinion of American verse and fiction. It was not easy to rid themselves of a long-established, binding tradition to which for a century and a half they had occupied a provincial position; it was far more difficult to free themselves of deference to the heritors of a brilliant line of critics. Establishment of American materials as fit for literature, however, provided a starting point of which they soon took full advantage. The 1831 *Mirror* bluntly admonished British critics that they were in no position to doubt the truth of delineations of American customs or scenery; when America was portrayed, America alone was competent to judge the representation. The *Mirror* advised Americans to write of American scenes: "our writers are never so happy as when at home"; for creation and criticism, first-hand knowledge was requisite. As the 1834 *American Monthly Magazine* wrote of Cooper, all inspiration seemed to leave him the moment he abandoned his native land or the seas encircling it.

Foreign figures were also anathema to the 1834 *Mirror*. In the work of American poetasters, it mourned: "Imaginary nightingales warble in very equivocal melody from non-existent thorns; supposititious deserts spread their burning sands amid the luxuriance of American vegetation. . . . Dying dolphins flounder in their comparisons; amber tears ooze from their similes, and renovated sphinxes spring from their tropes." Why reject either American scene or American simile? If you depict America, do it, as Howells was to say later, in as "Americanly" a manner as possible. So, using good eighteenth-century British style, argued the *Mirror;* but if its periods and irony were traditional, its doctrine was not.

Further implications in the doctrine of the superior veracity of American judgment on things American were not overlooked. The 1835 *Mirror* reprinted in full Irving's thoughtful essay on England and America, with the comment that Irving's ideas were as applicable to the current situation as when they had first appeared in the *Sketch Book*. A few numbers later it reflected that from such works as Mrs. Trollope's libel on the United States the British could derive little truth about American life and manners. British writers who perforce relied heavily upon such misleading sources were incompetent to express opinions about either the country or the literature which represented it. No other land, the *Mirror* declaimed shortly after this outburst in a mood rivaling Virgil's when he praised Italy, has local scenery and national recollections as inspiring to the artist in all media as are those to be found in America; here, therefore, the arts will find their most congenial habitation. In this panegyric other periodicals joined. The novels of William Gilmore Simms were regularly praised for their presentation of American materials. The 1835 *Knickerbocker* pontificated that an American literature must partake largely of national subjects and feelings, which by their patriotic overtones should distinguish the American product from alien works even in those works which did not deal specifically with subjects drawn from the Western world.

The patriotic note in the *Knickerbocker*, which was sounded also in other magazines, rang its full peal in the *Democratic Review*. A large part of its program was the promotion of American literary materials. In 1839 Parke Godwin, writing possibly in response to Cooper's *The American Democrat* and *Gleanings in Europe*, fulminated: "Some asinine individual, who must have been as partial to paradoxes as his long-eared archetype to thistles, has taken upon himself to remark that there are few or no materials for romance in America. . . . Nature has here granted everything to genius which can excite, exalt, enlarge, and ennoble its powers. . . . Our history, too, is poetical. Let time but wrap it in its mighty shadows, and what were the fables of old compared to our familiar story!" To the *Democratic Review*'s more fanatical writers, the historian's robe and the prophet's mantle seemed equally congenial.

The *Democratic Review* soon drew restrained support from other magazines which had briefly delayed their opposition to the proletarian evangel. The *Knickerbocker*, unwilling to fall behind its rabid new rival, felt that the United States was already making fair progress toward a literature of democracy [lower case]. Two years later, the far more conservative *New York Review* chimed in with the *Knickerbocker* in finding merit in what the United States had already produced that the *Democratic Review* had belittled. In our writing, it declared, we should employ "those ideas and sentiments which should form the basis of a grand national literature: our romantic origin, our magnificent position, and our matchless destiny, the regeneration of humanity." It seldom had expressed such glowing sentiments. The *New York Review*'s brief stand on the side of Democracy did not mean that it endorsed the florid chauvinistic program of democracy's mouthpiece; its position indicated, however, how widespread was the confidence in American literary materials.

By 1845, the fanatical *Democratic Review* had not only changed engineers, it had considerably lowered its steam pressure. Its more restrained writers, like Jones and Evert Duyckinck, had outlasted the fanatics, and it spoke more soberly although still championing literary reform. The *Broadway Journal*, an ably edited periodical that deserved a longer life, spoke for an influential segment of New York thought in declaring that we had carried too far our confidence in our ability to create and judge our own literature. By combining our common self-assurance with the ultranationalism of the Young Democrats of the *Democratic Review*, we had fallen into the trap of judging our literature by our own inadequate standards, by the work of men whom we had hastily elevated to the position of literary masters. We should never possess an American literature until we realized, first, that we did not yet have one, and secondly, that in the United States we did not have all that was necessary for it, excellent although our native materials undoubtedly were. We must come to the realization that literature is not merely national, but universal. By 1847 the *Democratic Review* was ready to concur with this position.

This former organ of the Young Americans now discussed the characteristics of a national literature; its stress upon the term "democratic" was far less in evidence than it had been five or ten years earlier. For this national literature the first requisite was naturally American writers, but even more significant was the description of the materials which they should present: "A due proportion of home themes, affording opportunity for descriptions of our scenery, for the illustration of passing events, and the preservation of what tradition has rescued from the past, and for the exhibition of the manners of the people, and the circumstances which give form and pressure to the time, and the spirit of the country; and all these penetrated by an intense and enlightened patriotism." The patriotic emphasis, though still important, is here relegated to the position of a seasoning; as Hazlitt said of wit, it was to be the salt of American literature, not the food itself.

The plea for universality made in the *Broadway Journal* was adopted in the 1848 *Holden's Dollar Magazine*'s defense of Lowell's poems. They were truly American, however far abroad their immediate subjects might range, in their "indomitable 'go-ahead' spirit of his Puritan forbears." It was unnecessary that the poet confine himself to American themes or dress them in a wealth of local allusion. It was now generally conceded that the *Democratic Review* in its first frantic years had overstated the case for American materials. It had nonetheless forced New Yorkers to think through the problem and to precipitate out of the flux a position that combined a thoroughly American with a more nearly universal concept of letters. This was a noteworthy advance, and a timely one.

As the 1850's began those archrivals the *Whig* and *Democratic* reviews both felt that the United States had finally emerged from its provincial chrysalis, after several previous abortive attempts, and was ready to spread its wings with a national literature that should also be a part of world literature. Of the two, the *Whig Review* took perhaps the slightly more international position. In it Tuckerman came out vigorously against literary isolationism. Far from denationalizing the American, he recognized that foreign ingredients which could be assimilated would enrich his truly national qualities by giving them form as well as adding to their substance. On this front the shooting war was nearly ended. The hundred–per cent nationalist snipers still occasionally attacked Longfellow for his use of European material. The 1853 *National Magazine* sneered that he would have been more at home in the Middle Ages; instead of portraying American life, "he always reminds us of, and insensibly lapses into books." In his compositions, "his themes and their manner of treatment are rather academical than natural; and even when they are natural, it is apt to be nature in a very high state of cultivation." The writer conceded that the whole world is the poet's proper range and that it includes past, present, and future; "but while we allow him this range, we would not have him abuse it; nor should he so far forget his own age as to sing of nothing but the ages before him." He should not be "a kind of scholastic Janus" who looks both ways, into future and past, while ignoring the present. Longfellow's remarks on what Henry Thoreau called the "sham-shaggy" in American thought evidently rankled.

Whitman's beating of the nationalist drum in his preface to *Leaves of Grass* did not represent the body of New York literati, who were rather firmly attached to an internationalist position through their concern with commerce and immigration as well as with letters. Even the militant nationalism and violent anti-British sentiment aroused by, and during the swiftly approaching civil conflict did not succeed in restoring any appreciable measure of the literary Anglophobia expressed by some factions in earlier decades.

LITERARY PROBLEMS

Amid the pressures generated by the contemporary local and national situations, the forces exerted by long-established literary principles must not be ignored. Naturally, they received less vigorous discussion than current problems unless they were in some way bound up with contemporary concerns such as national feeling. Among these timeless principles of importance to critics, the plotting and characterization in literary works received the lion's share of attention. The author's concern with these has already been discussed. Earlier chapters have considered other time-honored literary concerns.

The earlier novels of the period escaped severe criticism on their constructive merits or defects. Patriotic pride in the existence of American works which, as Bryant had remarked before coming to New York, were by an American and were not thoroughly bad, tended to blind reviewers to literary lapses of the authors. Early reviews of Cooper's *The Spy* discounted its poorly organized plot and generally wooden characters in order to focus their praise upon its

single well-drawn agent and its patriotic overtones. A novelist, declared the 1824 *Minerva*, should offer "a faithful and spirited delineation of human character," but it went into no specifications of this
requirement. Critical gratification at the existence of readable novels
by Americans drowned out the feeble adverse comments on construc-
tion.

One of the pioneers among New York periodicals to define its
position in its criticism of novels was the *New York Review* for 1826,
and it too mingled benevolence toward the work of a fellow-country-
man with discussion of principles of plot and characterization. Its
review of Cooper's *The Last of the Mohicans* indicates how it effected
this combination. "If any doubt remained as to the author's power as
an imaginative writer, it must be removed by this experiment. He is
a *poet;* and if his creations should not be immortal, it will be the work
of the perverse and incalculable accidents of time; for multitudes,
less worthy, have a niche in the temple of memory." The reviewer
proceeds immediately to dilate upon the requirement that the agents
act strictly within the limitations set by their natures and opportunities,
with adequate motives assigned to account for their several actions—
all of which Cooper has successfully performed. "There are no scenes
in modern romance which can surpass" seven of the major incidents
of the tale. Cooper knows the Indians and faithfully describes them,
and he obviously knows every foot of the terrain traversed by the
agents. "If he fails any where, it is in the management of his female
personages"; but he errs in the best company, "for Shakespeare before
him has been accused of want of knowledge in this province of
poetry." In fine, "our author stands alone among his countrymen, in
solitary and enviable distinction." His success is largely due to the
fact that, "like his favorite Hawkeye," he gathers his materials through
acute personal observation, not at second hand from books; and his
success with purely American materials is proof of their adequacy for
literary depiction. The writer skillfully blends patriotic with critical
principles.

The dramatic unities, though moribund, possessed still sufficient
vitality to extend their domain beyond the realm of the drama. The
1829 *Mirror* handled them respectfully in a critique of Thomas Moore.
Its writer did not indeed go beyond the erroneously conventional
notion that they had been enunciated by the ancient Greeks. With
all his respect for them, however, he valued them rather as expressions
of common-sense practice than as literary laws; whether the author
ultimately decided to abide by their admonitions or not, he should pay

respectful heed to the warnings implicit in them. The *Mirror* soon
went counter to its previously expressed respect for the rules. In an
article on the novels of John Neal and their author, it expressed
pleasure in their agents: admittedly they were sometimes unnatural,
yet they were powerfully drawn. The extravagant incidents, too, were
interesting. What if the rules were broken! Taken as wholes, his
novels were no doubt artistically bad, sometimes even unintelligible;
yet each contained parts worth reading and—a telling point in those
days—something worth learning. When interest and knowledge are
presented, the critic insisted, unity of plot or character may be
forgotten.

William Cox, the *Mirror's* drama critic and later its foreign correspondent, in 1833 re-emphasized a narrative principle for both drama
and the novel: the author may not merely describe his characters, he
must portray men and women and their manners. Men doing and
suffering were far more deeply affective of the emotions than were
men merely anatomized. In the following year the *American Monthly
Magazine,* applying Cox's principle, condemned Cooper's later novels
as inferior to those earlier works which had not only vividly portrayed
incidents but two deeply imagined characters, Long Tom Coffin and
Leatherstocking. These were genuine, living embodiments; his later
agents were shallowly conceived. This reviewer was in full agreement
with an earlier review of Cooper's *Heidenmauer* in the 1832 *Mirror:*
"The story hangs loosely together—the parts fit clumsily—the persons
of the drama are blurred by haste and their own native imperfections;
and the whole story might not improbably be traced in its real origin,
to the very tailor from whom, in his prefatory chapter, the author
affects to have received it." Many New York litterateurs were familiar
with Aristotle's four requirements for characters, and some had read
Lessing's refinements on Aristotle in his *Laokoön.* The *Mirror,* it
should be noted, was uniformly friendly to Cooper as many of its
contemporaries were not. Its strictures upon his novels were the faithful wounds of a friend, not the product of malicious spite or enmity.

The Aristotelian tradition of criticism was also paired with that
which stemmed ultimately from Aristophanes and Plato, who were
concerned over the possible moral influence of the agents. In 1834
Gulian Verplanck, although no strait-laced Puritan himself, professed
to see in Tasso's Tancred a far more desirable character than "the
coldblooded and perfidious Aeneas, or any of the butchering heroes
who have followed him." The novelist must of course display despicable persons, but he can turn them to moral advantage by making them

unattractive. Scott's villains, Verplanck believed, were much more properly presented than those pictured by "the profligate and sarcastic cynicism of Fielding." The subject of Verplanck's address, "The Influence of Moral Causes upon Opinion, Science, and Literature," no doubt evoked his severe handling of Fielding, whom liberal New Yorkers generally found worthy of their respect. A year later the *Knickerbocker* interrupted the general chorus of reprobation that Bulwer's novels had met on moral grounds. *The Last Days of Pompeii,* it announced, was free of that despicable moral obliquity so reprehensible in the earlier novels. The reviewer evidently preened himself on the generosity of mind which enabled him to see improvement in the morals of such a literary reprobate as Bulwer. New York reviewers, however they might feel their responsibility to indicate possible moral peril in literary works, were more concerned with other matters.

By the 1830's critical interest, in keeping with the romantic era, centered heavily upon the portrayal of the agents; matters of plot, though not overlooked, were relegated to a lower position. Some of the voices raised in defense of the traditional emphasis upon plot nonetheless deserve mention. The 1835 *American Monthly Magazine* declined to admit that literary perfection could be achieved without a principle of order and harmony to control the beauty of the work and guide the vigor, the taste, and even the genius of the author. This governing principle, it declared, lies in "the key-stone of the art, the well-adjusted plot, the clear arrangement of the characters, the *lucidus ordo* of old Horace." Romantic themes, the writer continued, do not exempt the author from his first duty, which is to form his plot, know what he will do before he puts pen to paper, and make every detail contributory to his end. The controlling power of plot, another article in the same volume affirmed, is the final touch that youthful artists seldom master. America being a youthful country, it is vain to expect such mastery of her artists; however much their taste may have improved and that of their readers, American work is still crude, unfinished, and immature.

Such preoccupation with the plotting of a work was, however, of rare occurrence. Writers and critics, concerned primarily with the agents, were inclined to let the action grow out of the personages. By the fifth decade, general concern with agents had been channeled into interest in their romantic representation. Before this shift had been fully accomplished, the 1837 *Mirror* had listed as indispensable elements of fiction "close discrimination of character" and "ingenious complication of plot, and above all, the close adherence to the realities of life and achievement." Lacking these, the doom of the hopeful novelist appeared to the *Mirror* to be as swift as it was certain. But adherence to the realities of life, as this writer failed to realize, brought with it attention to things as they are, with all their imperfections on their head in apparent lack of cause and effect. The interest in the agents came to surmount that in any unity of action. Emerson's 1844 echo of Spenser's "Soule is forme, and dothe the bodie make" would have been interpreted by the New Yorker of that decade to emphasize the importance of character rather than of plot. The romantic emphasis upon character was generally adopted in New York.

IMAGINATION

Although realism as they conceived of it had come to be of prime interest to the New York literary thinkers, they must not be accused of having forgotten the literary role played by the imagination. Their discussions of this power are of considerable interest. The first to treat of it in detail was probably William Cullen Bryant in his 1826 "Lectures on Poetry." Although he acknowledged his debt for his theory of the imagination to Samuel Johnson, he was an avowed follower of the Coleridgean doctrine concerning the imagination and its creative function in the making of poetry; and many of Bryant's contemporaries show their acquaintance with Coleridge's *Biographia Literaria* and other works on the imagination. Richard Henry Dana, Sr., a close friend and frequent visitor of Bryant in New York, also promulgated Coleridge's doctrines in his lectures and writings.

Other concepts of the imagination, some of them pre-Coleridgean, also appeared in New York periodicals. In 1829 George P. Morris based his assumption of the right to edit any verses he saw fit to print in the *Mirror* upon the assertion of Longinus that genius without method lets the imagination run wild; it often needs the checkrein of judgment. He advocated something less than strict control, however. A year later he scored Jeffrey's attempts, as he saw them, to regulate works of the imagination by established critical canons; to do this would "petrify the warmth and paralyze the energies of poets and poesy." A median between regulation and license must be discovered, inclined perhaps slightly toward license but not without decent restraint. Like a cultivated plant in need of pruning, the imaginative power of genius, "unaided by study and labour, never produced anything truly great."

Four years later, the *Mirror* declared that American poets had suffered much from "star-gazing, building castles in the air, and wild theory"; but he felt that they were now in process of emancipating themselves from license through the agency of imagination supported by sound information and good sense. Although, as noted in the case of John Neal, wayward eccentricity might be tolerated for the enjoyable fruits of its power, that share of divinity which Coleridge declared to be present in the imagination precluded the use of that power without a regard for the chief end of man. Morris, as a supporter of the older traditional knowledge buttressed by modern discovery, provides a good indication of the fairly rapid fusion of Coleridgean with previous imaginative theory.

New York writers were well aware of the literally image-making power of the imagination and of its power of deeper, clearer vision than that possessed by ordinary minds. He who possesses imaginative power, declared the 1836 *American Monthly Magazine*, stands above ordinary mortals. They must endeavor to see with his eyes, to receive beauty and power through his mediation, and to accept his vision, no matter how strange the form in which it has presented itself to him. His revelation, the 1837 *New York Review* asserted in less transcendental vein, may tax the higher powers of reason and invention to receive; but the mind of man must be open to discover new truths instead of stubbornly clinging to the old and accepted. The poet must even adopt the attitude of the prophet. Like any valid prophet, he will have learned from looking backward a sound perspective for viewing the future; but while knowledge of the past presumably aids him in plotting the right course for his imagination, it cannot exert perceptible pressure upon his vision nor definitively foretell what is to come, any more than it could have foretold the advances made in modern knowledge. The vision of the poet was not expected to blueprint knowledge. "The poetry of the age," the *New-Yorker* stated, "is the yearning of the spirit for the vast, the shadowy, the unattainable." The critic in his demand upon the poet for the fruits of his romantic insight will keep this indefinite quality of his vision in mind.

The imaginative principle was also envisioned as playing a large part in Young America's proposed democratic revision of society. "All old subjects of thought," averred the *Democratic Review* in its manifesto, "and all new questions arising, connected more or less directly with human existence, have to be taken up again and re-examined in this point of view." Although rational activity would share largely in this project, a wide-ranging imagination was to furnish its beginning and map its course. The critical processes that entered into the proposed literary activity were also imaginatively driven. Some of the critics who wrote for the *Democratic Review* were aware of new approaches to literary criticism emanating from German scholars and applied them to their own activities. It was the more conservative *New York Review*, however, which published the most ably worked out discussion of this new mode of criticism.

George Allen's essay, "Reproductive Criticism," in the 1838 *New York Review*, was undoubtedly the most detailed and thoughtful statement produced during this half-century in New York of the part played by the imagination in criticism. Allen who had been reading extensively in the works of modern German philosophers and critics took the opportunity of a review of works by Heine and the Schlegels to propound his theories. His title comes from Heine and much of his thinking from his three immediate German sources. He was no iconoclast in criticism. The somewhat mechanical rules of inquiry into aesthetic principles by which criticism had heretofore been regulated did not in his opinion merit full condemnation. The new school of the brothers Schlegel had, nonetheless, so fully supplemented them as in many aspects of criticism practically to supplant them. In following their critical procedure the critic ranges himself alongside the art-product under study "with the specific purpose of reproducing, step by step, the creative processes of the artist." He imaginatively regenerates in himself the creative experience of the artist. As one effect of this experience, he can appreciate what the author had in mind and in many instances can justify the position of elements in the work that seem misplaced to the less sympathetic reader. He can also give a reason for the inclusion of parts that to the outward view seem extraneous. Such an experience makes him able to show where the poet was obedient to his imaginative vision and where by reason of some pressure he abandoned his insight to the detriment of his poem. His sympathy is of course not that sentimental kind that suspends the judgment in a welter of emotional fellow-feeling; it stimulates and clarifies judgment.

No other critical process, Allen insisted, can so surely indicate the presence or absence in a work of that artistic unity which is the highest achievement of the constructive imagination. His ideas remind the modern reader forcibly of Walter Pater's concept of criticism in the later nineteenth century, and even more forcibly of Joel Spingarn's "creative criticism" in the twentieth. From 1838, when Allen presented his thesis, his German-derived theories pervaded the remaining four years of the *New York Review* and constituted one of the dominant critical attitudes in other periodicals in the city. Although New Yorkers were somewhat more selective in their acceptance of German thought than Perry Miller has indicated in *The Raven and the Whale*—they rejected with peculiar vigor that extreme transcendentalism so captivating to Concord—German romantic criticism was generally received with considerable interest. Within a few years, influenced presumably by Ruskin's *Modern Painters*, warnings were published that the sympathetic critic must not surrender his objective judgment; but the method met with general approbation.

New York critics frequently censured the restless American tendency to focus upon everything by turns and nothing long; the American was incompetent to study and appreciate works of art, for which an imaginative experience followed by long, deep thought is needed. Sam Ward in the 1839 *New York Review* found that without such concentration "our intellects . . . have hardly time to crystallize, to subside into that quiet so necessary to the exercise of the judgment, and the contemplation of the beautiful." Among the causes of this restlessness Ward mentioned the haunting fear of the American that his decisions are tainted with provincialism. No sooner do we attend to an American work, he added, than we are distracted by the emergence of some European art-product that is pressed upon us to obstruct our American view and hinder the growth of an American taste. Longfellow's *Hyperion*, the subject of Ward's review, merits the earnest, sympathetic criticism advocated by George Allen; but highly wrought European romances are poured over the American reader in a flood that prevents his reliving Longfellow's imaginative experience. The high seasoning of these importations also blunts American taste, which if uncloyed would savor *Hyperion* much more than the spicy novels which it now bolts *ad nauseam*.

Although Wordsworth and the Schlegels would have looked askance at their practice, American critics who followed the imaginative practice of criticism nevertheless concerned themselves chiefly with the content of what they read. This emphasis was perhaps stronger in New York even than elsewhere. Influenced strongly by Carlyle in spite of their loudly vocal disapproval of his works, and by others who held like ideas with him, they concentrated their attention upon the content rather than upon the embodying form. The idea that form and content are hardly separable had little weight with them. Metaphor and logic, declared the 1829 *Mirror*, should yield to correctness of opinion, brilliancy of thought, or beauty of sentiment; some idols of the previous century were to be cast down. Without wholly ignoring the old gods, the critic should now rather consider "the essence and peculiar life of the poetry itself." And the essence of the poetry, as he saw it, resided primarily in the content.

A more directly Coleridgean note on the imagination was added in the 1840 *New York Review* to its earlier Teutonic harmony. Art, it wrote, differs from metaphysics in going beyond abstract thought; its ideas are "clothed in a body borrowed from nature. In every genuine product of art, nature is taken up, and, as it were, recast. Such a work is the fusion of nature in thought. The arts, then, . . . are products of the imagination. . . . We look through the symbols at the thing signified; it acts upon us as a real and living object. . . . What a man shall see in a work of art, depends, in a great measure, on what he is in himself. For he is in his degree a second artist." The *New York Review*'s religious affiliations suggest here an obvious amalgamation of Coleridge with the psalmist's "as a man thinketh in his heart, so doth he express truth." It was easy also to combine Allen's reproductive concept of criticism with the ideas on the imagination from *Biographia Literaria*.

This "sage and meditative imagination," the next volume of the *New York Review* declared, "alone constitutes the inspiration of the greatest poets." Using it as his criterion, this reviewer flatly denied poetic excellence to Scott. The author of *Waverley* had wisely attempted only that description of a richly romantic period which lay within his powers; the vision and the faculty divine, which were lacking in him, were not requisite to the performance of such tasks. The author's mind, he continued, is no mere sponge to soak up and subsequently to emit whatever it encounters; it is a creative organ that imaginatively fuses and fancifully combines. To this unjustly severe devaluation of Scott, the *Knickerbocker* added a harmonizing Wordsworthian note, that the "veritable critic" studied the works of nature as his Bible, supplementing this discipline with equal application to works of art. He must view his subjects deep beneath their surfaces and "clear his vision of those films which ignorance and prejudice, and the imperfections of our individual nature, are continually casting before it." Only upon attaining such a depth of insight will he be competent to criticize.

For critic as for poet, William A. Jones developed the remarks of the *New York Review* upon the difference between art and philosophy. There is peril for the man of letters, he declared, in excessive devotion to the philosophical outlook. As Horace and Philip Sidney had insisted before him, Jones found the poets to be the "true masters and best expounders" of the philosophers. Exclusive pursuit of metaphysics can, if long indulged, injure the understanding—he no doubt had in mind Coleridge's debacle—which can be reinvigorated only through recourse to the poetic embodiments of truth. It must be severely held to its function as a critical tool.

The study of philosophy had suffered a loss of prestige through the works of practitioners who were not popular in New York. Carlyle was severely censured for his puzzling style and uncouth diction. The *Knickerbocker* delighted to ridicule the *Dial* as its numbers appeared. The *Democratic Review* satirized the "wise men from the East": Emerson was barely tolerable, the other transcendentalists almost beneath contempt. William Hazlitt's passion for philosophy, if known to his followers, was not mentioned.

After the regrettable demise of the *New York Review* in 1842 and the contemporary cooling off of the *Democratic Review*, New York critics saw in criticism an activity repressive of error and corrective of faulty expression rather than a creative force; the influence of George Allen was the chief opponent to this general view. Pleas for more attention to style frequently appeared. Reviewers were expected to consider the expression rather than, as the romantic trend required, the content. This emphasis was brief; to it the stir which Poe's reviews caused undoubtedly contributed. The 1842 *Arcturus*, though no lover of Poe, commended his articles in *Graham's Magazine:* he looked oftener at the letter than at the spirit; he took praiseworthy pains with details, and thereby arrived at a penetrating estimate of books. The 1845 *Whig Review* deplored "the acrimony and contempt which have often accompanied Poe's acuteness," but did not deny the value of his conclusions. Poe's support of stylistic criticism, however, as the *Whig Review*'s comment indicates, perhaps contributed as much to its downfall as to its brief flowering. His corrosive comments upon his avowed objects of scorn scandalized those who might have agreed with his judgments, and his left-handed or unsatisfactory comments on literary figures of the city in *The Literati* papers seemed to many New Yorkers to damn their lions with too faint praise. His personal relations with influential literary figures had further alienated New York literary circles from him. In short, since he was the protagonist of this critical method, it was forced to share part of his personal unpopularity. Being against the trend of the times in literary thinking, this method could hardly have endured in any case.

The reaction against stylistic criticism was as inevitable as rapid. Evert Duyckinck, himself a connoisseur of good writing, charged in the 1847 *Literary World* that few of those who sat in the seat of judgment were worthy to occupy it; they were "wanting in true literary feeling, in honest indignation, in independence, in knowledge" —in all the qualities that he believed would enable their possessors to accompany the author in his creative courses. Critical attention to style is significantly not listed. Duyckinck's anger had been kindled by his contempt for the venal reviewers and the cliques which they had formed; what he asked for, however, was a revival of the criticism to which George Allen's essay of a decade earlier had pointed the way. Supporting Duyckinck in 1848, the aged James K. Paulding declared that the competent critic must share the author's genius and even exceed him in taste and judgment. He must keep abreast of the author's experience, but—as Ruskin had recently shown—while in full sympathy with him must not lose sight of his merits and defects.

In 1849 the *Literary World*, with Duyckinck as its editor, rested literary criticism squarely upon Coleridge's method as illustrated in *Biographia Literaria*. The critique of Wordsworth, a noble specimen of the critical art, had not indeed fully revealed the fundamental laws determining the quality of any work of art. His brief comments analyzing the imagination had, however, pointed out the correct path that critics must travel if they are ever to arrive at immutable canons of taste. The *Literary World* found support across the East River from a Brooklyn newspaper editor, Walt Whitman, who strongly recommended *Biographia Literaria* as the critic's handbook: it "will reach the deepest thoughts of the 'choice few' among readers who can appreciate the fascinating subtleties of Coleridge." And the combination of Coleridge with the sympathetic criticism from Germany was about to be restored.

In 1850 Henry T. Tuckerman advocated the union of imaginative power and good sense and judgment as a source of great improvement in the literary art. Fantasy and feeling, he wrote, when combined bring the perfection of poetry—an idea earlier expressed also by Bryant in his unpublished "Lectures on Poetry." But the sort of fancy preferred by many reviewers in his day—mere dreamy, vague musing—produces nothing of worth; when functioning properly this faculty is energized by vigor and earnestness as well as genuine feeling. "Imagination is, indeed, an essential of poetry, but with it must blend thought enough," he added, "to give energy, and feeling sufficient to awaken a human glow, or the result is as coldly brilliant as frost by moonlight." The blame for this emotional vagueness Tuckerman laid at the door of

"German literature and the example of Shelley, Wordsworth, and other metaphysical writers"; however possible it might be for other races to support poetry with the unassisted fancy, the Saxon heart responds to imaginative effort only when combined with feeling, thought, and clear good sense. Philosophy does not deal in clear-cut images, which are requisite to good poetry.

Tuckerman revived in 1851 the earlier interest in Hazlitt's criticism. Hazlitt combined the above-mentioned essentials of literature in his literary judgments to effect a sympathetic analysis of an author's work. He hungered for truth as well as for beauty, and these appetites so combined the sensuous, the imaginative, and the purely intellectual that beyond other critics he could impart to his readers his enjoyment of and sympathy with genius, whose processes he clearly illuminated. Harking back to George Allen's essay of 1838, he characterized the best modern criticism as "a certain reproductive intelligence, that seems to fuse into new and more impressive combinations the elements of every subject" of which it treats. In thus following the steps of the author's creative experience, the critic must share in the author's secondary power of the imagination as Coleridge had defined it. The critic's essay thus becomes in its own right a new artistic creation; it embodies the reviewed author's, plus the sympathetic critic's, imaginative experience. "The creative and analytical now unite their forces, and mutually give birth to discussions on society, art, literature, and politics, which nominally appear as criticism—a word that has now quite eclipsed its original significance." The two activities, creation and judging, are by this theory almost united; they are the product of knowledge working in harmony with sympathetic imagination and governed by judgment.

It is evident that the concept of the sympathetic imagination, whether reproductive or not, was the highest critical achievement of the two decades prior to the Civil War. Criticism of its type was not indeed practiced widely in this era, nor is it frequently encountered in the long history of criticism. Its presence indicates nonetheless the high level of judging that was attained in New York among these critics who were not swayed by less literary considerations. Supplementing the few voices raised in defense of literary form, and levying upon the best then known and thought in the literary world, it provided a breadth and sanity of vision unequaled elsewhere in the United States and capable of holding its own in literary judgment with the best that England or the Continent could then offer.

PRIMITIVISM

The primitivistic romantic tendencies of the age also found enough support to arouse critical discussion. As a rule, primitivism was somewhat loosely construed as the quality resident in the past exclusive of the Greek and Roman flowering ages. Although it inevitably concerned itself with Indian times and lore, it was also confused with the romantic interest in the Middle Ages, on which in 1832 the *Mirror* published two opposing articles. The writer of the first declared that the medieval world had been correctly termed the Dark Ages but could not be accurately described as primitive. Although its products were rude, they lacked "that simplicity which among primitive and unsophisticated nations is often its companion, and gives grace." The medieval mind, this article implied, was a complex of repressions and frustrations.

The second article countered with the warning that concentration upon ancient classical literatures and our own had left a gap in our literary knowledge that we failed at our peril to fill. Medieval literature might possess slight intrinsic value as a whole; it yet deserved our study on the ground that it afforded the only instance in which the rise and development of a literature can be traced. It is moreover a literature from which modern literature has derived benefit. The available specimens indicate stages in literary progress which offer parallels profitable for our consideration. There exist also a few specimens of acknowledged literary merit, but in no sense are they truly primitive. The patronizing tone of the proponent of medieval literary study is clear. No more than his adversary would he have American writers take it for a pattern. It is however significant that he saw in this study a good paradigm for scholars to plot the course which American literature might conceivably be expected to follow. Other writers and periodicals added to the New Yorker's knowledge of medieval German and Italian literary times and letters, so that it was not long before the confusion of the medieval with the primitive was corrected.

In America primitivism encountered obstacles not met in Europe. For Americans the primitive man was predominantly the Indian, and they found it no easy matter to idealize the aborigines. In the first place, eastern Americans had for two centuries lived at anything but a romantic distance from their red neighbors; during the recent years those Indians whom they encountered had been debased by their association with white men who had pitilessly exploited them. Few on the seaboard had enjoyed Cooper's opportunities at Cooperstown to become acquainted with the aborigines in their natural state. Secondly, it was difficult to glorify the members of a race which had perhaps scalped your grandmother. Thirdly, as the 1838 *New York Review* confessed, thinking Americans could only feel shame at the treatment of Indians in the past and disgust at the current barbarous removals of southern tribes to lands in the west. They were not ancestors to be covered with a veil of the imagination, as were the former inhabitants of Europe; they were an alien race which many would not take the trouble to understand. In New England, which might with some justice claim to have been the cradle of American letters, Americans could look back a century and a half to perhaps the most ruthless instance of genocide on the continent. For such reasons, American writers and reviewers alike were unprepared to look upon the Indian with the romantic idealization he received in Europe.

Cooper tried valiantly to present the Indians as including, like other races, individuals of varying good and bad qualities. His works, although somewhat reservedly received in New England, where the *North American Review* among other strictures doubted the accuracy and propriety of his portrayal of Indians, at first found great favor in New York. The 1826 *United States Literary Gazette* was not indeed fully satisfied with his Indians: they were no doubt accurately depicted as far as the picture went and they were undoubtedly interesting. The reviewer added, however, "we should have preferred to see more of it [Indian character] in the social and domestic state, instead of being introduced to a few wandering and solitary individuals. Still it seems as successful as any which has been attempted, and is apparently the fruit of much pains and considerable attention to the subject." The reviewer seemingly did not share in the objections to Indian character as flat and monotonous which the *North American Review* had raised; the sole question apparent in his mind is the quality of Cooper's representation. So much from New England.

Five years later the *Mirror*, although generally friendly to Cooper, granted Charles Sealsfield space for a detailed attack upon the accuracy of his Indian pictures. Sealsfield charged that they were too sophisticated, were made, in fact, pretty much in the author's own image. This, he tartly added, was no doubt the reason why Cooper had made them talk far too much and do too little. The actual Indian is "a smoking, ruminating animal . . . a rough, cunning man of the woods," far more accurately portrayed in the novels of Miss Sedgwick. Significantly, Sealsfield preferred *The Pioneers* above Cooper's other tales; in it the sole Indian character is as debased as the most venomous

Indian-killer could have conceived him. He dismissed *The Prairie* as the skim milk left after *The Pioneers* had taken all the cream, and he categorically asserted that anyone who really knew the Indian would deny all truth to Cooper's general representation of him. But Sealsfield did not object to the Indian as a suitable subject for literary portrayal.

Cooper's attackers and defenders, and his own hot-tempered retorts to goading reviewers, constitute a story which still lacks its denouement. However the debate may ultimately be settled, it is unquestionable that his novels established the Indian as an accepted literary character. With the possible addition of Simms, Cooper was the principal portrayer of the Indian until Longfellow published his *Song of Hiawatha.*

The interest in primitivism found an explanation in the 1837 *New-Yorker.* The rudest states of society, it declared, do not foster the boldest, most original thinking; society, in fact, has little to do with the case. To the few minds which actually "give tone and character to the literature of each successive age," the state of the general mind is of little significance. Those men in primitive societies who express their thoughts are more independent and daring than more sophisticated writers simply because they are unbound by any preceding patterns of expression. The human mind either looks behind to collect and combine what is already established, or it looks forward to investigate new relations and express new truths. When it lacks a previous body of knowledge it perforce resorts to the second alternative. Such a course obviously stimulates the individual to become self-reliant. Freed from advice or restraining tradition, the primitive man "plunged fearlessly forward into the unexplored regions of philosophy and conjecture, and returned laden with rich rewards of adventure." But, the writer continued, such independent, questing temperaments have existed in all ages. However precedent may seek to bind them to conformity in more civilized times, the current state of society and tradition does not seriously affect them. The unbiased observer, the writer concluded, could find original minds outside of primitive society. The primitivistic dream of original heroes stemmed obviously from Carlyle —an antidemocratic tendency cavalierly dismissed by the *Democratic Review.*

Whether the American reviewer inclined toward the Young Americans or the conservatives, he generally looked coolly upon the assertions of the American primitivists. He claimed for the American the virtues associated with primitive man, but—as Cooper claimed to have done with Leatherstocking—he combined them with the advantages bestowed by ages of European tradition. To the reviewer the American was the heir of all the ages, although there was some disagreement as to how well he was using his patrimony. The public indeed demanded and devoured bales of primitivistic provender in the shape of Indian and frontier stories; the serious reviewer uniformly condemned such "romantic trash." If he gave it much attention, he usually worried about the degree to which it misrepresented the United States abroad through the circulating libraries. Whitman's remark that the past was good enough in its day and his patronizing mention of the small theater of the antique did not represent the consensus of literary thinking, although he had his forerunners. Critics did not confuse the common man with primitive man nor dismiss inherited culture with a flick of the wrist. The American had started and had lived in a new nation, and thus owned some of the primitive virtues; but in the eyes of Americans he was youthful rather than primitive.

SIX

LOCAL PROBLEMS OF

NEW YORK CRITICISM

During the decades between the two wars, in addition to the concerns already noted, New York critics faced four significant though unrelated problems. These were, first, the preservation of an independent outlook; secondly, the provision of publishing media for their essays and reviews; thirdly, their duty with respect to the public; and finally, their evaluation of American literary achievement. Although these problems have been mentioned in connection with previously discussed topics, they merit detailed treatment.

CRITICAL INDEPENDENCE

Both critic and reader were constantly exhorted in the journals to maintain their judgment unclouded by either inward or outward shading of the facts. One should not yield to his emotions after they have been excited by his reading. "To be overcome by surprise," declared the 1817 *American Monthly Magazine*, which felt no love of the new romantic writers, "by such 'bandits' as Scott and Byron, is an impeachment of no man's firmness—but to surrender one's judgment, at the summons of every footpad of Parnassus, is sheer dastardy." More liberal periodicals were inclined rather to look upon the author's problem as exploratory. They urged readers and critics to support him in striking out along untraveled paths and byways of the Muses. In so doing, they agreed, he might disregard tradition if it seemed to him advisable. The writer aware of these conventions—liberals declined to call them laws—would regard them as significant generalizations, to be taken into account but not slavishly to be obeyed. He must be granted even wider freedom than Pope allowed to deviate from the common track. The reader was not advised to act from mere caprice, nor was ignorance commended; but he should do his own thinking and form his personal conclusions.

The critic was likewise to perform his onerous duties on the basis of his own judgment. He should beware, warned the 1833 *Knickerbocker*, of overlooking moderate merit in a work: if not original and creative, it might possess the property of at least giving pleasure. He must remind himself that a book by an illustrious author must still stand upon its own feet and be judged without reference to its author. As E. S. Gould, echoing an earlier dictum of Bryant, warned New Yorkers in 1836, he must also remember that a book must stand in the open market of the world, not have a protective tariff of adulation reared about it because it is American and not unreadable. As the *New-Yorker* reiterated, he should judge the American product by universal standards: its power to excite the emotions, elevate the feelings, and enchain the attention. To be sure, the *New-Yorker* added, literature reflects its age and the culture in which it was produced, but there is no scale of values for any single period or locale. Such temptations from within, the critic must carefully avoid.

The critic, it was occasionally noted, would concern himself more profitably with examining a work by strictly literary standards, although as to these standards, periodicals differed. Early in 1839 the *Mirror* approved Carlyle's pronouncement that the primary business of criticism is not with matters of expression, decorum, logic, or psychology, but with something which includes all these matters and more: "properly and ultimately, a question on *the essence and peculiar life of the poetry itself.*" It comprehends the poem body, garment, and soul. "It gives the author his just deserts. It considers, rather the ideas, than the words in which they are clothed; it examines, more the correctness of opinion, the originality and brilliancy of thought, the beauty of sentiment, than the coherence of metaphor, or even the sequence of logick. Such a critic must possess a *mens divinior*, not merely a knowledge of the rules of Kames and Blair—he must have a kindred feeling with the poet—he must be a poet, and not a cold calculating measurer of words and sentences." Here George Allen's influence is clearly perceptible. Six months later, the *Mirror* applied its principle to blast a new work as "a demi-prose, demi-verse dramatic sketch; a sort of literary nondescript"; the writer should realize that improvement on established forms is impossible and devote himself to the content. Yet, as this stricture implies, an improperly garbed poem, although form was rated lower in importance, was branded a failure. Even such attention to form, however, became rarer as the period progressed; the romantic concern with content was reinforced with immediate national distractions to shift attention from such aesthetic matters.

External pressures were usually political, religious, or local. Under one or more of these heads criticism and reviewing were all too often censured. Until the mid-1830's political bias had little affected New York critical judgment; periodicals pointed with pride to their superiority in this respect to British reviews. With the animosities engendered by the Jacksonian modifications in political practice, however, as the founding of the *Democratic Review* indicates, the political spirit entered criticism under the guise of social reform. The subsequent establishment of the opposition's organ, the *Whig Review*, shows as clearly that the battle was openly recognized to be political. The attempts of religious pressure groups to sway the decisions of the *Mirror* and the *Knickerbocker* demonstrate the activity of sectarianism. It is refreshing to note that both periodicals successfully repelled these piratical boarders and that the most intelligently edited literary magazines of the day included the religiously affiliated *New York Review*.

As for local bias in New York, the outspoken contempt of New England expressed in the *Knickerbocker* and the *Democratic Review* indicates to what lengths it could be carried. Some hostility to New England, though on religious grounds, was also expressed in the *New York Review*. On the other hand, the *Mirror* and other periodicals welcomed numbers of the *North American Review* and speakers from New England on literary matters were fairly discussed. The loss of Southern sympathies after 1850, when Simms and others broke off relations with their New York associates, was a misfortune that the city suffered through no fault of her own.

Closely connected with these partisan rifts were those which engaged individual literary men. Evert Duyckinck's persistent effort to support Cornelius Mathews, which Perry Miller engagingly recounts in *The Raven and the Whale,* is one instance in which a staunch personal friendship entered into editorial policy and consequently into critical activity. The long-standing feud between the Duyckinck brothers and Rufus Griswold over their respective anthologies is another unpleasant episode. The *Mirror* likewise championed its contributor T. S. Fay against all challengers. A rift for a time divided Washington Irving and Fenimore Cooper, but it was happily closed. Poe's long squabble with Lewis Gaylord Clark and other editors, which has recently received detailed study, like Emerson's contemporary tempest in the Harvard "washbowl," was a disturbance that generated a great deal of heat. Poe's later reputation in American letters has made the episode loom larger in our eyes than it probably seemed to literary thinkers of his day. To these latter it no doubt gave a great deal of entertainment—unless they were of the relatively few persons who participated in it; it hardly changed the course of literary events beyond pointing up vigorously principles of criticism of which many were already aware. Poe was only briefly a New Yorker and was generally an outsider whose attacks were feared but, all too readily for his targets' good, overcome. Fortunately for the critical well-being of the city as a whole, literary men were concerned with more constructive matters than with personal disagreements, lively though these quarrels occasionally were. The better periodicals consistently showed a broad tolerance for diversity of opinion; the children of this world were wise enough to make progress amid disagreement. The *Mirror*'s welcome to the *New York Review* was perhaps the high-water-mark of such breadth. "Though differing with this work in some of its tenets, we are rejoiced to find so accomplished a champion of those tenets in the field; for the cause of truth is ever a gainer when opinions, worthy of examination, are ably set forth, in whatever light they may be placed."

The thorniest of all problems for New York critics was no doubt the maintenance of a proper relation with British criticism. Although it was troublesome to the country as a whole, New York felt it with peculiar force. The city's extensive commercial intercourse with Britain drew its inhabitants very close to the land across the Atlantic, for two peoples with such business ties naturally developed many common interests. Irving's prestige abroad as well as in New York further cemented friendly relations between literary men of the two countries; and Bryant and Willis were also popular in England, the one as poet, the other as *bon vivant*. There occurred, however, vitriolic outbursts of anti-British feeling, new irritations which fanned the smouldering enmity from the War of 1812 into occasional flame. The 1834 *Mirror* reprinted Irving's *Sketch Book* essay on Anglo-American relations with the remark that the ties noted by Irving were still binding. Cooper also tried during his years abroad, although seldom tactfully yet with insight and honesty, to inform the two nations about each other. Yet, despite the efforts of these and other well-informed Americans, New Yorkers were several times inflamed by real or fancied British slights.

New York magazines did not hesitate to inform the British that Americans were superior judges of foreign delineations of America and Americans. The 1832 *Mirror*, for example, contemptuously dismissed Mrs. Trollope's book on America as a "poor individual attack from an irresponsible female" whose combined ignorance and spleen deceived any British readers gullible or biased enough to entertain her assertions. If Americans should notice such work at all, they should also discount it as a mere money-making venture for writer and publisher. Enlightened folk on either side of the Atlantic, they must remember, regularly mingled with the greatest friendliness—a relation that it was to the best interests of both countries to preserve. American publishers, it pointedly added, could surely find foreign matter to reprint superior to Mrs. Trollope's spiteful outburst. A year later the *Mirror* warned New Yorkers that there could be no advantage from arousing once more the former violent feuds between Britain and the United States. Both sides would be well advised to rid themselves of hostile suspicions. The British must cease to patronize Americans as bumpkins—they were no longer provincial Britons or colonials. Americans must learn to hold their tongues when irritated, secure in the conviction stated earlier by Irving that time would plead their case in foreign courts of opinion. Moderate men on both sides should devote their efforts to the allaying of any springing enmity.

Mrs. Trollope continued to be the focus of contention in the late 1830's. According to the 1839 *Corsair*, the British were as much at fault as the irritated Americans for the existence of hard feelings: by printing five successive editions of her slanderous book, they had propagated British contempt for the new nation. It joined its voice to the *Mirror*'s earlier pleas for moderate American conduct. "There was a time when we could have been 'eloquently indignant' upon such a theme as this, but in common with most of our countrymen we feel that extreme sensitiveness to the opinion of strangers has passed away; nor are we necessarily hurried into a belief that the whole English people delight in national detraction, because a large portion of them have ignorantly adopted a vulgar compilation of slanders as a household book. Our emotions are only of surprise and sorrow. . . ." Steam navigation, the writer noted, had drawn the two nations so close that their actions would inevitably be more intimately knit than ever before. "The question arises whether those sympathies are to be woven merely between the factious of one country and the demagogues of the other"—the choice of terms indicated with which group in New York the *Corsair* thought the trouble was located—"or whether the world's cause of sound social principles and Christian feeling is to be advanced by mutual intelligence between the honest and the right judging of the two lands. Are shillings and pence, pick-pockets and political fanatics, to be the only commodities interchanged between us?" The settlement lay in the hands of the intelligent classes of the two countries—in the United States, he tacitly implied, it would not be found with the contributors to the *Democratic Review*. Nathaniel Willis' superficial lament, that the speedy steam packet had made America a suburban London, did not arouse any echoes in other New York writers.

Anglophobia in the periodicals followed regularly hard upon the flaring up of political disagreement between the two countries. Irving's essay in the *Sketch Book* attempted to soothe the hard feelings on both sides after the second war with England. The *Corsair*'s article obviously reflected the American irritation over the difficulties attendant upon the settlement of the boundary between Canada and New England. In 1847 anger at Britain's recent attempts to gain a second North American foothold in the former Texas republic required the pouring of more oil on the stormy waters.

The *Literary World* faced squarely this revival of the old feud. Evert Duyckinck, its editor, reminded his subscribers that Americans and Englishmen have much in common along with marked differences. Politically, Americans have a long lead on the road both are traveling, whereas the British far anticipate us in the common world of letters. The two peoples have much to learn from one another, which they can use to the best advantage of both while acting as independent entities. In literature they recognize the need for Americans to go their own gait; repeatedly they have urged the new nation of writers to be their natural selves and depict themselves in their works, not to affect some personality which they suppose Europeans will like better than the genuine American. The British cutting up of American pretensions to equality with them in letters, Duyckinck hailed as beneficial surgery; "only let us preserve a little self-respect, and while we profit by foreign advice, pay it back, not in foreign adulation, but in honest independence." Instead of keeping a timorous eye on the direction of British criticism, American reviewers must form and express their own judgments. In particular, they must assure American authors of a fair hearing amid the uproar caused by the myriad British importations for the American market. With a full awareness of his strength and weakness, the American could deliver just criticism.

Duyckinck added ruefully that most American critics were unequal to their task. They were insincere, hence unreliable; they were unjust because their methods lacked thoroughness; morally and intellectually their judgment was unsound. Those who were sitting in the seats of American criticism confused their position with the seat of the scorner. In fact their awkward attempt to occupy both chairs was an added cause of their ineptitude. "To be truly fair, the critic must have an intimate sympathy with his authors"—Allen's principle was well known to Duyckinck. The American critic must and can develop into the desired literary appreciator; until this should occur, the nation was without criticism.

Such depreciation of the nation's critics naturally met vigorous protest. Charles Fenno Hoffman declared that Americans had inherited from Britain a free spirit that made them competent and independent in judgment. The *Democratic Review*, despite the waning of its democratic emphasis, vitriolically condemned all who would concede British superiority in letters. Notwithstanding such chauvinist statements, the doctrine of intelligent cooperation with England in letters preached by Irving in 1819 which has been traced in the preceding pages was consistently upheld by the more influential papers.

With the furor of 1847, the Anglo-American literary question seemingly burned itself out. The quarrel over the Oregon question either followed too promptly the immediately preceding political disagreement, or it inspired political rather than literary eloquence; at any rate, comparatively little of literary antipathy to Britain appeared in New York subsequent to it. The prevailing literary attitude toward Britain in the fifties remained cordial yet courteously assertive of American literary and critical independence. Britain might excel America in letters; she must not therefore presume to dictate to us how we should write or criticize.

THE PUBLICATION OF CRITICISM IN NEW YORK

The most immediately pressing problem faced by the New Yorker who was interested in literary problems was the difficulty of publication. Then as now, critiques were essays rather than volume-length, and criticism found expression almost entirely in the periodicals. In the majority of cases it was immediately motivated by a book, in reviewing which the critic found his stimulus as well as his opportunity for expressing his ideas. It was in this way that criticism not only kept close to the reading provided for New Yorkers instead of speculating primarily on the art itself, but was also more immediately responsive to currents of interest than would have been the case had it been delayed in book-form. Excepting the quarterlies, the periodicals had to keep abreast of the times on account of their political articles and social comment. It is interesting to note that, contrary to the generalization made by William Charvat, the weekly *Mirror* was in criticism the organ of as competent criticism as were the monthlies and quarterlies. The quarterlies could offer the critic space for a more exhaustive treatment, to be sure; but in an age when literature was held to be the expression of society the short, more nearly contemporary comment was perhaps more effective; and a critic can judge with as much penetration in a short article as in a long one. In quarterlies like the *New York Review* are found accordingly the detailed discussions of the nature and proper practice of criticism, while monthlies and weeklies tend to apply the art to literary specimens. This distinction is not indeed always observed, but it is generally valid.

Although by the 1840's New York writers agreed that periodical literature represented most accurately the literary state of the city, they found its publication a precarious venture. Prior to 1829, the *Mirror* reported, no attempt to establish a purely literary magazine had succeeded. Even those magazines which tried to appeal to wider interests found constant difficulty in collecting the money due on subscriptions. Citizens would sign subscription lists to almost any new publication, the *Mirror* sadly noted, but would not pay up in many instances until the periodical had attained a degree of success that conferred prestige on the subscriber; and this delay made such success a near impossibility. The new publication feared to demand payment in advance for fear of turning away readers. Morris calculated in the same *Mirror* article that a publisher must be able to carry a deficit of at least ten thousand dollars—a nearly prohibitive sum for most literary entrepreneurs—before he could discover whether he had a successful venture. Even after the status of the magazine had been established, its numbers were likely to contain frequent appeals for payment from deadheads whose numbers were lethally large.

Since critics had a large stake in literary magazines as their media of expression, the high rate of mortality among them was a constant source of uneasiness. A year was normal life expectancy even for such competent ventures as those edited by Bryant in the 1820's and the later admirable *Corsair* and *Broadway Journal*. Still later, when the circle of cultured readers had considerably increased, *Putnam's* was able to survive for five years, but its demise left George William Curtis saddled with its heavy debts. A nation's reviews, the 1830 *Mirror* declared, are an accurate gauge of its intellectual status; it had been embarrassing to have reported a year earlier that the cultural interests of New Yorkers had never yet given a literary magazine adequate support to enable it to survive more than a few years at most.

In still another sense, editors admitted, the periodicals were an indication of the infirm literary and critical sense of the times. Magazine criticism, even when not corrupt, was frequently irresponsible. Readers are unreasoningly swayed by the printed page, the 1840 *Knickerbocker* noted; even the veriest blockhead of a critic can find a following if he can find a publisher. Although it agreed with the Jacksonian Democrats that the people are the sole and final tribunal, whose decisions in the long run will prove correct, they can be temporarily misled by unscrupulous judges. William A. Jones concurred: "there are almost as few judicious critics as original writers." From quarterly down to daily paper, and the newspaper reviewers were to *Arcturus's* thinking the most microscopic of all, there was a decline in the quality of criticism, the demise of the weekly *Mirror* having removed almost the sole specimen of critical merit in its category. But gradual relief was at hand.

Cheaper printing that lowered the cost of books effected a major revolution during this period in the practice of reviewing. Books which in 1820 had been out of the reach of most American purchasers were now made available to all through the invention of the rotary press. The flurry of cheap novels in newspaper format that developed in the 1840's, although it multiplied for the most part inferior literary works, nonetheless contributed to the general lowering of prices on books. With books now in the hands of the public, the long-established practice of excerpting long illustrative passages from the book under review became superfluous; and those incompetent or lazy reviewers who had taken refuge in quotation to fill their pages now found themselves faced with space which they had to fill by their own thoughts. The *Democratic Review*, which from the first had been as full of ideas as an egg of meat, had never admitted long quotation or summary of the works it considered; and in 1843 it noted with derisive satisfaction that some of its contemporaries were hard put to it to supply the new and more detailed criticism. The transition was especially difficult for the quarterlies with their long-drawn-out articles, but the monthlies also suffered. Once the reviewers had adjusted to the new method, however, the way was open for essays which not only adequately reviewed their subjects but, as Lowell was especially successful in doing after the war, added new contributions on the subject from the critic's stores of knowledge and opinion. Had the change been effected earlier, New York would have had either more constructive critical thought like George Allen's "Reproductive Criticism" or less ineffective and misleading reviews—in either case, a desirable consummation.

Before the thoughtful, detailed review could be achieved, another ruse of the old-time reviewer had to be smoked out and despatched. To this end the wider dissemination of good reading also contributed. The 1855 *Knickerbocker* gleefully attacked the practice of prefacing the discussion or quotation of the subject under review with a long-winded dissertation upon matters in general that sometimes bore but remotely if at all upon the immediate problem. "A double row of colossal sphinxes, a mile in length, and leading to nothing, would bring less sense of disproportion. In truth, the sphinxes themselves would be more intelligible than most of these profoundly empty essays." Discussions of a modern dramatist which commenced with windy arguments over interpretations of Aristotle's *Poetics* or speculations about the nature of primitive literature had to go, however the reviewer might bewail the loss of opportunity to display his erudition or the need to undertake some hard, pointed thinking. With these removed, the critic could be required to spread himself on the book and the problems immediately concerned with it, and the reader could anticipate at least an attempt at expression of considered judgment. The empty criticaster would soon be banished from the more reputable periodicals for lack of ideas. The transition to the new mode of criticism was here also difficult, but in its effects greatly rewarding. Neither of these objectives was fully achieved before the Civil War in New York, but at least the way was cleared for them.

As William A. Jones asserted in 1844, periodical writing had now become the staple of reading for most Americans; and it seemed likely that articles "short, to the point, interesting" would provide the principal source of intellectual entertainment and study for some time to come. This conviction, which was shared by many New Yorkers, partly accounts for their intense and sustained interest in the essay as a form and in Lamb, Hazlitt, Carlyle, and Macaulay as its practitioners. The 1854 *Democratic Review* even included an appreciation of the once hated Sydney Smith as the beau ideal of reviewer and essayist. Although some die-hard praiser of past times now and then raised his voice in lament for the passing of the eighteenth-century essay-writers, he was the exception. Tuckerman expressed the majority view in 1851 when he credited the modern review with the production of articles in which the writer first dissects fairly the work under examination and then adds his own scholarly and entertaining contribution to the field of that work. A biographer, S. A. Allibone remarked in the 1854 *Putnam's*, is usually so entangled emotionally in the fortunes of his subject that he can hardly produce a fair survey of an author's career and works. The periodical essay, on the other hand, may not only examine the subject objectively, but may also report dispassionately the opposition which his author excited as well as the praise bestowed upon him—a picture far better balanced and less stained by hero worship.

As in most literary areas, this first half of the nineteenth century did not so much firmly establish patterns of criticism of its own as thoroughly turn over for re-examination and adaptation critical and literary problems which present themselves to literary men in every lively age of letters. In this adaptation it mingled whatever new ingredients, such as those from Germany, it found available for use. In a nascent democracy with a free press, although it provided the greatest scope in expression of all literary milieus, this was perhaps all that could or should be undertaken. Such problems are the hardy perennials of literary history, which change with their habitat but survive as to species. Paradoxically, that very democratic principle which the Young Americans had asserted would force the rewriting of all literary history guaranteed the survival of previously existing literary problems and methods under conditions that permitted their freest development according to their own natures.

ACHIEVEMENTS AND PROSPECTS

Finally, what had American authors accomplished? What were the prospects of American literature? To both these questions New York critics offered outspoken responses throughout the period.

First, however, one literary failure was admitted, which some deplored as indicating the inability of Americans to create a literature: they had produced no epic or long narrative poem of any consequence. Gulian Verplanck had expressed the wish of many in his 1834 address, "The Influence of Moral Causes upon Opinion, Science, and Literature," for such a great American *Iliad* or *Aeneid*, or better yet, an heroic poem on the order of Tasso. It was presumed that a great literary artist would prove himself by the creation of such a poem. Renaissance theory as to the relative greatness of literary genres had not yet died in Verplanck's generation, and he rejected the modification of the traditional demand for a national epic which would substitute the historical novel as its modern replacement. The 1834 *Knickerbocker*, though disagreeing with Verplanck, admitted that he was not without company in his belief. It declared that the survival of ancient belief in the supremacy of the long poem had left competent American lyric poets without due honor in their own country. These poets had produced "matter which possesses all the elements of perpetuity; poems which, though short, are perfect; full of nature and life, without blemish or stain." On this head, however, tradition was stubborn and hard to dislodge.

In denying that primitive society, to which the epics of Homer were still ascribed, had fostered the boldest or most original thinking, the 1837 *New-Yorker* opened the attack upon the supremacy of the long poem. The present age, it asserted, reflects the revolutionary spirit, is violently emotional; instead of clearly representing heroic deeds, its poetry embodies the yearning for the vast, the shadowy, the unattainable. Poe was soon to develop this principle into his contention that the long poem is a contradiction in terms; since poetry expresses emotion at high temperature, the feeling which it represents soon burns itself out and the poem along with it. Somewhat inconsistently, the *New-Yorker* still hoped for the appearance of an American epic which it had just demonstrated to be an impossibility. No New York theorist produced a satisfactory retort to Poe's theory, which seemed to preclude the possibility of a long poem that was not a succession of short emotional ejaculations strung together with versified nonpoetic passages. Until Henry Timrod wrote it in South Carolina, such a response was not forthcoming in the United States.

In 1840 the *New York Review* advanced another salient against the supremacy of the epic by admitting the existence of several distinct species of poetic excellence—a concession that implied, whether the writer realized it or not, that the poet need not climb the ladder of poetry from pastoral to epic. The age's ruling passion for change, which he had noted as active in this matter, tended further from the traditional poetic path of ascent. Evert Duyckinck indeed seemingly reverted to traditional patterns when he declared: "It is in vain that a nation is said to live epic poems, if they do not write them." His remark, however, was probably directed against the cant phrase frequently read in liberal magazines and picked up fifteen years later by Whitman: "America is a poem in our eyes," rather than a reaffirmation of the renaissance classification of poetic genres. Although Duyckinck would no doubt have welcomed a great American epic with all the fervor that later critics expressed in their hopes for the great

American novel, he clearly did not hopefully expect it. His organ *Arcturus* admitted that poetry was then being written for the people, and it was common belief that the people would read only shorter works of any sort.

The conservative *Whig Review* in 1845, as was to be anticipated, held to tradition: the fugitive verse of American poets gives no indication whether its composers are true poets. To demonstrate such capacity, "there must be continuity, scope for variety of powers." By this time, however, Coleridge's skepticism concerning the long poem had been actively taken up by William Jones, then at the height of his reputation. Poe energetically seconded Jones's declarations. Jones's support against the long poem, it may be remarked in passing, was probably one cause of Poe's classifying him as one of the two or three really able American critics. The belief had long been held by Poe, who for once paid a debt. The demand for a long national poem did not survive this attack, aided as the onslaught was by the shift of public interest to prose fiction. Militant nationalism also played a significant part in the downfall of the epic. America was the acme of all things: America did not produce long poems; long poems, therefore, were not the acme of poetry. Although less baldly stated, this was the logic of many vociferous theorists. In fine, the dominant literary faction held that the lack of a national epic indicated no deficiency in American letters.

It was generally admitted, however, by New York critics, who mingled a realistic survey with their beliefs, that American literature had not accomplished anything like the literary potential of the country. One should, they felt, truthfully write of American letters in the optative mood of contingent futurity; they should, could, and would come into being, but had not yet done so. In 1824 the *Mirror*, assessing the literary property of the country in its early years, felt that American authors had indeed broken the literary ice but had not actually entered the waters. The *Mirror* had already found merit in Cooper's and Paulding's novels, which ably exploited American materials. Two years later Bryant declared the sole obstacle to American poetry lay in the inertia of American poets in the presence of abundant poetic materials. In condemning N. P. Willis for his failure to make full use of his talents and to develop according to his early promise, the 1830 *Mirror* adopted an attitude quite in line with the literary demands of many periodicals upon American authors. They were lenient in their judgment only when they were satisfied that the writer had employed the full capacity of his powers.

A foreshadowing of the twentieth-century production line in manufacture appeared in the quantity of writing produced at the expense of quality. E. S. Gould in 1836 described American authors as prolific but unsound. Theirs was, the 1837 *American Monthly Magazine* agreed, a "hot-bed growth" in need of the closest critical pruning. The *Democratic Review*'s proclamation of limitless manifest popular literary destiny appeared to more sober minds to reflect the American *auri sacra fames*, that accursed hunger for wealth that materialistically concerned itself with the multiplication and vending of products. According to the 1840 *Knickerbocker*, the itch to publish and profit had "blighted and scorched all those finer feelings, which are indispensable to poetic excellence." American writers, it was widely feared, had rushed too impetuously into print. The 1845 *Broadway Journal*, with the *Whig Review* concurring, was convinced that the tender plant of American letters had been excessively forced without at the same time having been adequately nourished. The resulting rank growth, both William Jones and Margaret Fuller asserted, was not a strong school of writers. Although the latter years of the era were lightened by somewhat more optimistic prophecies of the coming American novel, the consensus was that American literature had been forced into unhealthy growth by the demand for a national literature. The product would come with time and care, it was confidently asserted; but milder methods of development were needed to produce sound literary timber.

In the 1833 *Knickerbocker* Timothy Flint had enumerated the hindrances to development of an American literature. It received no encouragement or subsidy from the government, as literary men did abroad. It lacked a literary metropolis where writers could meet and strengthen one another's talents by mutual criticism of their products. Its continuing subservience to British opinion and models prevented development by its emphasis upon copying and deference. It was so deeply engulfed in the deluge of bad writing that the good disappeared in the flood; and "the vile spirit and fashion of puffing and reviewing" further choked true merit. Worst of all, literature ranked in public interest far below politics. Bent evidently upon a jeremiad, Flint included no ameliorating conditions in his picture.

Flint's summary of the situation, though pessimistic, was a fair list of adverse forces, which in the years that followed had mostly to be faced. His implied desire for literary patronage by the government, it is true, fell upon almost wholly deaf ears. Wordsworth's supposed defection from the cause of liberty "just for a handful of silver" still rankled in literary minds. New Yorkers, moreover, in many instances

agreed with Bryant's declaration in 1818 that American literary practitioners should receive not even the protection of a literary tariff in
the shape of favored positions at the bar of criticism, but should com-
pete in the open market of the world. They had the right only to expect the patronage of buyers and readers that a fair inspection of their
literary wares could bring them.

From all the other perils New Yorkers offered an escape. New York,
they declared, was the literary center where authors could rub shoulders and best develop their talents. Although Boston and Philadelphia
contested this claim, by the end of the era the latter city had given up
the struggle, and Boston was forced grudgingly to yield ground. Although enslavement to British models was a recurrent complaint, most
New York critics felt that with the passing years notable progress was
being effected toward the establishment of suitable literary relations
between British and American authors. The deluge of bad books that
poured out of the presses was without any remedy, but many New
York writers comforted themselves with the analogy that grain is not
gathered without the winnowing of vast amounts of chaff. The in-
effectiveness of the winnowing process worried critics and reviewers,
hampered as it was by the pervasive puffing and blackguarding tactics
of the publishers and their advertising henchmen; but, to resort to another analogy, all this obfuscating smoke indicated the presence of some
true literary fire.

The final objection on Flint's list, the ranking of literature as a pursuit below political activity, on the whole worried New Yorkers less
than the others. The democratic extremists naturally felt that the democratic principle which was to inform literature must be first established
before the literature which it inspired could arise; and the more conservative felt that America's first responsibility was her existence as a
nation with a stable government. Few critics in New York held themselves aloof from questions of the public welfare and national well-
being, and no one thought of literature as a pursuit withdrawn from
the practical pursuits of life.

In their assessment of the literary situation, then, New York critics
at nearly every opportunity throughout the period expressed a qualified
optimism. In keeping with the practical air of the city, they tended to
face their problems squarely, and they freely admitted their literary
weaknesses while recognizing the strength of their prospects. They
were uniformly skeptical of large claims; the *Mirror*, for example, reported with dead-pan irony the claim that there were a hundred competent poets in the country. At the same time, they felt that Ameri-

can authors had done well under their considerable handicaps; they thoughtfully evaluated American books for their better qualities while warning authors of their shortcomings and while studying foreign works for whatever good they might contain for American use or adaptation; and they plotted with care the course which the new literature seemed likely to follow.

SEVEN

CONCLUSION

The periodical criticism which has formed the staple of this study undoubtedly has certain limitations. The most generous concession of latitude to the reviewer could not fully compensate for the constant restraint inherent in his obligation to keep in mind the subject of his review. George Allen's "Reproductive Criticism," although probably one of the outstanding critical essays of the period, was itself basically an intelligent development of German concepts in the books he was reviewing. Even Poe's "The Poetic Principle" cannot be considered a rounded piece of literary theory. Three decades after Allen wrote, Lowell, with all his influential position as editor of the *North American Review*, was restricted to consideration of such works as came up for his attention.

Whether greater freedom, such as would have been provided by the opportunity to express one's thoughts in a scholarly volume, would have produced a rounded theory of literature or criticism, is an academic question. As matters stood the New York writers could hardly have had the opportunity for such expression, and it is unlikely that they felt the need of such an outlet for their ideas. The evidence is overwhelming that periodical publication appealed to them as a satisfactory medium of expression; they themselves believed that it provided the most nearly accurate expression of their times. The United

States, except perhaps in New England, was still too unorganized a society to furnish a fixed object for contemplation and literary or critical analysis; and by reason of its comparative racial homogeneity New England could not represent a country that was constantly and rapidly developing its human and cultural composition through the adding of new ingredients. The hordes of immigrants that entered the country were welcomed and assimilated in New York to a degree unknown in Boston. For such a society as New York's, which by 1840 closely approximated that of the country as a whole, the tentative and fragmentary statement afforded by the periodicals was adequate and fairly accurate expression. The Boston culture indeed produced more artistic literature in this era than did New York, but it was the expression of a region. It was neither national nor, as contemporary New Yorkers claimed, indigenous to the new nation.

The New Yorkers were from fairly early years fully aware of their literary position. The *Mirror* in 1829 and 1830, the *Knickerbocker* in 1838, and William A. Jones in the 1844 *Democratic Review*, recognized the services performed by the *North American Review* for American letters and criticism. Jones presented it as our *Edinburgh* and *Quarterly* without the latter magazine's bad qualities. As late as 1849 the *Knickerbocker* interrupted its frequent diatribes against the Yankees to print a strong plea by G. P. Fisher for preserving the virtues of the Puritans. In the same year Jones admitted that New England had produced fully two-thirds of the best authors the United States could show. New Yorkers were fully aware of their secondary rank in letters.

At the same time, New York saw much in New England that was unsatisfactory if not actually dangerous to American letters. Criticism of culture in the Boston area became especially violent at about the same time that the new surge for Jeffersonian democracy swept over the New York literary area. The *Knickerbocker*, however, and not the *Democratic Review*, led in condemning New England's literary and cultural ways. In 1837 it attacked Puritanism in its British and American manifestations as "religious charlatanry"; it had been disastrous to American religious life and by implication to literature as well. (The writer seems to have been only less inclusive than H. L. Mencken in the varieties of belief subsumed within the term "Puritan," but he blamed it for its radicalism, not its conservatism.) The next year it charged that the undeniable services performed by the *North American Review* were greatly diminished by its prejudice and sectional feeling. The *Knickerbocker*'s sniping at numbers of the *Dial* has already been noted. The 1847 *Literary World* took up the attack upon the *North*

American Review, "that calm old adder slumbering on the lawn of Harvard"; and the 1848 *Holden's Dollar Magazine*, pointedly ignoring the Boston quarterly, praised the *Knickerbocker* as "the father of all American magazines." Several magazines characterized New England writing as careful in performance—a romantic sin—didactic in tone, and without naturalness or spontaneity. And W. A. Jones summed up the charges: "New Englandism" in letters carried "taste in its lowest form (cold and cautious), to its point of perfection" by achieving a colonialism not in any full sense of the term American.

For the transcendentalists, Emerson was recognized as the ablest spokesman. The 1841 *New York Review* naturally took exception to his *Essays* as expressing "a semi-philosophical theory strangely blended with certain elementary notions of religion, making as large demands on the conduct as on the faith of those who receive it, and leading to principles and forms of social organization which have no basis in the nature of man, and which experience has already condemned as impracticable." It can claim relation to the Germans and Coleridge only as sprung from "some equivocal generation, a *lusus naturae*, feeble, and we trust short-lived." Emerson could, it was generally admitted, lay some claim to literary distinction: the 1847 *Literary World* called him "one of the finest, as he is certainly one of the most singular, poetical spirits of the time." This writer further qualified his praise by listing as many faults as merits in his poems, and though treated with respect, he won few supporters of his philosophy or his works.

With all their sharp censure of their Yankee neighbors, New Yorkers cherished few illusions about their own creative literary efforts. As businesslike children of this world, they were accustomed to accurate stocktaking, and unlike the Boston sons of light they did not indulge in mutual admiration societies. The *Mirror* about the year 1830 repeatedly assessed the literary situation of the city. In 1829 it commented on the good sense, enlightenment, and liberal views of the New York weeklies in general. A year later it noted that the taste of the newspapers in the city was improving and that their standards had always been higher than those observed in areas round about them. In 1831 it reported in some detail upon the standing of the city in intellectual matters compared with that of its neighbors. The general intelligence of New York, it asserted, was superior to that of all other cities in the United States; why, then, did the city lag behind them in letters and science? Although it possessed authors equal to any in the land and talent adequate to assure its pre-eminence, these authors were "insulated," given no opportunity for the encouragement of concentrated effort. The city was not a literary metropolis in the sense that London was. "All the elements of greatness abound in her," but to be brought into active production they must be assimilated and combined into a unified literary effort. Other cities, whose direction had been more consciously guided and whose citizens did not first have to be amalgamated into a homogeneous body, surpassed New York because their concerns, literary and other, were less dissipated into unrelated channels. As new generations should grow in New York, her heterogeneous population would become a single race, as indeed the editor felt was already occurring. As an encouraging sign for the future, he noted the dawning of a local feeling, distinct in many characteristics but free from spite and envy toward other regions, whose expression should give New York her rightful pre-eminence in letters and the arts. In another article the editor declared that New York, although so far unsuccessful in longtime support of a literary magazine, could support one as well as any other city. And in 1838 he welcomed the *New York Review* as the fulfillment of this expectation, although his belief as to its longevity was dashed four years later.

The adverse comments upon New England and her literature, already noted, often carried with them the tacit assumption that cultural matters were better managed in New York. A noticeable statement of this feeling was made in 1849 by W. A. Jones in his attack upon "New Englandism." After his charge that the Yankee states were the most provincial of all our regions because they still adhered so closely to British thought and ways, he added, "How different from New York, which is cosmopolitan, and truly a Metropolis, the city of the Dutch, and of the English, and of the native American, crossed by the French, German, Welsh, Scottish and Irish races—a city of the world like London, not the country town of litterateurs and bluestockings." It was only in New York, he asserted, that the British taproot of American letters can find truly American nourishment and produce an American literature. And the *Literary World* in 1853 exulted over the complaints emanating from Boston that Thackeray's lectures there cost more than they were worth. "They are counting the cost, the shrewd Yankees! and recommending the home manufacture, the cheap New England fabrics, the fustian and linsey-woolsey of Boston, and crying out for protection to Hillard, Wendell Phillips, Choate, and homemade stuffs! They are hardly equal yet in the provinces to the enjoyment of a foreign luxury, they have not come up to our metropolitan enjoyment of a choice thing, rare and costly." They would actually find Thackeray a good investment: "Think of the improvement in the home article by competition, and recollect that parsimony is not always the best economy." Maybe jealousy inspired their dislike: "New York gives the imprimatur, will not Boston enjoy the book?" It is noticeable that the writer lists in his attack only second- or third-rate Boston litterateurs. The *Literary World* stood on fairly good terms with Holmes and Lowell, and though sharply critical of Emerson and Longfellow, recognized their abilities in their literary fields.

Excepting the fanatical Young Americans of the late thirties and early forties, New York writers were uniformly skeptical of large literary claims. Nonetheless, it was this very group which centered its activities in the early volumes of the *Democratic Review* that produced as its ultimate expression the most significant writer of the century, Walt Whitman. Whitman circulated freely in the orbits of several New York magazines and found the rampant nationalism of the Young Americans a point of view sympathetic to his own. His "Preface" to his *Leaves of Grass* was the acme—and much more—of the things they accomplished. However his poems scandalized this very group and their satellites, Whitman's prefatory theses organized their ideas into one document and added scope and depth to them. Even his assertion that the United States was essentially the greatest of all poems repeated claims made fourteen years earlier in the *Democratic Review;* and his catalogue of the qualities in the greatest poets includes many of those proclaimed in the same periodical by W. A. Jones. The *Democratic Review*'s demand in its manifesto that all human thought and literary expression be reformulated in the light of the new democratic principle formed a basic element of Whitman's declaration. It is surely no instance of the *post hoc ergo propter hoc* fallacy to conclude that such congenial vigor of feeling and expression set its impress upon Whitman's literary attitudes. The student of Whitman will profit from detailed study of the periodical literature in his background, to which Gay Wilson Allen in *The Solitary Singer* has pointed the way.

The effect of these periodicals upon Herman Melville was somewhat less significant than their impress upon Whitman and cannot be readily assigned to specific sources. Perry Miller in *The Raven and The Whale* has already narrated Melville's fortunes with several of the editors and writers for New York magazines. It should be noted that Melville came to New York after the fanatical *Democratic Review* had spent its first force and that the Duyckinck brothers did much to guide his career. Although vigorously patriotic, these men were not fulminating nationalists, and their impact upon Melville was in all probability philosophical and literary as much as it was journalistic. The fact that Melville's philosophical reading in their library went to press as a rough, somewhat undigested mass, cannot be laid to their charge. Melville, on the whole, reflects the influence of the more cultivated forces in New York literary circles, just as Whitman is more nearly related to the firebrands. To go off half-cocked was one of the less desirable qualities in New York literary men as a whole, and both Whitman and Melville showed this defect. Melville, moreover, had received some of his literary shaping before New York litterateurs further molded him; Whitman had from adolescence been exposed to their pressures. Both men, however, though in varying degrees perhaps, must be interpreted in the light of this exposure.

In their haste, which is a defect that has constantly been the defect of New York activities, the literary wise men of Gotham creatively and critically all too often put to sea in bowls without waiting to build a more seaworthy transport. In their expressing and forecasting the course of American literary thought, however, they were wiser than those New England sons of light whom they ironically described as the "Wise Men from the East." There may be something almost grotesque in the combination of a Mother Goose rhyme with the biblical Parable of the Unjust Steward that underlies the thinking of this entire study. Their union, however, aptly expresses the situation indicated in the remark of Edmund Wilson with which this study began. As Van Wyck Brooks once remarked, for the fit though few, the New England writers produced works that are possessions for all time. Without perhaps subscribing in full to Brooks's subsequent statements, one who has studied the literary vicissitudes of New York prior to the Civil War can hardly deny that the literary course of America must be plotted from the data which its literary and critical luminaries provide.

DRAMATIS PERSONAE

Although the drama of literary development in pre–Civil War New York lacked unified action, it displayed an abundance of agents who provided the Renaissance literary virtue of variety. Among these actors must be included the periodicals themselves. Each magazine strove to present a personality, almost a persona; the *Knickerbocker* pretended to be Father Knickerbocker's mouthpiece. Contributions during this era were mostly unsigned, a circumstance contributing further to the personality of the periodical; the few signed articles detracted little from this impression. The pages of Frank Luther Mott should be consulted for descriptions of these magazines. A few, however, which played leading roles in our study, are presented here in order of appearance.

The first *American Monthly Magazine*, edited by H. Biglow and O. L. Holley, ran from 1817 to 1819. Biglow, John Neal wrote, was "one of those rolling stones that gather no moss, which are so common in America." Holley, a Harvard graduate, after his editorial experience became a New York lawyer. As their virulent antiromantic reviews indicate, their model in style and judgment was *Blackwood's.*

A more spritely publication, the New York *Mirror*, appeared in 1823 and ran for two decades. George P. Morris, its editor, came to New York as a youth from Philadelphia; he launched his weekly when only twenty-one. A diminutive man with curly hair and beard, he was a dynamo of energy. He wrote popular songs, of which "Woodman, spare that tree" is still known. Like Kipling's Bobs, he affected the military; in the militia he rode the tallest horse he could and was regularly nicknamed "the General." A down-to-earth businessman, Morris realized that a purely literary magazine would live precariously in New York; he accordingly varied his contents to suit diverse readers. He incorporated articles of travel, many by the popular Nathaniel Willis. His serial novels, by T. S. Fay and others, were geared to the taste of the average reader. Notes on the theater frequently appeared. There were fashions and toilet-hints aimed to attract women, and the last page often carried the words and music of a new song. Lyric verse was also featured; Morris wished to encourage American poets by furnishing an outlet for their effusions.

In literary matters, the *Mirror* belied the rule that the weekly magazine was inferior to the monthlies and quarterlies. Morris incorporated articles by competent writers, though unsigned, which in a few hundred words commented on current literature and criticism; occasionally more detailed analyses of authors or movements appeared. Opposed views, as in varied comment on Cooper, were freely admitted. The influence of the *Mirror* during its first fifteen years is incalculable, since it reached both literati and populace, and was read not only on the seaboard but also west of the Alleghanies.

A second *American Monthly Magazine*, begun in 1833, survived for five and one-half years. One of its first editors, H. W. Herbert, well-known under the pseudonym of Frank Forrester, was a grandson of the Earl of Carnarvon and after his education at Eton and Cambridge, came in 1830 to New York. He brought with him highly developed tastes in classical scholarship, dissipation, sports, and writing—three of which at least he amply exercised in New York. Irritated that the *Knickerbocker* had rejected his contributions, he started this rival magazine; the larger part of its early articles he himself wrote. After two years he was succeeded by Charles Fenno Hoffman and Park Benjamin, who gained the contributions of Paulding, Verplanck, and James Hall among other prominent men to add to the competence of its articles. Two notable interests were the magazine's concern for German literature and for matters relating to the American West.

Herbert's enemy, the *Knickerbocker*, enjoyed a long life, from 1833 to 1865. A year and a half after its founding, it passed into the hands of Lewis Gaylord Clark, an upstate New Yorker from Otisco. Clark drove the *Knickerbocker* down the middle of any debatable road that he treated. It catered to the sentimental reader in mildly humorous essays. It followed the safe course of promoting a national literature without at the same time being isolationist.

Clark was a friend of Irving and Dickens—the magazine's name was a graceful bow to Irving. He was a handsome man with a talent for making friends, made for membership in clubs; he was a charter member of the Century Club in 1846. He lined up the most imposing list of contributors of any magazine of the period: the New Englanders Longfellow, Hawthorne, Holmes, and Whittier, and the New Yorkers Paulding, Hoffman, Verplanck, and Halleck were known to write for him.

The *Knickerbocker*'s role in literature and criticism was lively rather than deep. Its most notable contribution was its insistence upon recognition of literature as akin to the other representative arts; it praised and defended American painters in much the same terms that it applied to writers. It continued the interest of a prior editor, Timothy Flint, in the cultural progress of the West. Its antipathies were such as were harmless to its subscription list: Thomas Carlyle, whom most New Yorkers considered a fair target; the generally unpopular transcendentalists; Cornelius Mathews, who was a protégé of Clark's *bêtes noires* the Duyckincks; and Edgar Allan Poe. Clark once described the transcendentalist *Dial* as turnip soup with precious few turnips. However shallow may have been the critical furrow he ploughed, his literary crop was good, and its quality warranted perhaps unduly the quality of his critical pronouncements.

In scholarship and depth of critical acumen, the *New York Review* (the second to bear that title) was unquestionably the best publication in New York. Appearing quarterly from 1837 to 1842, it was hailed at once by George Morris as fully the equal of the *North American Review*. Caleb Henry, its first editor, was later professor of philosophy at New York University, and a successor, J. G. Cogswell, had been educated in Germany. Both these men were deeply interested not only in English and American letters but also in German literature and philosophy, and they secured contributors who penetrated far more deeply into the latter subject than had the *American Monthly Magazine*. The quarterly was an organ of the resurgent Protestant Episcopal Diocese of New York; nevertheless it allowed its literary contributors extensive freedom in subject and expression on literary matters—a unique quality for New York's religious publications. It is difficult to identify many of its contributors, but among them were Evert Duyckinck, George Allen, Samuel Ward and his sister Julia.

Until the late thirties George Morris' warning held true: the alliance of a literary magazine with politics gave it the kiss of death. Less than three months, however, after Emerson's delivery of "The American Scholar," and serving in effect as complement to it, the *Democratic Review* appeared in Washington. Andrew Jackson was its first subscriber and politics its prime concern. By 1841 it had removed to New York, whose writers had been affiliated with it from its inception, and it had become in essence a New York mouthpiece before its removal thither. In New York its literary activities became more highly developed; Bryant gave it added prestige, aided by William A. Jones, Evert Duyckinck, and J. L. O'Sullivan. Its manifesto proposed to make all things new, including literature, in the Jacksonian Democratic image as Young America saw it. After due allowance for this bias, one finds in its pages penetrating reviews and intelligent criticism. William Jones, its leading critic, had been called by Poe one of America's best, and he justified Poe's estimate by transcending the magazine's limitations in several of his pronouncements. Its literary comment was timely, sometimes of lasting value; but one of its principal claims to merit was its influence in helping Emerson to bring Whitman to a boil, as Whitman later admitted.

The natural course of politics brought into existence the *Whig Review*, which ran from 1845 to 1852. Sumptuously printed, it provided in addition to its political message strong and usually intelligent critical articles. G. H. Colton, its first editor, was a young Yale graduate, J. D. Whelpley, his successor, a medical doctor who was also deeply interested in commercial exploitation of Central America. G. W. Peck, probably the third editor, was a New England lawyer with extensive previous experience as a musical critic in Boston before moving to New York. The interest of each of these affected the course of the *Whig Review*. With due correction for its political astigmatism, its literary and critical comment was of as high quality as that of its opponent. Its eight years of life gave an outlet to a number of competent literary thinkers.

In January, 1853, G. P. Putnam brought out in *Putnam's Magazine* one of the ablest and most readable of New York's monthlies. It took over the subscription lists of the defunct *Whig Review* and like many members of that party it adopted the new Republican party's politics. It was hailed immediately as "a sort of American *Blackwood's*," but it never equaled its prototype in either billingsgate or bias. Under the lively direction of Charles F. Briggs it prospered in every way except financially; the hard times of 1857 brought it to an end. Briggs had

Parke Godwin, Bryant's son-in-law, and George W. Curtis as assistants. Unlike the recently founded *Harper's Magazine,* it pointedly concentrated upon publishing original American writing, although it did not ignore British literature. In spite of *Putnam's* republican leanings, it did not ignore or otherwise attack Southern writers; and like the *Knickerbocker* it was attentive to the growing literature by western authors. New England writers, James Russell Lowell in particular, were painstakingly evaluated. Frank Luther Mott correctly gives it the highest level attained by any American magazine up to its time.

Other periodicals that played minor but significant parts in the drama of New York letters include the *Minerva* from the twenties; Horace Greeley's *New-Yorker* from the thirties; from the forties, Duyckinck's *Arcturus* and *Literary World, Brother Jonathan,* on a popular level, and Brigg's *Broadway Journal;* and from near the end of the period the *National Quarterly Review.*

Mott has calculated that by the year 1860 one-third of the periodical circulation in the United States emanated from New York, almost three times that issuing from its closest competitor Pennsylvania. With the variety of interests shown by New York's heterogeneous population, it is likely that the percentage of purely literary and critical output from New York is slightly smaller than the total national output. It still remains the largest in bulk emanating from any American literary center, and, as this study has undertaken to show, it presented American literary and critical opinion of singular significance to the nation as a whole.

NEW YORK CRITICS

Although most of the literary and critical pronouncements during pre–Civil War years were anonymous, some articles were signed. Industrious scholarship has discovered the authorship of many unsigned articles, so that a number of literary personages now emerge from the vast body of anonymity. A brief account of the literary figures whom these efforts have helped to resurrect will now be given. Persons will be introduced according to the decade of their first significant writing.

Prior to the 1820's three literary figures appear: Gulian Verplanck, John Bristed, and James K. Paulding. Bristed was born in England in 1778, attended Winchester College, and studied medicine at Edinburgh. He also read law and was admitted to the Inner Temple. Coming to New York in 1806, he practiced law, lectured, and wrote. In 1818, he published a thoughtful study, *The Resources of the United States of America,* in a long chapter of which he dispassionately reviewed the literary prospects of the new nation. He was the father of Charles Astor Bristed, a later well-known dilettante and critic.

Gulian Verplanck, one of several native New Yorkers who figured in Gotham's literary scene, has aptly been called the essential New Yorker. Born in 1786, he was graduated from Columbia in 1801, the youngest to receive the baccalaureate degree from that institution for many decades. He read law and practiced briefly, but his interests were political and literary. For several years he made the equivalent of the Renaissance grand tour of Europe. During Washington Irving's editorship of the Philadelphia *Analectic Magazine*, he contributed a few long reviews of current works, in which his conservative literary tastes clearly appeared. In 1819 his political warfare with DeWitt Clinton caused him to write satirical verses entitled "The Bucktail Bards," and a war of pamphlets ensued. He served in the New York legislature, the New York senate, and eight years in Congress. From 1821 to 1825 he was a professor in the Protestant Episcopal General Theological Seminary in New York, and for several decades he was in demand for public addresses in the city and afield. These dealt frequently with literary and educational topics, one of their pervasive themes being the duties of the American scholar and man of culture and letters. With his friends William Cullen Bryant and Robert C. Sands, he composed an annual, *The Talisman*, which was published from 1827 to 1829. Verplanck's scholarly activities culminated in his three-volume edition of Shakespeare, published in 1847, a labor of love to which he devoted years of earnest research. He was probably the most distinguished New Yorker of pre–Civil War days to actively participate in the literary scene, and his activities spanned a period shorter only than Bryant's.

Another New Yorker of Dutch extraction was the novelist-critic James Kirke Paulding. Born into a large, poor family in Dutchess County in 1778, he had only the formal training of a rural school. When he was about eighteen, his brother William, a successful lawyer and active literary force in the city, found him a clerkship; and his sister Julia, who had married William Irving, opened the way to his entry into the circles frequented by her husband and his brother Washington. By 1802 he was writing for Peter Irving's *Morning Chronicle*, and five years later he shared in *Salmagundi*. During these years, as relations with Great Britain worsened, he intensified one of his ruling passions, a violent Anglophobia which colored deeply his literary thinking. Following further his friendship with Irving, he contributed reviews to the Philadelphia *Analectic Magazine* while Washington was its editor.

From 1815 to 1823, Paulding lived in Washington, serving on the Board of Naval Commissioners, a connection that culminated in 1838 with three years service as Secretary of the Navy. The last twenty years of his life were spent in retirement as a gentleman-farmer near Hyde Park.

Paulding was perhaps the sturdiest survivor from the age of neo-classicism that the New York circles produced. In his first and best-known novel, *Koningsmarke* (1823), he copied Fielding's device from *Tom Jones* of writing critical interchapters introductory to each book. These chapters contain also some of Fielding's ironic outlook, which in fact came naturally to Paulding, who was frequently castigated by his reviewers for allowing a joke to interfere with the course of his tales. His Anglophobia combined with a dislike for the romantic in literature, whether in prose or in verse, and he bitterly satirized Scott as its protagonist in both media. His vigorous nationalism united with an equally vigorous but incipient realism that was aided, as in his early *Letters from the South*, by his keen though amused observation of men and manners. His position as one of the early American novelists to whom nationalists could point with pride—for some time he shared with Cooper and Bryant the fame of America's literary reply to European denigration of American letters—gave his literary and critical theories a wide audience during the 1820's.

Of William Cullen Bryant's career the leading events are generally known; his outstanding activities as literary theorist and critic have been overshadowed by his reputation as poet and editor. After laying the foundations of a critical reputation with contributions to the *North American Review*, in 1825 he came to New York to be joint editor of the *New York Review and Athenaeum Magazine*. Before the end of the decade, he had transferred his activities to the *Evening Post*, where his interests centered for the next half-century. Critically, he was soundly based in the classical tradition and in the neoclassical theorists; but "Johnson deep and Addison refined" were supplemented by Coleridge and the romantics, to whom were added later the critical essays of Sainte-Beuve. Bryant's penetrating "Lectures on Poetry," though delivered in 1826, were not printed until 1884, and most of his reviewing was done in magazine and newspaper columns. If these papers could be identified and collected in full (a number were edited by Tremaine McDowell), there is little doubt that Bryant's stature as a critic would stand second only to Poe's in the pre–Civil War era.

The thirties brought a notable increase in periodicals and in writers upon literary subjects. From New England came one of the most dashing figures in early American letters, Nathaniel Parker Willis. Born in Maine in 1806, he attended the Boston Latin School, Andover, and Yale, receiving his bachelor's degree in 1827. With this prestigious education, he came in 1831 to New York, where Morris made him foreign correspondent of the *Mirror*. Following five years of lionizing abroad, he returned in 1836 to New York, where two of his plays were moderately well received in the theater. For a year he was associated with the critical *Corsair*. He was, although he wrote little criticism, the subject of enough violent literary disagreement to be himself a literary force in the city until in 1852 failing health forced him out of the literary picture. Lowell in his *Fable for Critics* pictures Willis very closely after the general opinion of him.

Of the same age as Willis was a native New Yorker whose life was marred by two serious misfortunes. Charles Fenno Hoffman lost his right leg above the knee from an accident when only eleven years old. He attended Columbia for three years, attained only a low academic standing, and left in 1824 without taking his degree. After reading law in Albany, he was admitted to the bar in 1827 and practiced law for three years in New York. He edited the new *Knickerbocker* for nine months in 1833, but late in the autumn left for a horseback trip to the northwestern territories, from which came his *A Winter in the West* in 1835. For two years subsequently he edited with distinction the new *American Monthly Magazine*, writing many of its articles and reviews. In 1839 he published *Greyslaer*, a punctiliously documented novel of the Revolution in the Mohawk Valley, material later made famous by Harold Frederic's *In the Valley*. He became mentally deranged, and in 1849 was committed to a mental institution, where he remained until his death thirty-five years later, never regaining his sanity.

The mercurial Samuel Ward was another native New Yorker, born in 1814 and graduated from Columbia in 1831. Several years of study in France and Germany prepared him for a stirring career of ups and downs as intellectual liberal, student of French and German literature, gold-seeker in California, and speculator and promoter in many grandiose schemes, not all of them quite respectable. Like his sister, Julia Ward Howe, he contributed intelligent articles on Continental literature to the *New York Review*. His knowledge contributed considerably to New Yorkers' awareness of Continental writers.

Another native son became the center of vicious literary controversy. Cornelius Mathews, born in nearby Port Chester in 1817, received his bachelor's degree in 1834 from New York University, was admitted to the bar in 1837, but like so many others soon abandoned the law for letters. He had by 1836 contributed articles to the *American Monthly Magazine* and the *Knickerbocker*, and he was soon to write for the *New York Review*. With Evert Duyckinck he founded and edited *Arcturus* in 1840, and wrote critical articles for it. A vigorous nationalist and champion of international copyright, he lectured and wrote in floods of words. His activities earned him the dislike of Lewis Gaylord Clark of the *Knickerbocker*, he was vigorously defended by Duyckinck, and a long-drawn-out warfare of vilification started. "The Centurion," as his enemies dubbed him, had with singular lack of humor published in 1843 *Poems on Man*, versified propaganda for the common man in his varied activities; and he ventured also into the field of satire with disastrous results. He was, however, a hard worker in critical reviewing and possessed some ability; his influence was considerable.

An important but less attractive figure from the 1830's was Park Benjamin. Born in Demerara, British Guiana, in 1809 he was brought to the United States at the age of four in the hope that he might be cured of the effects of a crippling disease. The hope was vain; he was painfully lame throughout his life. Perhaps as a result of his physical state, he was unusually restless. He attended Harvard for two years, a member of Oliver Wendell Holmes's famed "Class of '29," but received his degree from Trinity College in Hartford. He studied law briefly at Harvard, but finished the course at Yale. By 1836 he had come to New York, where until 1838 he edited the *American Monthly Magazine* with Hoffman. Briefly thereafter he was literary editor of Greeley's *New-Yorker*. His reputation for caustic critical comment was by this time thoroughly established. With his founding of the *New World* in 1839, together with a companion broadside, other unlovely qualities became increasingly evident. He reprinted the novels of current British authors without payment and seriously undermined the publishing business by issuing "extras"—entire novels printed on newspaper-size sheets for a few cents per copy. Until the postal regulations caught up with him, he could mail these at magazine rates. Some American stories were also printed in this form, among them a temperance tale, *Franklin Evans*, by a young Brooklyn journalist named Walter Whitman. He got up vituperative quarrels with rival editors, attacked American writers savagely, and joined the numerous band of those sued for libel by Fenimore Cooper, even that more select number against whom Cooper's suits were sustained by the courts. Upon the demise of the *New World* in 1845, his activities in the writers' world decreased, and in 1848 he married and retired until his death in 1864. He was also a fairly well-known minor poet. One of his poems, *Poetry: A Satire* (1842) dealt with literary and critical matters. Of his sort New York produced relatively few literary men. Occasional quarrels flared up, with a good deal of name-calling; these were, however, seldom charged with the venom that tainted Park Benjamin.

Although far from being the deepest critical mind of the age, Evert Augustus Duyckinck was prepared by heritage, training, habitual industry, and good sense to be a focus of literary activity. Born in the city in 1816, the son of a publisher and bookseller, he was thus from childhood associated with books and periodicals. He was graduated in 1835 from Columbia as a sound classical scholar with a taste for elegant literature. He was admitted to the bar two years later, like so many of his fellow-litterateurs, but never practised law. He made a Continental grand tour in 1838–39. In England he heard Carlyle lecture on the French Revolution with mixed emotions; all Carlyle's views, he wrote in his diary, were true in some way, yet Carlyle carried most of them too far. Europe and England gave him an awareness of the world and a breadth of view that in later years were to stand him in good stead.

Before sailing to Europe, Duyckinck had contributed articles on Crabbe, Herbert, and Goldsmith to the *New York Review*. Late in 1840, with his friend and later protégé Cornelius Mathews, he edited *Arcturus*, which, although it proved to be a meteor rather than a fixed star, during its eighteen months was a notable light on the New York literary landscape. Five years later he undertook to edit a comparable magazine, the *Literary World*. Through disagreement with the Wileys, who owned the periodical and objected to his use of Mathews' services, he gave up the editorship after two months, and C. F. Hoffman took it over; but in October, 1848, he bought the magazine and with his brother George conducted it till it came to an end with the year 1853. It was unquestionably the best literary weekly of its time.

Before undertaking *Arcturus*, Duyckinck had indicated his breadth of outlook by declaring that American literature must now be "practical for the masses, original and ingenious for the educated." This statement implied no attempt to carry water on both shoulders; it was an intelligent attempt to amalgamate the leveling tendencies of the Young Americans with the scholarly interests of those who had been conducting the *New York Review*. Duyckinck was himself attached to both groups: although a liberal in politics, he was an ardent member of the Protestant Episcopal Church. He thus was able to contribute articles to both the *Democratic* and *New York* reviews, for he belonged to the right wing of the former and the left wing of the latter.

His personal probity and unflinching honesty carried over into his editorial work, and although he was not free from prepossessions in literary matters, his work shows a remarkable fairness and justice. Less scrupulous men like Rufus Griswold, repelled by him, might refer to him slightingly as "one of our great little cliquists and claquers," and he could retort in kind; but he remains one of the most respected figures of the New York scene by modern readers as well as by his contemporaries.

One of Duyckinck's literary efforts, that capped his career, remains to be mentioned. With his brother George, he published in 1855 the *Cyclopaedia of American Literature* in two massive volumes. It far surpassed Griswold's earlier anthologies in both organization and execution, for the brothers were better trained, better connected, and more honestly concerned to include the entire American literary panorama with fair comment than was their Yankee competitor. It remains today a useful and readable work.

Duyckinck was personally a stimulus to American letters. His home became a resort for American writers in New York, and his library of 17,000 volumes was a resource for them. His encouragement of Herman Melville to read, think, and write is probably the best known of his many assists to young writers. The effervescent but rather young, touchy James Russell Lowell liked and admired him; in his *Fable for Critics* Duyckinck is pictured as shepherding a flock of young American authors. A gentle, meditative man, he was nonetheless excellent company, and New York was incalculably the gainer for his literary services.

To a young New Yorker went the honor of being rated by Poe among the ablest American critics. Poe's praise was probably inspired by the fact that William Alfred Jones agreed with him on several critical principles; it was nonetheless not unmerited. Born in the city in 1817, Jones was graduated from Columbia in 1836, and being the son of a judge dutifully tried to read law, but he bitterly disliked it and soon embarked upon a literary career. He became one of the leading contributors to the early *Democratic Review*. Although he shared that periodical's reform principles, he seems never to have been completely swept off his feet by its insistence that the world put on a democratic face that would give to all literary things a completely new look. As a devout Episcopalian, he was attracted rather to the more restrained, scholarly liberalism of Evert Duyckinck, for whom he wrote extensively in the *Literary World*. A small, nervous, lively man, he possessed vigorous literary style and remarkably clear insight. Unfortunately, great expectations for years stood in the way of his using to the full his considerable literary powers; and when these hopes proved to be vain, he broke under the disappointment. Upon the imminent demise of the *Literary World*, he became librarian of Columbia College, where he served with energy and distinction until 1865. During his ten to fifteen years as practicing critic and reviewer, he was a highly articulate and trenchant writer on American letters and deserving of Poe's high acclaim.

A happy variation from the regular pattern of relations between the churches and letters deserves mention here. The already noted free hand given to reviewers by the church-affiliated *New York Review* was made possible largely through a vigorous program of education fostered by the Protestant Episcopal Church in which the diocese of New York played a prominent part. By a lucky coincidence, several of the outstanding New York editors and writers were Episcopal laymen. Gulian Verplanck occupied probably as influential a position in his church as in letters, and he lent his scholarly services to teaching in the new General Theological Seminary besides lecturing and writing on secular subjects. George Morris, the vital editor of the *Mirror*, was also a member of the Episcopal Church, and the brothers Duyckinck were active in its affairs.

Evert Duyckinck found in the diocesan organ the *New York Review* means of publishing his long articles on the English poet-clergymen Herbert and Crabbe. The mercurial Sam Ward, whose major escapades were still to come, contributed to it an article on Balzac and a review of Longfellow's *Hyperion;* and his sister Julia wrote on lyrics by Goethe and Schiller. Its first editor, Caleb Henry, was interested in both clerical and secular sides of the quarterly and fostered both to a degree rare in church-affiliated publications.

As the half-century wore on, members of evangelical communions increasingly contributed to the literary and critical scene. One of the most significant articles of the period, a careful analysis of the novel as an art-form in the 1854 *Putnam's*, was written by a Presbyterian theological student, William Swinton. It would be some decades, however, before cultural concerns would greatly concern evangelical denominations. Melville's ironic reference to the "infallible Presbyterian church" in which he had been bred and his reactions to his religious training, were shared no doubt by many literary aspirants.

Duyckinck belongs to the forties as well as to the thirties. Another figure prominent in the fifth decade was Charles Francis Briggs, a transplanted Yankee jack-of-all-trades. Born in 1804 on Nantucket, he made several voyages before the mast to Europe and South America. After a brief period as a merchant in New York, he published in 1839 *The Adventures of Harry Franco*, which made his literary reputation, and four years later *The Haunted Merchant*. In 1844 he founded the *Broadway Journal*, an ably edited literary organ which enjoyed Poe's and Lowell's editorial services. Briggs, who was a friendly soul, entertained Lowell while the latter underwent treatment in New York for iritis. His literary connections were wide and intimate; they stood him in good stead later as editor of *Putnam's*. His literary judgments, which are difficult to isolate, appear to have been sound and practical rather than brilliant, and were of great service to his literary associates.

Charles Astor Bristed, son of John Bristed, was the New Yorker turned cosmopolitan. A graduate of Yale, he received a second bachelor's degree from Trinity College, Cambridge, and followed this with several years of travel on the Continent. His convivial tastes had earlier led him to contribute to the New York *Spirit of the Times* and other sporting journals. Several critical articles by Bristed appeared also in the *Whig Review*, in particular a dialogue discussing Tennyson's poetry. In 1855 he wrote "The English Language in America," and in 1858 collected some of his critiques in *Pieces of a Broken-Down Critic*. Beside the earnest vigor of the New York critics, he appeared as the world-weary dilettante. He was devoted to classical learning, and in some respects he paradoxically allowed the scholar's love of qualified statement to weaken the impact of his literary papers. It was rumored that he kept a mistress abroad, a suspicion that titillated and scandalized the more upright like George Washington Peck.

A late-transplanted Bostonian was Henry Theodore Tuckerman. He had attended Harvard but illness forced him to travel for his health without taking a degree; he came to New York in 1845. He joined W. A. Jones in championing Hazlitt's criticism and wrote essays in profusion for periodicals in various cities which he later collected in numerous volumes. Appreciative rather than critical, few of his essays have stood the test of time, although his comments on *The Scarlet Letter* in the 1851 *Southern Literary Messenger* seemed to Hawthorne to be deeply perceptive. In spite of Lowell's complaint that his countless pages made the literary scene "one vast Tuckerman," his works were widely read.

Many of the critics already mentioned carried over their activities into the fifties. To be perhaps classed as partially belonging to New York is George Ripley, who had already shared actively in the transcendental movement as manager of Brook Farm before he moved in

1847 to Flatbush and served as literary critic for the *Tribune* from 1849 until his death in 1880. William Swinton, a young theological student born in Edinburgh in 1833, who came to New York in 1855 via Canada and North Carolina, contributed to *Putnam's* a thoughtful study, "Novels—Their Meaning and Mission," which sharply classified and systematized the study of novels and romances. A hard worker but irregular in his periods of production, he took a position in 1858 with the New York *Times* and gave up his preparations for the Presbyterian ministry. The fifties offered so many confusing problems that threatened the life of the nation and were thrown into such difficulties by the panic of 1857 that younger men had to devote their energies to more pressing or more lucrative pursuits than writing on literature or criticism.

Colorful characters in abundance adorned and enlivened the New York literary scene of which the men previously discussed were the major figures. As writers, editors, or otherwise interested figures, they each left an imprint—cultural, social, financial, even lurid—upon the New York literary record.

John Wakefield Francis, a poor boy of German parentage, was graduated from Columbia in 1809, studied medicine in New York and Edinburgh, and built up a practice that made him wealthy. A frequent public speaker, his less formal conversation was, as he liked to call it, Rabelaisian; and his anecdotes, the more printable of which have been preserved, were the life of stag gatherings. Although he wrote as well as spoke in public, his personal impact upon society and letters was the more significant; he did much to relax any tendency toward the less lovely aspects of Puritanism which might have infiltrated even the Knickerbockers without such liberalizing forces as Dr. Francis.

Another hedonist was Henry Cary, who contributed articles to the *Knickerbocker* under the pseudonym of John Waters. Born in Grenada in the West Indies, where his family had extensive properties, he was brought up in Massachusetts. The family having lost their fortunes in a slave uprising in Grenada, Cary entered business in Boston, but in 1809 the ruin wrought by Jefferson's Embargo moved him to New York. Within a few years he had amassed a fortune. Having literary aspirations, he supplemented his truncated education by careful reading, and, as his means increased, by foreign travel, until he became an influence parallel to Dr. Francis in the cultural and epicurean life of the city.

More directly related to letters was William Cox, who came as a young man from England, wrote for the *Mirror* literary and dramatic articles, and under the pseudonym of "An Amateur" satirized the literary weaknesses of the day. About 1830 he returned to England, whence for some time he contributed to the *Mirror* accounts of current life and letters in London. Another young man, Louis Tasistro, after receiving a liberal education in Ireland and traveling extensively, came to the United States. He edited papers in New York and Boston and contributed to New York periodicals. He was also an accomplished actor. Subsequently he became a translator for the Department of State in Washington.

Two other Irishmen were colorful contributors to the literary scene. John Louis O'Sullivan was the son of an American sea-captain; born reputedly on a British man-of-war in Gibraltar, he had been educated in a French military school and Westminster School in England before his graduation in 1831 from Columbia. With Samuel Langtree he founded the *Democratic Review* in 1837 and four years later brought it to New York. A man of large ideas and incurable optimism, he is credited with having coined the phrase "manifest destiny." After selling the *Democratic Review* in 1846, he served in politics in New York state and later entered the diplomatic service. He was a warm friend of Nathaniel Hawthorne but, unlike him, engaged in vigorous public activity, not always strictly within legal limits. He backed the filibustering activities of Narciso Lopez in Cuba; twice indicted for violation of neutrality laws, he both times escaped conviction. Any pot he tended was sure to boil, and literary New York seethed whenever he fed the fires.

A wild Irishman, born in County Limerick about 1828, was Fitz-James O'Brien. He received a good education and when about twenty-one went off to London with an 8000 pound patrimony, which he squandered there and in Paris. Coming to New York in 1852 with letters to prominent literary men, he soon became the light of the Bohemian set. He contributed to several magazines, in particular a detailed discussion of Herman Melville's work for *Putnam's*. Although he was versatile, he could never remain solvent; in spite of an impressive front, he was constantly in debt to his landladies and survived pecuniary crises by moving in temporarily with friends. At the outbreak of the war, his big cavalry mustache led him into the Seventh Regiment, where he evidently belonged: he was cited for gallantry in action, but was wounded in 1862 and died of tetanus. His impact moved New York from succumbing to the pressures of Victorian propriety that had been transmitted to the city.

Other American regions also contributed to the excitement of New

York literary life. George Nicholas Sanders, born in 1812 in Kentucky, came from a family that dealt in livestock; he arrived in New York in 1845 ready for metaphorical horsetrading. He served as lobbyist for several dubious enterprises, among which a project to sell forty thousand old muskets to the French revolutionists of 1848 is representative. In the early fifties he joined the ranks of the political Young Americans and purchased the *Democratic Review* for advancing the presidential candidacy of Stephen A. Douglas, thereby giving the periodical added impetus toward its downfall. In 1853 he got himself appointed as consul to London and set out thither without awaiting Congressional ratification of his appointment. By the time the appointment came up for a vote he had involved himself in so many European subversive schemes that he failed of approval. He had a gargantuan appetite to go along with the Rabelaisian conversation of the day, and his enthusiasms swept people temporarily off their feet in a way Colonel Sellers would have envied. During the Civil War he was a Confederate agent in Europe. His brief stay in New York greatly stirred the magazine world.

More patriotic and reputable but equally adventurous was another Kentuckian, Charles Wilkins Webber. Born in 1819, he was informally educated at home. At nineteen he joined the Texas Rangers. Five years later he enrolled as a student in Princeton Theological Seminary, but in 1845 took up journalism in New York. He is believed to have edited the *Whig Review* for two of its early years. In 1849 he undertook an expedition to the Colorado and Gila rivers, but Comanches stole his horses before he could start from Corpus Christi. Some years later, he got a charter from the New York legislature to form a camel transport company across the plains, which failed because of certain reproductive eccentricities of camels and other misfortunes. In 1855 he joined William Walker's filibustering expedition into Nicaragua, and was killed at the battle of Rivas.

Several Yankees played minor parts in the New York literary drama. Rufus Wilmot Griswold, the anthologist, shuttled back and forth between Philadelphia and New York, dividing his activities between the two. Although he engaged in many literary activities, his chief impression was left by his several anthologies of American literature which appeared in the 1840's and were frequently reprinted. He made enemies easily, and lost prestige first for his shameless conduct as Poe's literary executor and later for his attacks upon the Duyckincks and their superior *Cyclopaedia of American Literature*.

Margaret Fuller and Edgar Allan Poe, whom she detested, were both influential upon the critical activities of the city, but neither was ever fully endenized there. They have accordingly received only passing consideration as forces acting upon, rather than belonging to, the city's literary life. Margaret Fuller was highly regarded for her work on the *Tribune*, as W. A. Jones attested. Poe made powerful enemies and was repeatedly attacked, on one occasion through fear of his *The Literati* papers before they appeared and resentment afterward.

George Washington Peck, born in 1817, was graduated in 1837 from Brown and migrated westward. After a few years of practicing journalism and schoolteaching in Ohio and Indiana, he read law and was in 1843 admitted to the Massachusetts bar; but journalism recalled him as musical and dramatic critic for the Boston *Post*. By 1847 he had come to New York, where he wrote for the *Whig Review* until 1850, contributing articles on Cooper, Dana, Poe, Lamb, Longfellow, and a condemnation on moral grounds of *Wuthering Heights*. He was one of the few New York critics who let moral grounds decide their literary opinions. In 1853 he left for Australia as correspondent of the New York *Times*, but returned to die of tuberculosis in Boston six years later.

After a checkered career that included selling real estate in South Carolina, Seba Smith came to New York with his poetess wife Elizabeth Oakes Smith about 1840. He engaged in various editorial occupations, and contributed articles to the *Southern Literary Messenger*. At various times between 1854 and 1859 he edited *Emerson's Magazine*. In 1860 he retired to Patchogue, Long Island.

The older generation, except as the subject of occasional eulogy, had chiefly Bryant as its surviving literary force after 1835. Irving was busy with his histories and biographies. Paulding was still alert to literary trends, as his recently published letters show, but he was disregarded as a literary figure. Verplanck had turned to politics and was editing Shakespeare rather than figuring in literary debate. It was the younger generation that developed later critical theory in this era.

Youth is in fact the first striking characteristic of these men. Morris undertook the *Mirror* at twenty-one; Clark took over the *Knickerbocker* at twenty-six; Sands edited the *Atlantic* at twenty-five. Of the others, Mathews began to publish articles at nineteen; Duyckinck, Jones, and Swinton started their careers at twenty-two; O'Sullivan and Ward were twenty-four; Hoffman and Willis, twenty-six; Benjamin and Colton, twenty-seven; and Curtis, twenty-nine. Others who began their New York careers later in life had previously engaged in literary or editorial activities elsewhere. Not only would youth be served in New York; it did the serving.

Geographical origins of the leading litterateurs were also varied. Native to New York were Verplanck, Sands, C. A. Bristed, Evert and George Duyckinck, Mathews, Hoffman, Jones, and Ward. From upstate came Lewis and Willis Gaylord Clark and James Brooks. New England furnished Bryant, Willis, Peck, Briggs, H. T. Tuckerman, Seba Smith, G. W. Curtis, and George Ripley. With the partial exception of the cosmopolitan Tuckerman, these became endenized New Yorkers, their Yankee heritage fairly thoroughly overlaid with the patina of Gotham. From states to the south representatives also came to live: George Morris from Pennsylvania, Parke Godwin from New Jersey; and from the west George Sanders and Charles Webber of Kentucky. Among the unidentified contributors were probably representatives from other states. From across the Atlantic came John Bristed, William Cox, Fitz-James O'Brien, J. L. O'Sullivan, Louis Tasistro, and William Swinton.

Temporary literary residents were also influential. Margaret Fuller and Poe have already been mentioned. R. H. Dana, Sr., was a frequent visitor, as was also J. R. Lowell. William Gilmore Simms came fairly often, before 1850, from South Carolina; nearly all his novels were published in New York. Timothy Flint from the west served briefly in the city as a magazine editor. New York drew these men for longer or shorter visits, and they left their imprint.

From whatever place men came and however long they lingered as residents, these new citizens of the city did not alter the fundamental nature of New York; they were rather absorbed into the city, for in most cases it was sympathy that had led them thither. Those who became part of the literary life of the city did enrich its quality without basically changing it; and those who were not accepted also left their mark, because rejection required forceful action that further developed elements already present. Such activity of acceptance or rejection had produced by 1860 many of the salient characteristics of an American literature and had sprouted the seeds of more. It was an American literature that was emerging.

ABBREVIATIONS

USED IN THE NOTES

AL	*American Literature*
AMM (1)	*American Monthly Magazine and Critical Review* (1817–1819)
AMM (2)	*American Monthly Magazine* (1833–1838)
AMM (3)	*American Monthly Magazine* (Boston, 1829–1831)
An	*Analectic Magazine* (Philadelphia)
Arc	*Arcturus*
At	*Atlantic Magazine*
BJ	*Broadway Journal*
Bro Jon	*Brother Jonathan*
Col	*Columbian Magazine*
Cor	*Corsair*
DR	*United States Magazine and Democratic Review*
E	*Emerson's Magazine*
H	*Harper's Magazine*
HDM	*Holden's Dollar Magazine*
K	*Knickerbocker Magazine*
LR	*Ladies' Repository*
LSR	*Literary and Scientific Repository*
LW	*Literary World*
M	*New York Mirror*
Min	*Minerva*
NAR	*North American Review* (Boston)
NM	*National Magazine*
NQR	*National Quarterly Review*
NW	*New World*
N-Y	*New-Yorker*
NYLG	*New York Literary Gazette*
NYQ	*New York Quarterly*

NYR   *New York Review*
NYRA   *New York Review and Athenaeum*
P   *Putnam's Magazine*
PMLA   *Publications of the Modern Language Association of America*
USR   *United States Review*
USRLG   *United States Review and Literary Gazette*
WR   *American Magazine and Whig Review*

BIBLIOGRAPHICAL

NOTES

These notes refer to studies of the problems discussed, to biographies of persons concerned, and to source materials. Titles of books, after their first appearance, are recorded by author and short title; titles of articles, after their first mention, by author (when known), by abbreviated title, and by abbreviated title of periodical as in the list of abbreviations. The number following the colon gives the specific page-reference. When a single number is given, it indicates a one-page article.

INTRODUCTION

Edmund Wilson, "Van Wyck Brooks on the Civil War Period," *Classics and Commercials* (New York, 1947), 423–24; Luther Mansfield, "Diversity and Innovation in the Middle States," *Literary History of the United States* (3 vols.; New York, 1948), I, 270; William Charvat, *Literary Publishing in America* (Philadelphia, 1959), 7–16; H. H. Clark, "Changing Attitudes in Early American Literary Criticism," in *The Development of American Literary Criticism* (Chapel Hill, 1955), 15–73; Floyd Stovall, "Introduction," in *ibid.*, 4–5, 7; John Allen Krout, and Dixon Ryan Fox, *The Completion of Independence* (New York, 1944); Allan Nevins, *The Evening Post: A Century of Journalism* (New York, 1922); "The Protestant Vindicator," *M*, XII (1834), 175; "Religious Charlatanry," *K*, X (1837), 20–27, 136–45: 24–25, 140–41; Stockton Axson, "Washington Irving and the Knickerbocker Group," *Rice Institute Pamphlets*, XX (1933), 178–95; Philip Appleman, W. A. Madden, and Michael Wolff (eds.), *1859: Entering an Age of Crisis* (Bloomington, 1959). Throughout this study an indispensable, constant aid has been *A History of American Magazines*, by Frank Luther Mott (3 vols.; Cambridge, 1930–1938).

ONE

Review of Bulwer-Lytton's *The Disowned*, in AMM (3), I (1829), 108–22: 112–13; "Whittier," *NM*, II (1853), 97–103: 99; H. T. Tuckerman, "The Poetry of Bryant," *DR*, XVI (1845), 185–91: 185; "Choosing a Subject," *M*, VI (1829), 214–15: 214; "Inspiration," *NW*, II (1841), 62; W. C. Bryant, "Lectures on Poetry," *Prose Writings of William Cullen Bryant* (2 vols.; New York, 1884), I, 3–44: 12–13, 15–16, 17–19; G. W. Peck, "The Works of Edgar A. Poe," *WR*, XI (1850), 301–15; "The Present State of German Literature," *AMM* (2), n.s. II (1836), 1–13: 6; "Goethe," *NYR*, III (1838), 397–442: 437; "The Literary Remains of Samuel Taylor Coleridge," *NYR*, II (1838), 96–111; "American Poetry," *K*, XII (1838), 383–88: 383; H. T. Tuckerman, "Goldsmith," in *Rambles and Reveries* (New York, 1841), 191–210: 210; "A Few Hints about Genius and Talent," *K*, XXXIX (1852), 299–305.

THE AUTHOR AS THINKER. W. A. Jones, "Aesthetical Fragments," *Essays upon Authors and Books* (New York, 1849), 174–84: 174; Jones, "The Culture of the Imagination," *ibid.*, 129–39; review of Catherine Sedgwick, *Redwood*, in *HDM*, VII (1851), 135–36; "Lessing," *NYR*, VI (1840), 323–68: 353–54; G. P. Morris, "Editorial Prerogative," *M*, VII (1829), 167; review of *Lexington*, in *M*, VIII (1830), 106–107; "Lord Byron's Childe Harold and Prisoners [*sic*] of Chillon," *AMM* (1), I (1817), 3–12: 4–5, cf. review of Walter Scott, *Harold the Dauntless*, in *AMM* (1), I (1817), 161–74: 165; review of *George Mason*, *M*, VI (1829), 333–34; "Goethe," *NYR*, III (1838), 440–41; "Novelties and Quackeries," *K*, XVII (1841), 359–62: 360, cf. "Corrupt Literary Taste," *NW*, III (1841), 142; review of recent poetry, *LW*, II (1847), 130–31; Jones, "Traits of American Authorship," *Authors and Books*, 23–28: 25–26; Park Benjamin, "Bryant's Poems," *DR*, VI (1839), 273–86: 274, 283; "Poetry and Philosophy," *M*, VI (1829), 270; G. C. Verplanck, Memoir of R. C. Sands, *The Writings of Robert C. Sands* (2 vols.; New York, 1834), I, 13; review of Miller's *Rural Sketches*, in *NYR*, VI (1840), 170–97: 170–71; notice of *Probus*, in *K*, XII (1838), 156–64: 156; notice of Emerson, *The Method of Nature*, in *K*, XVIII (1841), 559 (cf. *K*, IX (1837), 432; *K*, XIV (1839), 90, 189; *M*, XVI (1838), 126–27; *DR*, II (1838), 323–26; *DR*, VIII (1840), 13–30; *DR*, XXIII (1848), 139–49; *NYR*, IV (1839), 179–81; *NW*, III (1841), 223; *H*, XVI (1858), 554); "Cooper's Works," *DR*, XXV (1849), 51–55: 52; Parke Godwin, "American Authorship," in *Out of the Past: Critical and Literary Papers* (New York, 1870), 176–95; J. K. Paulding, "National Literature," in K. B. Taft, *Minor Knickerbockers: Representative Selections* (New York, 1947), 17; review of Wordsworth, *The Excursion*, in *LW*, V (1849), 463–64; "Robert Browning," *P*, VIII (1856), 372–81, cf. review of Browning's poems, in *LW*, V (1849), 487–88; Tuckerman, "Goldsmith," in *Rambles*, 191–92; "Authors and Authorcraft," *Bro Jon*, I (1842), 296–97; "A Chance for the Critics," *LW*, I (1847), 77; Elbert Slingerland, "Literature," *American Literary Gazette*, Albany, N.Y., I (1847), 293–97: 296; review of Bryant's Poems, in *LW*, I (1847), 5–6; "Periodical Literature," *NM*, I (1852), 1–3, cf. "American Art," *NYQ*, I (1852), 229–51: 231; "The American Drama," *E*, VI (1858), 304–12: 305; Parke Godwin, "Recent American Poetry," *DR*, V (1839), 523–41:

525 ff.; "The Portico, no. 5," *K*, IX (1837), 47–51; C. A. Bristed, "A Tale about the Princess," *WR*, VIII (1848), 71 ff.; Jones, "American Authorship," *Authors and Books*, 25–26; H. T. Tuckerman, "The Novelist: Manzoni," in *Characteristics of Literature* (2 vols.; Philadelphia, 1849, 1851), II, 13–37: 19; review of Longfellow's *Ballads*, in *NW*, IV (1842), 46–47; review of J. G. Lockhart's *Memoirs of the Life of Sir Walter Scott*, in *NYR*, VII (1840), 137–85: 153; J. S. Holme, "Harmony of Philosophy with Poetry," *K*, XXXI (1848), 534–36; J. G. Brooks, "Lord Byron," *Min*, I (1824), 250–52; "John Neal," *M*, XI (1833), 117–18; "Miss Sedgwick's Novels," *AMM* (2), n.s. I (1836), 15–25: 19–20; "The Frailties of Genius," *M*, XVI (1838), 167; "*The Scarlet Letter*," *HDM*, V (1850), 337–44; "Infirmities of Genius," *H*, III (1851), 327–29; "Bayard Taylor's *Poems*," *WR*, XV (1852), 30–35; "Chatterton," *M*, IX (1832), 305; H. T. Tuckerman, *Thoughts on the Poets* (London, 1850), 44–53: 44; "What Is Poetry?" *P*, VIII (1856), 368–80; Tuckerman, *Thoughts*, 5–28: 23–24; "The Earl of Carlisle on Pope," *LW*, VIII (1851), 454–55.

THE CREATIVE IMAGINATION. Review of Coleridge's *Kubla Khan*, in *AMM* (1), I (1817), 12–16; review of Coleridge's *Biographia Literaria*, in *AMM* (1), II (1817), 105–14; R. H. Dana, Sr., "Preface" to *The Idle Man, Poems and Prose Writings* (2 vols.; New York, 1850), I, 147–52; "Wordsworth, Byron, Scott, and Shelley," *H*, III (1851), 502–505; "Moore," *M*, VI (1829), 292; "Francis Jeffrey," *M*, VII (1830), 340–41; notice of *Poems* by W. D. Gallagher, in *AMM* (2), n.s. II (1836), 89–92: 90; "The Literature of the Age," *N-Y*, III (1837), 257; "Life of Scott," *NYR*, VII (1840), 137–85: 153; "Lessing," *NYR*, VI (1840), 323–68: 353–54; "Coleridge," *NYR*, II (1838), 96–111: 96–97; W. A. Jones, "On the Value of Metaphysical Studies," *The Analyst: A Collection of Miscellaneous Papers* (New York, 1840), 73–74; "Harmony of . . . Poetry," *K*, XXXI (1848), 534–36; "Taylor's Poems," *WR*, XV (1852), 30–35; "What Is Poetry?" *P*, VIII (1856), 368–80; "Ideals in Modern Fiction," *P*, X (1857), 90–96.

THE AUTHOR AS PROPAGANDIST. "American Art," *NYQ*, I (1852), 229–51: 229–31; "American Literature, No. 2," *K*, V (1835), 378–84; review of Dickens' *Pickwick Papers*, in *AMM* (2), n.s. V (1838), 288–89; "Democracy and Literature," *DR*, XI (1842), 196–200; "Petrarch," *DR*, XI (1842), 277–82: 278; "Boz and Democracy," *Bro. Jon.*, I (1842), 243–44; review of Bryant's *The Fountain*, in *NW*, V (1842), 63; "Mr. Mathews's Poems on Man," *NW*, V (1842), 63; "Mr. Mathews's Poems on Man," *DR*, XIII (1843), 415–25; Taft, *Minor Knickerbockers*, 18. Paulding's nationalism is discussed at length by Teut Riese, *Das englische Erbe in der amerikanischen Literatur* (Bochum-Langendreer, Germany, 1958), 150–69; see also *The Letters of James Kirke Paulding*, ed. R. M. Aderman (Madison, 1962). "The Literature of the Age," *N-Y*, III (1837), 257; "The American Reviews," *K*, XVIII (1841), 457–59; "A Chance for the Critics," *LW*, I (1847), 77; "Current Poetry," *LW*, II (1847), 130–31; "Nationality in Literature," *DR*, XX (1847), 264–72: 267; "Poets and Poetry of Europe," 121–28: 122; review of Miss Sedgwick's *Clarence*, in *LW*, V (1849), 297–98; Philarète Chasles, "The Actual and Fantastic Voyages of Herman Melville," *LW*, V (1849), 89–90, 101–103; "The Encouragement of Young Artists," *M*, XII (1835), 351; J. F. Cooper, *Notions of the Americans* (2 vols.; Philadelphia,

1833), II, 111–12; "Mr. Paulding's New Novel of Westward Ho!" *M*, X (1832), 122–23; notice of J. H. Ingram's *The Quadroone*, in *M*, XVII (1840), 327; "American Authors and American Subjects," *M*, XVII (1840), 247.

THE AUTHOR AS REALIST. E. A. Duyckinck, "The Poetical Remains of the Reverend George Crabbe," *NYR*, I (1837), 96–109; "A Few Plain Thoughts on Poetry, by a Business Man," *K*, IX (1837), 225–35: 226; W. A. Jones, "Horne's *New Spirit of the Age*," *DR*, XV (1844), 49–62: 51; "Nationality in Literature," *DR*, XX (1847), 264–72: 267; C. A. Bristed, "Thackeray's *Vanity Fair*," *WR*, VIII (1848), 198–99; review of Thackeray's *Pendennis*, in *LW*, VIII (1851), 45–46. On Thackeray's reception in the United States and especially in New York, see G. N. Ray, *Thackeray: The Age of Wisdom* (New York, 1958), 195–221. Parke Godwin, review of Thackeray's *The Newcomes*, in *P*, VI (1855), 283–90: 284: Parke Godwin, "Ruskin's Writings," *P*, VII (1856), 490–500: 499; "The Moral and Artistic in Prose Fiction," *WR*, XIV (1851), 105–15: 107; review of R. B. Kimball's *The Romance of Student-Life Abroad*, in *K*, XLI (1853), 66–68; William Swinton, "Novels: Their Meaning and Mission," *P*, IV (1854), 389–96: 395.

SUPPLEMENTARY WORKS. William Cox, *Crayon Sketches* (2 vols. bound in one; New York, 1833); E. A. Duyckinck, and G. L. Duyckinck, *Cyclopaedia of American Literature* (2 vols.; New York, 1856); J. W. Francis, *Old New York* (New York, 1866); L. E. Fuller, "The United States Magazine and Democratic Review" (Unpublished Ph.D. dissertation, University of North Carolina, 1936); R. W. Griswold, *The Female Poets of America* (Philadelphia, 1848); R. W. Griswold, *The Poets and Poetry of America* (Philadelphia, 1842); R. W. Griswold, *The Prose Writers of America* (Philadelphia, 1847); George Kummer, "Anonymity and Carlyle's Early Reputation in America," *AL*, VIII (1937), 297–99; H. W. Mabie, *The Writers of Knickerbocker New York* (New York, 1912); Tremaine McDowell, *William Cullen Bryant: Representative Selections* (New York, 1935); Perry Miller, *The Raven and the Whale* (New York, 1956); G. E. Mize, "The Contributions of Evert A. Duyckinck to the Cultural Development of Nineteenth Century America" (Unpublished Ph.D. dissertation, New York University, 1954); Allan Nevins, *The Diary of Philip Hone* (New York, 1936); Annabel Newton, *Wordsworth in Early American Criticism* (Chicago, 1928); R. E. Riegel, *Young America: 1830–1840* (Norman, Okla., 1949); H. E. Spivey, "The Knickerbocker Magazine: 1833–1865" (Unpublished Ph.D. dissertation, University of North Carolina, 1936); W. S. Vance, "Carlyle in America before *Sartor Resartus*," *AL*, VII (1936), 363–75; G. E. Verplanck, *The Advantages and Disadvantages of the American Scholar* (New York, 1836).

TWO

Morris, "Editorial Prerogative," *M*, VII (1829), 67; review of *Lexington*, in *M*, VIII (1830), 106–107; "Moore," *M*, VI (1829), 292; "A Few Plain Thoughts," *K*, IX (1837), 225–26; Henry Reed, "William Wordsworth," *NYR*, IV (1839), 1–70: 4–5, 7; "Edgar Allan Poe," *NM*, II (1853), 193–200: 198–99; "Poetry and Poets," *LR*, XVI (1856), 170–74; "Poets," *M*, VI (1829), 211; Bryant, *Prose Works*, I, 4–6; "Mrs. Mary E. Brooks," *M*, VII

(1830), 229–31: 230; "Literature of the Age," *N-Y*, III (1837), 257; review of R. W. Griswold's *Prose Writers of America*, in *K*, XXIX (1847), 344–66: 343; Bryant, *Prose Works*, I, 4–5; J. B. Sheys, "A Chapter on Poetry and Painting," *M*, VIII (1830), 168; W. A. Jones, "Mr. Forrest's Oration," *DR*, III (1838), 51–55; Julia Ward, "Poems from the German," *NYR*, IV (1839), 393–400: 393–94; S. D. Burchard, "The History of Poetry," *K*, XXIX (1847), 523–32: 523; "Carlisle on Pope," *LW*, VIII (1851), 454–55.

THE AIMS AND ENDS OF POETRY. E. A. Duyckinck, "George Herbert of Bremerton," *NYR*, II (1838), 111–33: 112; George Allen, "Reproductive Criticism," *NYR*, II (1838), 49–75: 73; E. A. Duyckinck, "Cornelius Mathews's Writings," *NYR*, VII (1840), 430–39: 430; "Ideals in Modern Fiction," *P*, X (1857), 90–96: 91; "A Few Plain Thoughts," *K*, IX (1837), 226; notice of J. W. Pabodie's *Calidore: A Legendary Poem*, in *NYR*, VI (1840), 247; C. A. Bristed, "The Princess," *WR*, VIII (1848), 171 ff.; Duyckinck, "Crabbe," *NYR*, I (1837), 105; Burchard, "History of Poetry," *K*, XXIX (1847), 529; "Bryant's *American Poets*," *Arc*, I (1840), 24–29: 25–26; W. A. Jones, "Poetry for the People," *DR*, XIII (1843), 266–79: 266; "What Is Poetry?" *P*, VIII (1856), 368, 373; Verplanck, *American Scholar*, 37–38; "Descriptive Poetry," *K*, XXIII (1844), 1–10: 2–3; review of *The Excursion*, in *LW*, V (1849), 463–64; notice of R. W. Griswold, *The Works of the Late Edgar Allan Poe*, Vol. I, in *LW*, VI (1850), 81; "A Few Words about Tennyson," *WR*, XII (1850), 176–81; J. D. Bell, "The Inspired Man," *LR*, XV (1855), 1–4; "Alfred Tennyson," *P*, VI (1855), 385–92: 385.

SUBJECTS AND MATERIALS.

Nature.—Notice of W. L. Bowles, *A Final Appeal to the Literary Public Relative to Pope*, in *NYLG*, I (1825), 5–6; Duyckinck, "Crabbe," *NYR*, I (1837), 101; review of *Wahrheit aus Jean Pauls Leben*, in *NYR*, I (1837), 251–79: 277–78; on defining poetry, *M*, VII (1829), 230; "The Taste for Poetry," *DR*, VI (1839), 523–32: 523; cf. Parke Godwin, "Bryant's Poems," *DR*, VI (1839), 273–86; Reed, "Wordsworth," *NYR*, IV (1839), 4–5; "Descriptive Poetry," *K*, XXIII (1844), 2; "Tennyson," *WR*, XII (1850), 176.

Ideas.—"Bryant's *American Poets*," *Arc*, I (1840), 25–26; "What Is Poetry?" *P*, VIII (1856), 369–80; "Percy Bysshe Shelley," *NYLG*, I (1825), 53–54; review of *The Year*, in *M*, IX (1832), 234–35; Duyckinck, "Mathews's Writings," *NYR*, VII (1840), 430; Tuckerman, "Bryant's Poetry," *DR*, XVI (1845), 185–86; "Alfred Tennyson," *P*, VI (1855), 385.

Imagery.—Bryant, *Prose Works*, I, 9–10; "Portico, no. 5," *K*, IX (1837), 49–50; "The Poetry of Charles Sprague," *M*, XVI (1839), 253; Tuckerman, *Thoughts*, 23–24; review of Longfellow's *The Golden Legend*, *LW*, IX (1851), 441–42, cf. "Longfellow," *NM*, III (1853), 1–6: 3; Fitz-James O'Brien, "Our Young Authors—Melville," *P*, I (1853), 155–64: 157; George Ripley, "Our Authors and Authorship—Melville and Curtis," *P*, IX (1857), 384–93: 389–90 (this essay was triggered by Melville's *The Confidence Man*).

Beauty.—Notice of Ruskin, *Modern Painters*, in *K*, XXX (1847), 346–47: 346; Godwin, "American Authorship" (1853), reprinted in *Out of the Past*, 186–87; Godwin, "Ruskin," *P*, VII (1856), 490–500; review of English

Poetry of the Present Day, in *K*, XXV (1845), 534–46; "Robert Browning," *LW*, V (1849), 193; "Browning's Poems," *LW*, V (1849), 487–88; "Robert Browning," *P*, VII (1856), 372–81; Bryant, *Prose Works*, I, 12–13; "Bowles's *Final Appeal*," *NYLG*, I (1825), 5–6; "A Few Plain Thoughts," *K*, IX (1837), 226; Tuckerman, "Bryant's Poetry," *DR*, XVI (1845), 186; "Tennyson," *WR*, XII (1850), 176; "Poe," *NM*, II (1853), 193–200; "Poetry and Poets," *LR*, XVI (1856), 170–74.

Verse.—G. C. Verplanck, "Life and Writings of William Clifton," *An*, III (1814), 479–88; "Life and Writings of Joel Barlow," *An*, IV (1814), 130–53; Morris, "Editorial Prerogative," *M*, VII (1829), 167; notice of Maria James, *Wales*, in *M*, XVI (1839), 272; Jones, "Thomas Moore," in *Authors and Books*, 191–95: 192–93; notice of W. T. Bacon, *Poems*, in *K*, X (1837), 352; "American Poetry and Foreign Reviews," *NYQ*, II (1853), 71–94: 78; notice of E. W. Ellsworth, *Poems*, in *K*, XLVI (1855), 289–95: 291.

Diction.—G. C. Verplanck, review of Waterman's *Life of Calvin*, in *An*, IV (1814), 42–49: 46–47; review of Moore's *Lalla Rookh*, in *AMM* (1), I (1817), 333–47: 342; review of Cooper's *Lionel Lincoln*, in *NYRA*, I (1825), 39–50: 40–41; "George Mason," *M*, VI (1829), 333–34; review of *Folchetto Malaspina*, in *K*, IV (1834), 311–13; review of Maria Edgeworth's *Harrington and Ormond*, in *AMM* (1), I (1817), 413–20: 415; "Probus," *K*, XII (1838), 156; "Editor's Table," *K*, XIX (1842), 495; "Germanic Infections: Dr. Channing," *K*, XIV (1839), 90–92; *Niles' Weekly Register*, quoted in Maurice Clavel, *Fenimore Cooper and His Critics* (Aix-en-Provençe, 1938), 17; notice of W. G. Simms, *The Partisan*, in *AMM* (2), n.s. I (1836), 101–104: 103; "Portico, no. 5," *K*, IX (1837), 48–50; notice of Halleck, *Poetical Works*, in *LW*, XI (1852), 9; "Poetry and Poets," *LR*, XVI (1856), 172; *Port Folio*, February, 1824, and *USLG*, April 1, 1824, cited in Clavel, *Fenimore Cooper*, 20–21; review of Cooper's *The Pilot*, in *M*, I (1824), 301; Verplanck, in Sands, *The Writings*, I, 13; C. C. Felton, "Modern Transcendentalism," *K*, XVII (1841), 469–75 (from *The Christian Examiner*); "Browning," *LW*, V (1849), 193; "How to Write a Fashionable Novel," *M*, XIII (1835), 203; "Portico, no. 5," *K*, IX (1837), 49; R. C. Sands, "Domestic Literature," *At*, I (1824), 130–39: 136–37; "Willis's Poems," *AMM* (2), n.s. II (1836), 209–24: 219; Benjamin, "Bryant's Poems," *DR*, VI (1839), 273–74; "A Distinguished Visitor," *M*, XVII (1839), 79; "Emerson, *The Method of Nature*," *K*, XVIII (1841), 559; notice of Cornelius Mathews' Works, in *K*, XXII (1843), 473–78; G. W. Peck, review of *Wuthering Heights*, in *WR*, XI (1848), 230–34: 230; O'Brien, "Melville," *P*, I (1853), 157; R. C. Sands, "Wordsworth's Poems," *At*, II (1825), 334–48: 334; "George Mason," *M*, VI (1829), 333; "Miller's *Rural Sketches*," *NYR*, VI (1840), 170–71; Walter Channing, "On American Language and Literature," *NAR*, I (1815), 307–14; "Lexington," *M*, VIII (1830), 106–107; review of Grenville Mellen's *Works*, *AMM* (2), n.s. III (1837), 73–84: 73–74; Tuckerman, "The Philologist: Horne Tooke," *Characteristics*, II, 107–43: 112, cf. "My Musing-Ground," *K*, XVI (1840), 117–22: 119.

Style.—Sands, "Domestic Literature," *At*, I (1824), 136; "Portico, no 5," *K*, IX (1837), 48, 51; notice of Hawthorne, *Twice-Told Tales*, in *K*, IX (1837), 422–25: 422; "Bryant's *Poems*," *LW*, I (1847), 5–6; review of Melville's *Pierre*, in *LW*, XI (1852), 118–20: 119; "Browning," *P*, VII (1856), 375; review of John Neal's *Rachel Dyer*, in *M*, VI (1829), 342–43; "A Few Plain Thoughts," *K*, IX (1837), 227; "Cooper's Works," *DR*, XXV (1849), 52; Swinton, "Novels," *P*, IV (1854), 390–91; "My Musing-Ground," *K*, XVI (1840), 117–22, cf. "The English Language," *K*, XV (1840), 212–20; Godwin, "Recent American Poetry," *DR*, V (1839), 535; review of Melville's *Redburn*, in *HDM*, V (1850), 55–56; review of Melville's *Moby-Dick*, *LW*, IX (1851), 402–404; "George Mason," *M*, VI (1829), 333; "Probus," *K*, XII (1838), 156; Emerson, *Method of Nature*, in *K*, XVIII (1841), 559; "Cooper's Works," *DR*, XXV (1849), 52; Godwin, "American Authorship," *Out of the Past*, 190–91; notice of J. R. Drake, *Poems* in *M*, XIII (1835), 164–65; notice of G. H. Colton, *Tecumseh*, in *DR*, XI (1842), 643–44; "Portico, no. 5," *K*, IX (1837), 47–51; Jones, "Thomas Moore," *Authors and Books*, 192–93; Tuckerman, "The Magazine-Writer: Wilson," *Characteristics*, II, 133–43; notice of Longfellow, *Outre-Mer*, in *AMM* (2), V (1835), 247–48; notice of Longfellow, *Ballads*, in *NW*, IV (1842), 46–47; "Longfellow's *Golden Legend*," *LW*, IX (1851), 441–42; R. H. Stoddard, "Thomas Buchanan Reid," *NM*, VI (1855), 289–94; Walt Whitman, "My Tribute to Four Poets," in *Complete Prose Works* (Philadelphia, 1892), 173–74.

SUPPLEMENTARY MATERIALS. Park Benjamin, *Poetry: A Satire* (New York, 1842); J. O. Eidson, *Tennyson in America* (Athens, Ga., 1943); W. E. Leonard, *Byron and Byronism in America* (Boston, 1905); Julia Power, *Shelley in America in the Nineteenth Century* (Chicago, 1928); H. E. Rollins, *Keats' Reputation in America to 1848* (Cambridge, 1946); J. G. Wilson, *Bryant and His Friends* (New York, 1886).

THREE

Review of W. G. Simms's *The Yemassee*, in *AMM* (2), V (1835), 171–81; "Early English Poetry," *NYR*, VII (1840), 366–77: 376–77; "Bulwer-Lytton as a Novelist," *WR*, XII (1850), 312–19: 313–14; Swinton, "Novels," *P*, IV (1854), 389–96.

THE END OF THE NOVEL. Notice of Royall Tyler, *The Algerine Captive*, in *Min*, I (1824), 331–32; review of Catherine Sedgwick's *Redwood*, in *Min*, I (1824), 186–88; review of *Maxwell, A Tale of the Middle Ranks*, in *M*, VIII (1831), 310; review of W. G. Simms's *The Damsel of Darien*, in *K*, XIV (1839), 457–58; *Columbian*, January 14, 1847, cited in Clavel, *Fenimore Cooper*, 93; notice of *The Factory Girl* and *Filial Affection*, in *Min*, II (1824), 29–30; W. A. Jones, "Children's Books," *DR*, XV (1844), 537–38; "Imaginative Writers," *M*, XVI (1838), 157–58; "Bores in Writing and Reading," *M*, XVII (1839), 76; notice of Bulwer-Lytton, *Falkland*, in *M*, VII (1830), 252, cf. "An Evening at the Theatre," *M*, VII (1830), 252, and "On Gay and *The Beggar's Opera*," *M*, VIII (1830), 43; "A Word in Favor of Novels," *M*, XI (1834), 269–70; review of J. P. Kennedy's *Rob of the Bowl*, in *K*, XIII (1839), 162–63; review of *The Scarlet Letter*, in *HDM*, V (1850), 312–14, 337–44; Charles Sealsfield, "The Works of the Author of *The Spy*," *M*, VIII (1831), 252–54: 253; "Dramatic Fictions," *K*, IX (1837), 587–93: 588; review of Hawthorne's *The Blithedale Romance*, in *WR*, XVI (1852), 417–24: 417–18, cf. "Longfellow's *Golden Legend*," *WR*, XV

(1852), 432–33; J. F. Cooper, review of Catherine Sedgwick's *A New England Tale*, in J. F. Beard, Jr., *James Fenimore Cooper: Early Critical Essays, 1820–1822* (Gainesville, Fla., 1955), 98–100; "Simms's *Yemassee*," *AMM* (2), V (1835), 172.

THE TREND TOWARD REALISM. J. K. Paulding, in Taft, *Minor Knickerbockers*, 15; J. K. Paulding, *A Sketch of Old England* (2 vols.; New York, 1822), II, 149–50; notice of J. K. Paulding, *The Dutchman's Fireside*, in *M*, VIII (1831), 380–82; review of Paulding's *Koningsmarke*, in *M*, I (1823), 108; Paulding, *Koningsmarke*, II, 14 ff.; review of *Francis Berrian, or the Mexican Patriot*, in *USRLG*, I (1826), 94–98: 97–98; notice of *Continental Adventures*, in *USRLG*, I (1827), 389–90; John Inman, "A Caution to Novelists," *M*, XIV (1837), 372–73; "English Standard Literature," *Cor*, I (1839), 233–34; review of Cooper's *Homeward Bound* and *Home as Found*, in *NYR*, IV (1839), 209–21: 210; notice of E. A. Poe, *Tales of the Grotesque and Arabesque*, in *M*, XVII (1839), 207, 215, cf. notice of Mary Clavers, *A New Home—Who'll Follow?* in *M*, XVII (1839), 127; "Early English Poetry," *NYR*, VII (1840), 366–77; Tuckerman, "Goldsmith," *Rambles*, 191–92; E. A. Duyckinck, "Dana's Life at Sea," *Arc*, I (1841), 40–42; review of Bulwer-Lytton's *Night and Morning*, in *Arc*, I (1841), 259–60; "Spenser's Poetical Works," *NYR*, VIII (1841), 50–73: 57–58; "Jottings," *New Mirror*, I (1843), 239; review of Catherine Sedgwick's *Redwood*, in *HDM*, VII (1851), 135–36; Tuckerman, "The Philosopher: Sir Thomas Browne," *Characteristics*, II, 13–37; "Student Life Abroad," *K*, XLI (1853), 66–68; "The Late Reverend Sylvester Judd," *NYQ*, II (1853), 278–312: 303–304; Swinton, "Novels," *P*, IV (1854), 389–96; Godwin, "Thackeray's *Newcomes*," *P*, VI (1855), 284.

THE NOVEL'S AGENTS. Review of Walter Scott's *The Lord of the Isles*, in *AMM* (1), III (1818), 274–85: 274; notice of *Percy Mallory*, in *Min*, I (1824), 76–77; "Cooper's *Lionel Lincoln*," *NYRA*, I (1825), 39–50: 40, 49; review of *National Tales*, *NYRA*, II (1825), 32–38: 37; review of Cooper's *The Last of the Mohicans*, in *NYRA*, II (1826), 285–92: 287; notice of Bulwer-Lytton, *Falkland*, in *M*, VIII (1830), 15; review of Cooper, *The Pathfinder*, in *K*, XV (1840), 344–45; notice of James or Horace Smith, *Gale Middleton*, in *M*, XII (1834), 94; "American Literature, no. 1," *K*, V (1835), 317–26: 320; "*Rob of the Bowl*," *K*, XIII (1839), 162–63; Bristed, "*Vanity Fair*," *WR*, VIII (1848), 198–99; review of *Northwood*, in *USRLG*, II (1827), 33–39: 33–34; "In Favor of Novels," *M*, XI (1834), 269–70; review of *Miriam Coffin*, in *M*, XII (1834), 3; "English and American Literature," *DR*, XXII (1848), 207–15: 208; "English Standard Literature," *Cor*, I (1839), 233–34; "Ideals in Modern Fiction," *P*, X (1857), 90–96: 92; William Cox, "Bulwer and Walter Scott," *M*, VII (1829), 132–34; "Bulwer-Lytton," *WR*, XII (1850), 314; "The Novels of John Pendleton Kennedy," *NYR*, X (1842), 144–52: 144–45; "James Fenimore Cooper," *NQR*, I (1860), 279–316: 279–80; notice of G. P. R. James, *Henry of Guise*, in *K*, XV (1840), 72–73; "The Reception of Mr. Dickens," *DR*, X (1842), 315–20; "*The Scarlet Letter*," *HDM*, V (1850), 341; "*The Blithedale Romance*," *WR*, XVI (1852), 417–18; Cooper, "Preface to the Leather-Stocking Tales," *The Writings of James Fenimore Cooper* (Iroquois ed.; 33 vols.; n.d.), I, vi–vii; "The Waverley Novels," *M*, I (1823), 35; "Spenser," *NYR*, VIII (1841), 59; "Kennedy's Novels," *NYR*, X (1842), 144–45; notice of Thackeray, *The Virginians*, *H*, XIX (1859), 124–25.

AMERICA AS MATERIAL FOR FICTION. John Bristed, *The Resources of the United States of America* (New York, 1818), 304–72: 355–56; review of Paulding's *Koningsmarke*, in *M*, I (1823), 108; "*Northwood*," *USRLG*, II (1827), 33–34; review of *The Rivals of Acadia*, in *USR*, II (1827), 94–102; "*Miriam Coffin*," *M*, XII (1834), 3; "Simms's *Damsel of Darien*," *K*, XIV (1839), 457–58; review of Rufus Dawes's *Nix's Mate*, in *K*, XIV (1839), 460, cf. "Desultory Thoughts on the Philosophy and Process of Civilization," *K*, XVI (1840), 1–9: 1–2; "American Subjects," *M*, XVII (1840), 247; notice of Cooper, *Mercedes of Castile*, in *M*, XVIII (1840), 191; "The American Reviews," *K*, XVIII (1841), 457–60; "The Life and Character of John Adams," *NYR*, X (1842), 1–67: 13–14; review of Melville's *Mardi*, in *HDM*, III (1849), 370–73: 370; Bryant, *Prose Works*, I, 311–12; "The Poetry of the West," *DR*, IX (1841), 23–44: 24–25.

PLOT VERSUS CHARACTERIZATION IN THE NOVEL. "*Percy Mallory*," *Min*, I (1824), 76–77; Verplanck, Memoir of R. C. Sands, *The Writings*, I, 13; review of Cooper's *The Headsman*, in *AMM* (2), II (1834), 194–200: 194; review of R. M. Bird's *Calavar*, in *AMM* (2), IV (1835), 172–82: 175; W. C. Bryant, *Prose Works*, I, 310; review of *The Adventures of a Young Rifleman*, in *USRLG*, I (1826), 178–90: 178–80; review of Cooper's *The Prairie*, in *USR*, II (1827), 306–308, cf. "*Lionel Lincoln*," *NYRA*, I (1825), 39–50: 44–45; Sealsfield, "The Author of *The Spy*," *M*, VIII (1831), 252–54; Paulding, "National Literature," in Taft, *Minor Knickerbockers*, 15–16; "*Francis Berrian*," *USRLG*, I (1826), 97–98; notice of Mary Shelley, *Frankenstein*, in *M*, X (1833), 390; "Simms's *The Partisan*," *AMM* (2), n.s. I (1836), 103; notice of *East and West*, *K*, IX (1837), 87; "*Nix's Mate*," *K*, XIV (1839), 460; "*Night and Morning*," *Arc*, I (1841), 259–60; "Spenser," *NYR*, VIII (1841), 57–58; "Poe's Works," *WR*, XI (1850), 313–14; notice of W. H. Ainsworth, *Crichton*, in *AMM* (2), n.s. IV (1837), 79–82: 79; "Poe's *Tales*," *M*, XVII (1839), 215; notice of Thomas Millar, *Lady Jane Gray*, in *M*, XVII (1839), 383.

SUPPLEMENTARY MATERIALS. R. M. Aderman, "James Kirke Paulding on Literature and the West," *AL*, XXVII (1955), 97–101; Marius Bewley, *The Eccentric Design: Form in the Classic American Novel* (New York, 1959); W. B. Cairns, *On the Development of American Literature from 1815 to 1833* (Madison, 1898); Richard Chase, *The American Novel and Its Tradition* (New York, 1957); O. S. Coad, "The Gothic Element in American Literature before 1835," *Journal of English and Germanic Philology*, XXIV (1925), 72–93; Alexander Cowie, *The Rise of the American Novel* (New York, 1948); James Grossman, *James Fenimore Cooper* (New York, 1949); H. W. Hetherington, *Melville's Reviewers, British and American* (Chapel Hill, 1961); H. M. Jones, *Ideas in America* (Cambridge, 1944); H. M. Jones, *Theory of American Literature* (Ithaca, N.Y., 1948); L. P. Leland, "Theories of Fiction in America: 1789–1870" (Unpublished doctoral dissertation, Ohio State University, 1940); T. R. Lounsbury, *James Fenimore Cooper* (Boston, 1882); G. H. Orians, "The Rise of Romanticism, 1805–1855," in *Transitions* (Durham, 1954), 161–244; A. H. Quinn, *American Fiction: An Historical and Critical Survey* (New York, 1936); B. T. Spencer, "A National Literature: 1837–1855," *AL*, VIII (1936), 125–59; B. T. Spencer, *The Quest for Nationality* (Syracuse, 1957); Dorothy Waples, *The Whig Myth of James Fenimore Cooper* (New Haven, 1938).

FOUR

Bryant, *Prose Works*, I, 1–44; Allen, "Reproductive Criticism," *NYR*, II (1838), 49–75; "Humbug in Criticism," *NW*, VII (1843), 691; E. W. Johnson, "American Letters—Their Character and Advancement," *WR*, I (1845), 575–80: 575–76; S. A. Allibone, "A Review of Reviews," *P*, III (1854), 408–15: 408–409; "Modern Criticism," *E*, VI (1858), 82–83; G. P. Morris on abusive criticism, *M*, X (1832), 127; "Introduction," *K*, I (1833), 1–14: 11–12; "The Art of Making Poetry," by an Emeritus Professor, *K*, I (1833), 107–13: 113; "American Poets and Their Critics," *K*, IV (1834), 11–24: 12–13; "Criticism," *M*, XII (1835), 335; "English Writers on America," *M*, XII (1835), 239 f. (a reprinting of Irving's essay from the *Sketch Book*); R. S. Mackenzie, "The Anatomy of English Criticism," *M*, XII (1835), 314–15; "Professor Wilson and Mr. Willis," *M*, XIII (1835), 102–103; "Mr. Bulwer and the Criticks," *M*, XIII (1835), 239; "Bulwer," *N-Y*, V (1838), 66; "Criticism and Poetry," *N-Y*, VI (1838), 183; Reed, "Wordsworth," *NYR*, IV (1839), 4–5; Washington Irving, "Desultory Thoughts on Criticism," *K*, XIV (1839), 175–78; "Lessing," *NYR*, VI (1840), 323; Duyckinck, "Mathews's Writings," *NYR*, VII (1840), 432; E. A. Duyckinck, "Prologue," *Arc*, I (1840), 1–3: 1; W. A. Jones, "Newspaper Criticism," *Arc*, I (1841), 148–53; Abel Smith, Jr., "Authors and Critics," *Col*, I (1844), 17–21; W. A. Jones, "Criticism in America," *DR*, XV (1844), 241–49; "Corrupt Literary Taste," *NW*, III (1841), 142; "The Curse of Criticism," *BJ*, I (1845), 92; "A Spicy Cut-Up of an Author," *LW*, III (1848), 41–42; "Wordsworth's *Excursion*," *LW*, V (1849), 463–64; "Read's Poems, or A Caution to the Critics," *WR*, XI (1850), 287–91; Tuckerman, "The Critic: Hazlitt," in *Characteristics*, II, 216–38; "Herman Melville's *Moby-Dick*," *HDM*, VIII (1851), 267–72: 271; "William Wordsworth," *DR*, XXXVII (1856), 363–76: 365; Swinton, "Novels," *P*, IV (1854), 389–96; "What Is Poetry?" *P*, VIII (1856), 368; W. A. Jones, *Characters and Criticisms* (2 vols.; New York, 1857), I, 261–64.

THE MORAL YARDSTICK. "Childe Harold," *AMM* (1), I (1817), 3; "Harrington," *AMM* (1), I (1817), 414–15; J. K. Paulding, *Koningsmarke*, II, 14–19; R. C. Sands, "Conversation between the Publisher and the Editor," *At*, I (1824), 1–8; J. G. Brooks, "*Redwood*," *Min*, I (1824), 186–88; Brooks, "Lord Byron," *Min*, I (1824), 250–52; J. G. Brooks, "Swift," *Min*, III (1825), 124–25; notice of Hawthorne, *Fanshawe*, in *Critic*, I (1828), 53–55; notice of Bulwer-Lytton, *Pelham*, in *Critic*, I (1828), 25–27, 68–69; "Beaumont and Fletcher's *Faithful Shepherdess*," *M*, IX (1832), 277–78; "Fashionable Literature," *M*, XV (1837), 7; "Falkland," *M*, VIII (1830), 15, cf. notice of Bulwer-Lytton, *Devereux*, in, *M*, VII (1829), 71; review of Bulwer-Lytton's *The Last Days of Pompeii*, in *K*, IV (1834), 495–98: 495; Samuel Ward, "Modern French Romance," *NYR*, IV (1839), 441–56: 441–42; review of William Godwin's *Fleetwood*, in *BJ*, I (1845), 361–62; "Usefulness the Motto of the Present Times," *M*, XI (1833), 71; Samuel Ward, review of Longfellow's *Hyperion*, in *NYR*, V (1839), 438–57; "Cooper's *Homeward Bound*," *NYR*, IV (1839), 210; notice of *Phantasmion, Prince of Palmland*, in *NYR*, V (1839), 249–50; review of *Richard Hurdis, or the Avenger of Blood*, in *K*, XII (1838), 367–69; "Wordsworth's Excursion," *LW*, V (1849), 463–64; Ripley, "Authors and Authorship," *P*, VIII (1857), 384–87.

DEMOCRATIC CRITICISM. "Moral Poets," *M*, I (1823), 110–11; review of Cooper's *Lionel Lincoln*, in *Min*, III (1825), 75–77, cf. "*The Pilot*," *M*, I (1824), 301; "Shelley," *NYLG*, I (1825), 53–54; "Original Papers from the Attic—Scribblers," *M*, XI (1834), 373–74; "Editorial Prerogative," *M*, VII (1829), 167; "Literature of the West," *M*, XII (1835), 239; "American Poets," *K*, IV (1834), 160; "American Literature, no. 1," *K*, V (1835), 317–26; review of J. P. Kennedy's *Horse-Shoe Robinson*, 2nd ed., in *AMM* (2), V (1835), 466–72; E. S. Gould, "American Criticism on American Authors," *M*, XIII (1836), 321–23; "American Periodicals," *N-Y*, III (1837), 81; "Criticism and Poetry," *N-Y*, VI (1838), 183; Park Benjamin, "American Criticism," *N-Y*, VII (1839), 45; "Introduction," *DR*, I (1837), 1–15; "Liberty vs. Literature and the Fine Arts," *K*, IX (1837), 1–11; Duyckinck, "Crabbe," *NYR*, I (1837), 96–109; "English Standard Literature," *Cor*, I (1839), 233–34; "*Phantasmion*," *NYR*, V (1839), 249–50; "Longfellow's *Hyperion*," *NYR*, V (1839), 438–57; Irving, "Desultory Thoughts," *K*, XIV (1839), 175–78; H. S. Leigh, "Thoughts on Contemporaneous Criticism," *M*, XVI (1839), 412; "Lessing," *NYR*, VI (1840), 323; "University Education," *NYR*, VII (1840), 109–36: 109–10; Duyckinck, "Mathews's Writings," *NYR*, VII (1840), 432; "A Letter to Critics of the Art of Painting," *K*, XVI (1840), 230–33; Jones, "Newspaper Criticism," *Arc*, I (1841), 148–53; "Corrupt Literary Taste," *NW*, III (1842), 142; Henry Ware, Jr., "The Yucatan Ruins," *DR*, XII (1843), 491–501: 491; Abel Smith, Jr., "Authors and Critics," *Col*, I (1844), 17–21; W. A. Jones, "Literary Portraits," *DR*, XV (1844), 196–206: 196–98; "Politics and Literature," *NW*, IX (1844), 656–57; review of Halleck's *Alnwick Castle*, in *BJ*, I (1845), 281–83; E. A. Duyckinck, "Literary Prospects of 1845," *WR*, I (1845), 146–51: 148–49; W. A. Jones, "Miss Fuller's *Papers on Literature and Art*," *DR*, XIX (1846), 198–202; "A Chance for the Critics," *LW*, I (1847), 77; E. A. Duyckinck, "Home Criticism," *LW*, I (1847), 269; W. A. Jones, "Essay Writing—The Champion," in *Authors and Books*, 13–22: 13; "J. Fennimore [*sic*] Cooper," *HDM*, III (1849), 13–22: 13; Tuckerman, *Thoughts*, 5–6; "Wordsworth's Excursion," *LW*, V (1850), 463–64; "Francis Jeffrey," *LW*, VI (1850), 217; "The American School of Art," *WR*, XVI (1852), 138–48; G. N. Sanders, "Fogy Literature," *DR*, XXX (1852), 396–400; "American Poetry," *NYQ*, II (1853), 79–80; "Lowell, the Poet," *P*, I (1853), 547–58; "Editor's Easy Chair," *H*, XII (1856), 262; "What Is Poetry?" *P*, VIII (1856), 368; R. H. Stoddard, "Alfred Tennyson," *NM*, IX (1856), 408–15: 410–13; Ripley, "Our Authors," *P*, IX (1857), 384–93; "Editor's Table," *K*, L (1857), 95; "Modern Criticism," *E*, VI (1858), 82–83.

FIVE

EMOTION AND CRITICISM. "Bulwer's *Devereux*," *M*, VII (1829), 71; "The Poetry of Keats," *M*, IX (1831), 82–83, cf. "American Periodicals," *M*, VIII (1830), 247; "America and England," *AMM* (2), I (1833), 34–42: 40; notice of Paulding, *The Dutchman's Fireside*, in *M*, VIII (1831), 380; "Kennedy's *Horse-shoe Robinson*," *AMM* (2), V (1835), 466; Allen, "Reproductive

Criticism," *NYR* (1838), 49–75; Peck's review of Emily Brontë's *Wuthering Heights*, in *WR*, VII (1848), 572–85: 572–73; notice of E. A. Poe, *Works*, in *K*, XXXV (1850), 164, cf. "Rufus Wilmot Griswold," *K*, XXXVI (1850), 162–72; Tuckerman, "The Critic: Hazlitt," *Characteristics*, II, 216.

ORIGINALITY. Paulding, "National Literature," in Taft, *Minor Knickerbockers*, 17–18; review of J. W. Eastburn and R. C. Sands's *Yamoyden*, in *LSR*, II (1821), 51–68: 67–68; J. K. Paulding, *John Bull in America* (New York, 1825), cited in Riese, *Das englische Erbe*, 150–69; W. C. Bryant, review of J. G. Percival's Phi Beta Kappa Poem, in *NYRA*, II (1826), 245–52: 250–51; "Shakespeare," *Min*, II (1824), 108–109; Bryant, *Prose Works*, I, 42; "Continental Literature," *M*, X (1834), 213–14; "American Literature, no. 3: Criticism," *K*, V (1835), 473–80: 477; "American Poetry," *K*, XII (1838), 383–88; Walter Channing, "On American Language and Literature," *NAR*, I (1815), 307–14; Duyckinck, "Mathews's Writings," *NYR*, VII (1840), 430; Duyckinck, "Miss Barrett's *Poems*," *Arc*, I (1841), 171–76; Abel Smith, Jr., "Authors and Critics," *Col*, I (1844) 17–21; Jones, "Critics and Criticism of the Nineteenth Century," *DR*, XV (1844), 153–62: 156–57; Johnson, "American Letters," *WR*, I (1845), 575–80; Jones, "Miss Fuller's *Papers*," *DR*, XIX (1846), 198–202; E. A. Duyckinck, "A Chance for the Critics," *LW*, I (1847), 77 and "Home Criticism," *LW*, I (1847), 269; E. A. Duyckinck, "Nationality," *DR*, XX (1846), 266–67; Chasles, "Herman Melville," *LW*, V (1849), 89–90, 103–105; Godwin, "American Authorship," in *Out of the Past*, 186–87.

AMERICA AS LITERARY MATERIAL. "Eastburn and Sands' *Yamoyden*," *LSR*, II (1821), 61–62; Paulding, "National Literature," in Taft, *Minor Knickerbockers*, 15–19; Sands, "Domestic Literature," *At*, I (1824), 130–39; "Paulding's *Koningsmarke*," *M*, I (1823), 108; "Cooper's Novels," *M*, V (1827), 31, 39; "Cooper's *Lionel Lincoln*," *NYRA*, I (1825), 39–50. For opinions concerning *The Pioneers*, see Waples, *The Whig Myth of Cooper*, 65–69; "Cooper's *Lionel Lincoln*," *Min*, III (1825), 75–77; "Cooper's *Mohicans*," *NYRA*, II (1826), 292; Sealsfield, "The Author of *The Spy*," *M*, VIII (1831), 252; "John Neal," *M*, XI (1833), 117–18; review of Cooper's *The Headsman*, *AMM* (2), II (1834), 195; "Literature of the West," *M*, XII (1835), 239–40; "Young Artists," *M*, XII (1835), 351; "American Literature, no. 2," *K*, V (1838), 378–84: 378–79; Godwin, "Recent American Poetry," *DR*, V (1839), 541; J. R. Tyson, "The American Revolution," *K*, XII (1838), 217–23: 219; "Portico, no. 5," *K*, IX (1837), 51; Ward, "Longfellow's *Hyperion*," *NYR*, V (1839), 440; "Halleck's *Alnwick Castle*," *BJ*, I (1845), 281–83; review of J. R. Lowell's *Poems*, in *HDM*, I (1848), 117–19; Tuckerman, "American Art," *WR*, XVI (1852), 138–48; "Longfellow," *NM*, III (1853), 3.

LITERARY PROBLEMS. Brooks, "Miss Sedgwick's *Redwood*," *Min*, I (1824), 186–88; "Cooper's *Mohicans*," *NYRA*, II (1826), 285–92; "Moore," *M*, VI (1829), 292; "John Neal," *M*, XI (1833), 117–18; Cox, "Imitation," in *Crayon Sketches*, II, 101–102; "Cooper's *Headsman*," *AMM* (2), II (1834), 194–200; notice of Cooper, *The Heidenmauer*, in *M*, X (1832), 107; G. C. Verplanck, *Influence of Moral Causes, Upon Opinion, Science, and Literature* (New York, 1834), 40–41; "Bulwer's *Last Days of Pompeii*," *K*, IV (1834), 495–98, cf. review of Bulwer-Lytton's *The Last Days of Pompeii*, in *AMM* (2), IV

(1835), 198–208; "Simms's *Yemassee, AMM* (2), V (1835), 175; John Inman, "Caution to Novelists," *M*, XIV (1837), 372–73, cf. rev. of Bulwer-Lytton's *The Duchess de Lavalliere*, in *loc. cit.*, 223.

IMAGINATION. Morris, "Literary Prerogative," *M*, VII (1829), 167; "Francis Jeffrey," *M*, VII (1830), 341; notice of *Zophiel, or The Bride of Seven*, in *M*, XI (1834), 334; "The Literature of the Day," *M*, XII (1835), 55; "Current Literature," *M*, XIII (1835), 7; "German Literature," *AMM* (2), n.s. II (1836), 6; Samuel Ward, "*Jean Pauls Leben*," *NYR*, I (1837), 263–64; "Literature," *N-Y*, III (1837), 257, cf. "The Eras of Literature," *N-Y*, IV (1837), 451; "Introduction," *DR*, I (1837), 14; Ward, "Longfellow's *Hyperion*," *NYR*, V (1839), 438–57; "Poetry and Philosophy," *M*, VI (1829), 270, cf. "*George Mason*," *M*, VI (1829), 333–34, and "Poetry," *M* VII (1829), 20; "Lessing," *NYR*, VI (1840), 353–54; "Lockhart's Life of Scott," *NYR*, VII (1840), 153; "A Letter to Critics," *K*, XVI (1840), 230–33; Jones, *The Analyst*, 71–75. *The Dial* received caustic notices in *K*, XVI (1840), 190, 451–52, XVII (1841), 171–74, and XIX (1842), 495–96, cf. W. A. Jones, "Unitarian Portraits," *DR*, XV (1844), 389–96. "New Poetry in New England," *DR*, XX (1847), 392–98; "Criticism in America," *Arc*, III (1842), 401–406; review of E. A. Poe's *Tales of Ratiocination*, in *WR*, II (1845), 306–309; Duyckinck, "Home Criticism," *LW*, I (1847), 269; for Paulding's remark, made in 1848, see A. L. Herold, *James Kirke Paulding: Versatile American* (New York, 1926), 118; "Wordsworth's Excursion," *LW*, V (1849), 463–64; Walt Whitman, *Uncollected Poetry and Prose* (2 vols.; New York, 1921), I, 131; Tuckerman, *Thoughts*, 175–76; Tuckerman, "The Critic: Hazlitt," *Characteristics*, II, 216–38.

PRIMITIVISM. "French Literature," *M*, X (1832), 37–38; "Continental Literature," *M*, X (1832), 53–54; "Stone's *Life of Brant*," *NYR*, III (1838), 195–225: 208; "Cooper's Novels," *NAR*, XXIII (1826), 150–97; review of Cooper's *The Red Rover*, in *NAR*, XXVII (1828), 139–54; on Cooper, *NYRA*, January, 1826, cited in Clavel, *Fenimore Cooper*, 300–301; Sealsfield, "The Author of *The Spy*," *M*, VIII (1831), 252–54; Samuel Ward, "Modern French Romance," *NYR*, IV (1837), 451; Cooper, "Preface to the Leather-Stocking Tales" (Iroquois ed.), Vol. I, v–vi.

SIX

CRITICAL INDEPENDENCE. "*Harold the Dauntless*," *AMM* (1), I (1817), 165; "Art of Making Poetry," *K*, I (1833), 107–13; Gould, "American Criticism," *M*, XIII (1836), 321–23; "American Poets," *N-Y*, I (1836), 49–50; "Charles Sprague's Poetry," *M*, XVI (1839), 55; "Religious Charlatanry," *K*, X (1837), 20–27, 136–45; notice of *Pocahontas: A Tragedy*, *K*, X (1837), 180–82; "A Defence of Acted Drama," *M*, V (1828), 207; "Infidelity," *M*, VII (1829), 55; "*The Beggar's Opera*," *M*, VIII (1830), 43; "Protestant Vindicator," *M*, XII (1834), 175; "Mr. Forrest's Oration," *DR*, III (1838), 54; "*The New-York Review*, no. 3," *M*, XV (1838), 247; "Literature of the West," *M*, XII (1834), 239 f.; "England and the United States," *M*, IX (1832), 351; "Original Letters from Eminent Writers," *M*, XI (1833), 25–26; "English Standard Literature," *Cor*, I (1839), 233–34; for summary of articles on American Literature in the 1835 London *Athenaeum*, see Hassold, *American Literary History before the Civil War* (Chicago, 1935), 62–64;

Duyckinck, "A Chance for the Critics," *LW*, I (1847), 77, and "Home Criticism," 269; C. F. Hoffman, "Preface," *LW*, II (1847), 5.

PUBLICATION OF CRITICISM IN NEW YORK. "The Critic," *M*, VI (1829), 407; L. G. Clark on the demise of the *AMM* (2), in *K*, XII (1838), 471; "American Periodicals," *M*, VII (1830), 247; "My Musing-Ground," *K*, XVI (1840), 117–22, cf. "The English Language," *K*, XV (1840), 218–19; Jones, "Critics and Criticism," in *The Analyst*, 126; Jones, "Newspaper Criticism," *Arc*, I (1841), 148–53; Ware, "The Yucatan Ruins," *DR*, XII (1843), 491; "Ellsworth's *Poems*," *K*, XLVI (1855), 289–94; Jones, "*Spirit of the Age*," *DR*, XV (1844), 55–58; Allibone, "Review of Reviews," *P*, III (1854), 408–409.

ACHIEVEMENTS AND PROSPECTS. Verplanck, *Influence of Moral Causes*, 41–42; "American Poets," *K*, IV (1834), 11–24; "Literature of the Age," *N-Y*, III (1837), 257; "Lessing," *NYR*, VI (1840), 323; "Bryant's *American Poets*," *Arc*, I (1840), 24–29; "Edward Everett," *Arc*, II (1841), 221–25; review of Longfellows' *Ballads, and Other Poems*, in *Arc*, III (1842), 214–20: 214; Johnson, "American Letters," *WR*, I (1845), 578–79; "American Literature," *M*, I (1824), 252; Bryant, *Prose Works*, I, 34–35; G. P. Morris, on the *American Monthly Magazine* and N. P. Willis, *M*, VII (1830), 287; Gould, "American Criticism," *M*, XIII (1836), 321–23; "The English Language," *K*, XV (1840), 215–16; "Grenville Mellen's Works," *AMM* (2), n.s. III (1837), 73–74; "Halleck's *Alnwick Castle*," *BJ*, I (1845), 282; Duyckinck, "Literary Prospects of 1845," *WR*, I (1845), 146–51; Jones, "Miss Fuller's *Papers*," *DR*, XIX (1846), 198–202; Timothy Flint, "Obstacles to American Literature," *K*, I (1833), 161–70; "Literature in New-York," *M*, VI (1829), 247.

SUPPLEMENTARY MATERIALS.

Chapters Four–Six.—John Bristed, *An Oration on the Utility of Literary Establishments* (New York, 1814); William Charvat, *The Origins of American Critical Thought: 1810–1835* (Philadelphia, 1936); J. F. Cooper, *The Letters and Journals*, ed. J. F. Beard, Jr. (Vols. I and II; Cambridge, 1960); E. H. Eby, "American Romantic Criticism: 1815 to 1860" (Unpublished doctoral dissertation, University of Washington, 1927); Hassold, *American Literary History before the Civil War;* M. F. Heiser, "The Decline of Neoclassicism," in *Transitions*, 91–159; J. C. McCloskey, "The Campaign of Periodicals after the War of 1812 for National American Literature," *PMLA*, L (1935), 262–73; Cornelius Mathews, *Various Writings* (New York, 1843); S. P. Moss, "Poe and His Nemesis—Lewis Gaylord Clark," *AL*, XXVIII (1956), 30–46; S. P. Moss, *Poe's Literary Battles: The Critic in the Context of His Literary Milieu* (Durham, 1963); J. P. Pritchard, *Criticism in America* (Norman, 1956); J. P. Pritchard, *Return to the Fountains: Some Classical Sources of American Criticism* (Durham, 1942); J. W. Rathbun, "The Development of Historical Literary Criticism in America" (Unpublished doctoral dissertation, University of Wisconsin, 1956); Joseph Rocchietti, *Why a National Literature Cannot Flourish in the United States of America* (New York, 1845); W. E. Sedgwick, "The Materials for an American Literature: A Critical Problem of the Early Nineteenth Century," *Harvard Studies and Notes in Philology and Literature*, XVII (1935), 141–62; H. E. Spivey, "Poe and Lewis Gaylord Clark," *PMLA*, LIV (1939), 1124–32; L. H. Tharp, *Three Saints and a Sinner: Julia Ward Howe, Louisa, Annie, and Sam Ward* (Boston, 1956); A. J. Stafford, "The Literary Criticism in Three New York Political Periodicals" (Unpublished doctoral dissertation, University of Texas, 1948); John Stafford, *The Literary Criticism of Young America* (Berkeley, 1952); G. C. Verplanck, *Discourses and Addresses* (New York, 1833); G. C. Verplanck, *On the Right Moral Influence and Use of Liberal Studies* (Edinburgh, 1835); G. C. Verplanck, *The Influence of Moral Causes upon Opinion, Science, and Literature;* F. C. Watkins, *James Kirke Paulding: Humorist and Critic of American Life* (Nashville, 1951); J. G. Wilson, *Bryant and His Friends* (New York, 1886); J. G. Wilson, *Life and Letters of Fitz-Greene Halleck* (New York, 1869).

CONCLUSION

Notice of the *NAR* for April, 1829, *M*, VI (1829), 326–27; "*The North American Review,*" *M*, VIII (1830), 346; notice of *NAR* for July, 1838, *K*, XII (1838), 77; Jones, "Criticism in America," *DR*, XV (1844), 244; G. P. Fisher, "Macaulay and the Puritans," *K*, XXXIII (1849), 508–16; "Religious Charlatanry," *K*, X (1837), 20–27, 136–45; review of Emerson's *Poems, LW*, I (1847), 197; C. F. Briggs in *HDM*, cited by Perry Miller, in *The Raven and the Whale*, 227; Jones, "The Two Everetts," in *Authors and Books*, 32–37; Felton, "Modern Transcendentalism," *K*, XVII (1841), 469–75, from the *Christian Examiner;* notice of Emerson, *Essays*, in *NYR*, VIII (1841), 509–12; "The Weekly Papers of This City," *M*, VII (1829), 15; "Editorial Courtesies," *M*, VII (1829), 324; notice of the *Proceedings of the Literary and Scientific Convention, Held in New-York, October, 1830*, in *M*, VIII (1831), 235; "On Establishing a New Literary Magazine," *M*, IX (1831), 23, cf. Bryant, "The Writings of Fitz-Greene Halleck," *M*, XIV (1838), 97; "*The New-York Review*, no. 7," *M*, XV (1838), 247; "Thackeray in America," *LW*, XII (1853), 20–21.

APPENDIX

The materials for this appendix have been collected from a great many sources, including many of the articles and volumes already cited. F. L. Mott's *History of American Magazines* provided much of the information about the periodicals, together with the unpublished dissertations previously listed by L. E. Fuller, G. E. Mize, H. E. Spivey, and A. J. Stafford. The following special studies of personages, supplemented by the *Dictionary of American Biography*, have been informative: H. F. Barnes, *Charles Fenno Hoffman* (New York, 1930); E. A. Duyckinck, *Memorial to Henry Theodore Tuckerman* (New York, 1872); Parke Godwin, *A Biography of William Cullen Bryant* (2 vols.; New York, 1883); A. L. Herold, *James Kirke Paulding: Versatile American;* M. M. Hoover, *Parke Benjamin: Poet and Editor* (New York, 1948); R. W. July, *The Essential New Yorker: Gulian Crommelin Verplanck;* Gordon Milne, *George William Curtis and the Genteel Tradition* (Bloomington, 1956); S. P. Moss, *Poe's Literary Battles* (Durham, 1963); Samuel Osgood, *Evert Augustus Duyckinck: His Life, Writings, and Influence* (Boston, 1879); W. I. Paulding, *Literary Life of James K. Paulding* (New York, 1867); J. G. Wilson, *Life and Letters of Fitz-Greene Halleck* (New York, 1869).

INDEX